...u uas

Decommissioning Risk Management

Applied Project Management
Book Series

Applying Monte Carlo Risk Simulation, Strategic Real Options, Stochastic Forecasting, Portfolio Optimisation, Data and Decision Analytics

IIPER Press

Liam Jackson, ChPP
Elvis Hernandez, Ph.D.
Johnathan Mun, Ph.D.

ROV Project Economics Analysis Tool

Copyright © 2020 by IIPER. All rights reserved.

No part of this publication may be reproduced, stored in a retrieval system, or transmitted in any form or by any means, electronic, mechanical, photocopying, recording, scanning, or otherwise, except as permitted under Section 107 or 108 of the 1976 United States Copyright Act, without the prior written permission of the Publisher. Requests for permission should be addressed to the Permissions Department, IIPER Press, 4101F Dublin Blvd., Ste. 425, Dublin, California 94568 USA, +1 (925) 999-9397.

Limit of Liability/Disclaimer of Warranty: While the publisher and Authors have used their best efforts in preparing this book, they make no representations or warranties with respect to the accuracy or completeness of the contents of this book and specifically disclaim any implied warranties of merchantability or fitness for a particular purpose. No warranty may be created or extended by sales representatives or written sales materials. The advice and strategies contained herein may not be suitable for your situation. You should consult with a professional where appropriate. Neither the publisher nor Authors shall be liable for any loss of profit or any other commercial damages, including but not limited to special, incidental, consequential, or other damages.

Designations used by companies to distinguish their products are often claimed as trademarks. In all instances where IIPER Press is aware of a claim, the product names appear in initial capital or all capital letters. Readers, however, should contact the appropriate companies for more complete information regarding trademarks and registration. IIPER also publishes its books in a variety of electronic formats. Some content that appears in print may not be available in electronic books. For more information about ROV products, visit our website at

www.realoptionsvaluation.com or www.rovusa.com.

Printed in the United States of America

ABOUT THE AUTHORS

Liam Jackson is a multi-disciplined project manager with over 10 years of management experience across large corporations such as British Petroleum and Bilfinger. Currently working in the Offshore Oil & Gas sector (the Southern North Sea region) for an operated gas storage company, he has managed various complex projects, which include brown-field modifications, oil and gas platforms, gas terminals, maintenance programs, decommissioning projects, and well plugging and abandonment (P&A) activities for various company-owned assets, both onshore and offshore.

Before working in the offshore oil and gas industry, Liam Jackson started his career studying building and construction (National Certificate in Construction and Higher National Certificate in Construction) while completing an apprenticeship as a civil engineer. He went on to hold other management roles, including delivery manager, site manager, and project engineer, for a number of businesses within a wide range of industries including onshore petrochemical refineries, chemical plants, pharmaceutical sites, dock-lands and construction sites, and for both residential building and large civil engineering projects. He is continuously incorporating the risk management culture into project management, and currently he is accountable for the safe and efficient delivery of projects in accordance with the agreed upon process and business objectives throughout the project's management from initial inception to final closure.

Liam Jackson is a Fellow member (FAPM) and a Chartered Project Professional (ChPP) through the APM (Association for Project Managers). He has obtained both the APM Practitioner Qualification and the APMP, the APM Project Management Qualification issued via the APM. He holds a business management degree from the University of Essex. Other key leadership and management qualifications include the Level 4 Award in Management, Level 4 Diploma in Management, and the Level 5 Diploma in Management, all issued through the Institute of Leadership and Management (ILM). Jackson has a passion for volunteering and coaching at career conferences for school-leavers who are looking for careers within project management.

LinkedIn: Liam Jackson ChPP FAPM
Email: liam.jackson@projectmanagementservices.co.uk
Grimsby, United Kingdom

 **Prof. Dr. Elvis Hernandez-Perdomo** is the co-founder and Executive Director of OSL Risk Management Ltd., an IT-based consulting, executive training, and software customisation firm specialising in strategic real options, financial and project valuation, Monte Carlo risk simulation, stochastic forecasting, optimisation, decision-making analytics, business intelligence, engineering risk services, enterprise risk management (ERM), project risk management, corporate governance, and risk analysis located in the United Kingdom. OSL Risk Management has partners in Spain, Italy, Portugal, Germany, Ghana, Nigeria, South Africa, Saudi Arabia, and elsewhere.

Dr. Hernandez is an associate director of OSL Consulting Engineering, a firm specialising in engineering services for oil and gas, petrochemicals, renewables, and energy companies. He is also a board member of multiple risk management organisations including the International Institute of Professional Education and Research (IIPER), AFRisk Convention, and EURisk Convention. He is also a senior executive trainer for the Certified in Quantitative Risk Management (CQRM Accreditation), and a program director for various executive trainings in Project Risk Management, Multicriteria Decision-Making, Enterprise Risk Management, Risk Quantification and Real Options Analysis, Reliability Engineering and Operational Risk, Decommissioning Risk, Company and Project Valuations, Portfolio and Asset Management, Financial Risk Management, and other related topics.

A Member of the Institute of Directors (*IoD*, UK) and of the Portuguese Economic Association, Dr. Hernandez has been a Senior Consultant in several international engineering and energy projects in countries across Latin America, Europe, and Africa, and in numerous industries including oil and gas, energy, logistics, telecommunications, financial and insurance, and SMEs. Additionally, he holds public seminars on risk analysis and CQRM programs. He was a former Central Banker's Economist, Founder and Executive Director of a Latin-America IT-based consulting firm, and Senior Executive Consultant at Real Options Valuations, Inc. (ROV) working on real options, risk management, Monte Carlo risk simulation, optimisation, and business intelligence analytics.

Currently Dr. Hernandez is a risk and engineering lecturer and has taught courses in financial management, investments, research methods, real options, project management, and statistics at the undergraduate and graduate MS and PhD levels. He is a Senior Executive Trainer in quantitative risk management at the Energy Institute and Institute of Risk Management in the United Kingdom. During his tenure at OSL Risk Management, Real Options Valuations, OSL Consulting Engineering, ONUVA Technologies, and Central Bank of Venezuela, he taught and consulted on a variety of real options, risk analysis, decision making, data analytics, project management, and financial valuation aspects for a large number of international clients, for example, E.ON, Petrobras, Centrica, PDVSA, ECOPETROL, Saudi Telecom Company, Wood, INEOS, CRODA, Orsted, ADNOC, AECOM, ERYC, GasMeth, Huawei, AXA, KIER Group, KPMG, Deloitte, Ministry of Defence, MTN Ghana, Vanguard, Vodafone, Department of International Trade (DIT UK), Telefonica, Mitsubishi Chemicals, Saudi Aramco, and many others.

He holds a PhD in Finance from the University of Hull (UK), and a PhD in Engineering Science, where his research and academic interests were corporate governance, multi-criteria decision analysis, risk management, project valuations, and real options in energy projects. He also has an MS in Statistics and Operations Research (*Distinction*), an MS/MIF in Finance (*Top Five*), and a BS in Economics (*Honours – Magna Cum Laude*), is Certified in Quantitative Risk (CQRM) by the IIPER (member of the prestigious AACSB), and is an Associate in Business ERP by SAP Corporation.

Dr. Hernandez belongs to the Academy of Higher Education in the UK as an Associate Fellow. He has written many academic articles published in the *Journal of the Operational Research Society, Journal of Reliability Engineering & System Safety, Applied Energy, Journal of Central Bank, Journal of Risk and Uncertainty in Engineering Systems (Part A: Civil Engineering), Journal of Engineering, Partial Order Concepts in Applied Sciences* (Springer International Publishing), and *Journal of the International Council on Systems Engineering.*

LinkedIn: Dr. Elvis Hernandez-Perdomo
Email: elvis.hernandez@oslriskmanagement.com
Hull, United Kingdom

Prof. Dr. Johnathan C. Mun is the founder, chairman, and CEO of Real Options Valuation, Inc. (ROV), a consulting, training, and software development firm specialising in strategic real options, financial valuation, Monte Carlo risk simulation, stochastic forecasting, optimisation, decision analytics, business intelligence, healthcare analytics, enterprise risk management, project risk management, quantitative research methods, and risk analysis located in northern Silicon Valley, California. ROV has partners around the world including Argentina, Beijing, Chicago, China, Colombia, Ghana, Hong Kong, India, Italy, Japan, Malaysia, Mexico City, New York, Nigeria, Peru, Puerto Rico, Russia, Saudi Arabia, Shanghai, Singapore, Slovenia, South Africa, South Korea, Spain, United Kingdom, Venezuela, Zurich, and others. ROV also has a local office in Shanghai.

Dr. Mun is also the chairman of the International Institute of Professional Education and Research (IIPER), an accredited global organisation staffed by professors from named universities from around the world that provides the Certified in Quantitative Risk Management (CQRM) and Certified in Risk Management (CRM) designations, among others. He is the creator of many powerful software tools including Risk Simulator, Real Options SLS Super Lattice Solver, Modeling Toolkit, Project Economics Analysis Tool (PEAT), Credit Market Operational Liquidity Risk (CMOL), Employee Stock Options Valuation, ROV BizStats, ROV Modeler Suite (Basel Credit Modeler, Risk Modeler, Optimizer, and Valuator), ROV Compiler, ROV Extractor and Evaluator, ROV Dashboard, ROV Quantitative Data Miner, and other software applications, as well as the ROV risk-analysis training DVD. He holds public seminars on risk analysis and CQRM courses. He has over 21 registered patents and patents pending globally. He has authored over 26 books published by John Wiley & Sons, Elsevier Science, IIPER Press, and ROV Press, including multiple volumes of the Applied CQRM Series (IIPER Press, 2019–2020); *Modeling Risk: Applying Monte Carlo Simulation, Strategic Real Options, Stochastic Forecasting, Portfolio Optimisation, Data Analytics, Business Intelligence, and Decision Modeling,* First Edition (Wiley, 2006), Second Edition (Wiley, 2010), and Third Edition (ROV Press, 2015); *The Banker's Handbook on Credit Risk* (2008); *Advanced Analytical Models: 250 Applications from the Basel Accords to Wall Street and Beyond* (2016, 2008); *Real Options Analysis: Tools and Techniques,* First Edition (2003) and Second Edition (2005); *Real Options Analysis Course: Business Cases* (2003); *Applied Risk Analysis: Moving Beyond Uncertainty* (2003); and *Valuing Employee Stock Options* (2004). His books and software are being used at over 350 top universities around the world, including the Bern Institute in Germany, Chung-Ang University in South Korea, Georgetown University, ITESM in Mexico, Massachusetts Institute of Technology, U.S. Naval Postgraduate School, New York University, Stockholm University in Sweden, University of the Andes in Chile, University of Chile, University of Hull, University of Pennsylvania Wharton School, University of York in the United Kingdom, and Edinburgh University in Scotland, among others.

Currently a risk, finance, and economics professor, Dr. Mun has taught courses in financial management, investments, real options, economics, and statistics at the undergraduate and the graduate MS, MBA, and PhD levels. He teaches and has taught at universities all over the world, from the U.S. Naval Postgraduate School (Monterey, California) and University of Applied Sciences (Switzerland and Germany) as full professor, to Golden Gate University (California) and St. Mary's College (California), and has chaired many graduate research MBA thesis and PhD dissertation committees. He also teaches weeklong Risk Analysis, Real Options Analysis, and Risk Analysis for Managers public courses where participants can obtain the CRM and CQRM designations on completion. He is a senior fellow at the Magellan Center and sits on the board of standards at the American Academy of Financial Management.

He was formerly the Vice President of Analytics at Decisioneering, Inc., where he headed the development of options and financial analytics software products, analytical consulting, training, and technical support, and where he was the creator of the Real Options Analysis Toolkit software, the older and much less powerful predecessor of the Real Options Super Lattice software. Prior to joining Decisioneering, he was a Consulting Manager and Financial Economist in the Valuation Services and Global Financial Services practice of KPMG Consulting and a Manager with the Economic Consulting Services practice at KPMG LLP.

He has extensive experience in econometric modeling, financial analysis, real options, economic analysis, and statistics. During his tenure at Real Options Valuation, Inc., Decisioneering, and KPMG Consulting, he taught and consulted on a variety of real options, risk analysis, financial forecasting, project management, and financial valuation issues for more than 100 multinational firms (current and former clients include 3M, Airbus, Boeing, BP, Chevron Texaco, Financial Accounting Standards Board, Fujitsu, GE, Goodyear, Microsoft, Motorola, Northrop Grumman, Pfizer, Timken, U.S. Department of Defense, U.S. Navy, Veritas, and many others). His experience prior to joining KPMG included being department head of financial planning and analysis at Viking Inc. of FedEx, performing financial forecasting, economic analysis, and market research. Prior to that, he did financial planning and freelance financial consulting work.

Dr. Mun received a PhD in finance and economics from Lehigh University, where his research and academic interests were in the areas of investment finance, econometric modeling, financial options, corporate finance, and microeconomic theory. He also has an MBA in business administration, an MS in management science, and a BS in biology and physics. He is Certified in Financial Risk Management, Certified in Financial Consulting, and Certified in Quantitative Risk Management. He is a member of the American Mensa, Phi Beta Kappa Honor Society, and Golden Key Honor Society as well as several other professional organisations, including the Eastern and Southern Finance Associations, American Economic Association, and Global Association of Risk Professionals.

In addition, he has written many academic articles published in the *Journal of Expert Systems with Applications; Defense Acquisition Research Journal; American Institute of Physics Proceedings; Acquisitions Research (U.S. Department of Defense); Journal of the Advances in Quantitative Accounting and Finance; Global Finance Journal; International Financial Review; Journal of Financial Analysis; Journal of Applied Financial Economics; Journal of International Financial Markets, Institutions and Money; Financial Engineering News;* and *Journal of the Society of Petroleum Engineers.* Finally, he has contributed chapters in dozens of books and written over a hundred technical whitepapers, newsletters, case studies, and research papers for Real Options Valuation, Inc.

JohnathanMun@cs.com
San Francisco, California

ACCOLADES AND PRAISES

"Due to the significant costs and multiple risks involved in decommissioning, learning from others' experience is essential in managing projects effectively. This work by the authors provides project managers a structured guidance on the considerations and risks associated when planning, executing, and completing decommissioning activities. The use of analytic models against real-world examples underpins the importance of managing cost and timescales whilst supporting the identification of variation in the project's cost and confidence intervals. For any project manager or company facing future decommissioning projects, I would recommend reading this work to help them understand, quantify, and manage the risks they will face."

Adam Beardmore, CEng, MEng, CQRM
Business Development Lead
Centrica Storage Limited (CSL)

"Decommissioning of an oil and offshore infrastructure presents both technical and commercial challenges. In a world that is now moving away from fossil fuels, there is a need to be able to make informed decisions about decommissioning programmes; not just when to do it, but what to do. This book combines deep experience in decommissioning with the methods and tools of Risk Management and Real Options Valuation that will enable asset owners to explore options and make the right decision at the right time. This isn't just a dry discourse on the topics; it is one that explains the issues and how to approach them, and illustrates the tools needed."

Mike Tooke, CEng, MEI
Director
2G BioPOWER

"This book describes the analytical methods and concepts that can be used to assist decision makers in mitigating the risk of a project overspending and/or experiencing a delay. It is an important piece of work for experienced project managers involved in decommissioning offshore oil and gas platforms, and I recommend it and the tools outlined within the book to anyone working in this field."

David Talbot, FEI
Chief Executive Officer
CATCH UK

"This book is essential reading for project managers involved in decommissioning large and technical structures. The authors introduce the reader to the concepts of quantitative risk management as a way of maximising the social, economic, and environmental outcomes associated with industrial-scale decommissioning. The book, through the use of practical examples, illustrates how applying the latest data modelling techniques combined with Real Options approaches to corporate decision-making processes can lead to quicker and more robust decommissioning decisions. In a nutshell before you take it apart read this first!"

Phil Glover, CQRM
Business Development Manager
Humber Local Enterprise Partnership UK

"This book combines real decommissioning challenges faced by the global O&G industry with a simple yet powerful method of visualising, quantifying, and analysing decommissioning risks and mitigating them using real option assessments. The authors give managers and stakeholder the tools to make smarter decisions when considering the decommissioning challenges by identifying the critical success factors for the desired outcome. There is focus on real options analysis, which gives stakeholders clear visibility of each strategic decision path available to them and the ability to optimise these decisions by combining elements of each path – this is very powerful when considering the potential financial implications of making the wrong decision. The book provides simple examples to illustrate the various real options strategies and how they can be applied to decommissioning strategies. The authors demonstrate the fantastic PEAT-DECOMM software, developed to perform risk-based decommissioning cost analysis of all real options. PEAT (Project Economic Evaluation Tool) makes Monte Carlo simulation easily accessible to all managers via an extremely user-friendly interface. Overall, the book uniquely combines expertise in Oil & Gas project management with successful quantitative risk management tools and techniques that gives readers powerful methods for managing any number of decommissioning challenges."

Jayesh Parekh, CEng, CQRM
Engineering Business Manager
ENGIE Fabricom UK

"A timely book that introduces industry-leading risk management approaches to a new industry: offshore decommissioning. As the sector builds its experiences in offshore decommissioning, we need robust approaches to managing risk and to ensure that we learn from other industries as well as ourselves. Liam, Elvis, and Johnathan share in this book their combined experiences from both hands-on management of offshore decommissioning as well as from other industries to provide us with a solid step towards safer and better implementation. Thanks!"

Martin Bjerregaard, MBA, BSc, MCIWM
Director
D3 Consulting Limited

"Oil and Gas Decommissioning Risk Management gives managers and directors in any industry the tools they require to understand the risks and opportunities associated with achieving an objective in a project. The real options tool allows you to analyse a wide range of variables to make quantitatively backed business decisions. As projects mature, real-world data can be fed in so that an organisation can identify and react quickly to emerging trends. The techniques in this book can be applied to any risk type."

James Bird, CQRM
Senior HSE Manager
KIER Group

CONTENTS

FOREWORD 19

INTRODUCTION 21

CHAPTER 1: DECOMMISSIONING IN A NUTSHELL 25

    PROCESS OF DECOMMISSIONING 26
        Project Management 26
        Engineering and Planning 27
        Permitting 28
        Platform Preparation 29
        Well Plugging and Abandonment 30
        Conductor Pipe Removal 32
        Platform Removal 33
        Pipeline and Power Cable Removal 34
        Materials Disposal and Site Clearance 36
        Monitoring 36
        Final Considerations 36

    REFERENCES 37

CHAPTER 2: DECOMMISSIONING CHALLENGES 39

    ASSET INTEGRITY 39

    WELL PLUGGING AND ABANDONMENT 42

    INFORMATION MANAGEMENT 43

    HEALTH, SAFETY, AND THE ENVIRONMENT 44

    OPTION AWARENESS 44

SUPPLY CHAIN MANAGEMENT VS. TALENT
MANAGEMENT 45

REFERENCES 46

CHAPTER 3: DECOMMISSIONING STAKEHOLDERS AND DECISION MAKERS 47

INTERNAL STAKEHOLDERS IN
DECOMMISSIONING 49
  Senior Leadership Team (Directors/Board) 49
  Project Team 50

EXTERNAL STAKEHOLDERS IN
DECOMMISSIONING 52

ENGAGEMENT WITH STAKEHOLDERS IN
DECOMMISSIONING 56

REFERENCES 57

CHAPTER 4: RISK MANAGEMENT AND STRATEGIC OPTIONS 59

WHY IS RISK MPORTANT IN MAKING DECISIONS? 60

DEALING WITH RISK THE OLD-FASHIONED WAY 63

WHAT ARE STRATEGIC REAL OPTIONS? 67
  The Real Options Solution in a Nutshell 69
  Issues to Consider 70

IMPLEMENTING REAL OPTIONS ANALYSIS 72

TYPES OF REAL OPTIONS STRATEGIES 74

EXECUTION TYPES 77

INDUSTRY LEADERS EMBRACING REAL OPTIONS 78

Expansion and Compound Options: The Case of an Asset Integrity System 83
Expansion and Switching Options: The Case of the Oil and Gas Exploration and Production 86
Abandonment Options: The Case of the Manufacturer of Oil and Gas Vessels and Equipment 88
CONSIDERATIONS WHEN IMPLEMENTING REAL OPTIONS VALUATIONS 90

FINAL COMMENTS 91

REFERENCES 92

CHAPTER 5: RISK-BASED STRATEGIC DECISIONS IN DECOMMISSIONING 93

DECOMMISSIONING STRATEGIES 94
Timing in Decommissioning Strategies 94
Conventional Decommissioning Strategies 96
Emerging Decommissioning Strategies 100
Emerging Decommissioning Strategies and Real Options 105

ACCOUNTING AND AUDITING IN DECOMMISSIONING 107
Measuring and Recognising Decommissioning Provisions 107
Depreciation Analysis and Residual Value 111
Capital Allowances, Taxes, and Decommissioning Reliefs 115
Auditing Decommissioning Costs 117

RISK-BASED ANALYSIS IN DECOMMISSIONING 119
Decommissioning Costs 120
Residual Value 122

HANDS-ON PEAT-DECOMM FOR PROJECT
VALUATIONS 124

Quick Interpretation of Some Economic
Measures 125
Navigating PEAT-DECOMM Software for
Project Valuations 126

DECOMMISSIONING STRATEGIES — RISK AND
LEARNING 142

REFERENCES 143

CHAPTER 6: PROJECT RISK MANAGEMENT IN DECOMMISSIONING 145

TRADITIONAL PROJECT MANAGEMENT IN
DECOMMISSIONING 146

Traditional Schedule Management 146
Traditional Cost Management 149

MODERN PROJECT RISK MANAGEMENT IN
DECOMMISSIONING 151

Schedule and Cost Risk Modeling 151
Monte Carlo Simulations and Risk Profiles 153

HANDS-ON PEAT PROJECT MANAGEMENT 154

Projects with Complex Tasks and Critical Path 155
Applied Analytics: Tornado Analysis 157
Applied Analytics: Scenario Analysis 157
Risk Identification and Risk Quantification 158
Risk Simulation: Risk Profile 167
Risk Simulation: Sensitivity Analysis 168

DECOMMISSIONING PROJECT STRATEGIES,
CONTROL, AND MONITORING 174

Strategies and Critical Path 174
Control and Monitoring 175

DECOMMISSIONING RISK AND LEARNING................... 186

REFERENCES.. 187

CHAPTER 7: ENTERPRISE RISK MANAGEMENT IN DECOMMISSIONING 189

APPLYING ERM IN DECOMMISSIONING 191

COMPREHENSIVE QUANTITATIVE ERM 192

HANDS-ON ENTERPRISE RISK MANAGEMENT MODELING 193
- Global Settings (Risk Classifications) 193
- Risk Groups (Segmentation and Taxonomy) 194
- Risk Mapping (Risk Structure) 194
- Risk Registers 199
- Risk Dashboards 200

HANDS-ON PEAT-DECOMM FOR ENTERPRISE RISK MANAGEMENT 208
- Applied Analytics: Tornado Analysis 208
- Applied Analytics: Scenario Analysis 209
- Risk Simulation (Risk Profile) 215
- Risk Simulation (Sensitivity Analysis) 216

INTEGRATED RISK MANAGEMENT AND DECISION SUPPORT 228

REFERENCES 230

APPENDIX: PROJECT VALUATION 231

NET PRESENT VALUE 234

INTERNAL RATE OF RETURN 234

MODIFIED INTERNAL RATE OF RETURN 235

PROFITABILITY INDEX 236

PAYBACK PERIOD 236

DISCOUNTED PAYBACK PERIOD 237

EXAMPLE COMPUTATIONS 237
    Payback Period (PP) 237
    Discounted Payback Period (DPP) 239
    Net Present Value (NPV) 241
    Internal Rate of Return (IRR) 243
    Modified Internal Rate of Return (MIRR) 246
    Profitability Index and Return on Investment
    (PI and ROI) 247

GLOSSARY 251

SOFTWARE DOWNLOAD & INSTALLATION 255

INDEX 261

FOREWORD

Oil and Gas Decommissioning was inspired by the authors who worked together on a UK North Sea decommissioning project where they undertook a rigorous and structured approach to assessing the risks involving safety and technical uncertainty associated with aged as-sets. This uncertainty is what ultimately impacts the schedule and the cost of decommissioning. Their realisation of the benefits of the approach to reduce risk and save cost lead them to document and share their collective knowledge on this important topic. In addition to describing all of the elements, stakeholders, and decision makers involved in decommissioning, this book introduces techniques, methodologies, and processes to promote better under-standing of the decommissioning process and of quantifying the risks associated with working in hazardous environments such as those surrounding the decommissioning work. It is also intended to help decision makers understand the technical risks and the impact they may have on the schedule and, ultimately, the cost of decommissioning. Managing these risks effectively is an important factor in minimising the overall spending, which is, after all, a sunk cost to the business. Having documented their first-hand knowledge as well as reference material, the authors have used supporting software tools to dynamically quantify the impact of the identified risks, giving organisations the ability to maintain safety and mitigate risks to cost and schedule. They have highlighted the benefits of the approach in being able to understand the subtleties of the individual project. The book provides guidance on where to focus resources, what key decisions will need to be taken, what information and options are available to the decision maker, and when to make the decisions.

Because decommissioning projects are highly risky (cash and liquidity constraints, capital expenditure uncertainties, and health and safety considerations), and they have high volatility (budget, schedule, operational costs), the value of incorporating real options analysis into the process cannot be underestimated. Real options, integrated into a proper risk management process, helps agile decision makers to create and obtain better decommissioning strategies while enhancing company performance value, reducing the downside risk, and taking advantage of the upside uncertainties. Overall, *Oil and Gas Decommissioning* provides an excellent over-view of the risks involved in decommissioning projects and how they can be managed. In addition, the references cited provide a helpful list of supporting information for the reader to gain a full understanding of offshore decommissioning, as well as its extrapolation to other industries (nuclear, chemicals, petrochemicals, renewables, marine, manufacture, mining, etc.).

Alastair Robertson, BSc (ChemEng), FIChemE, MEI, MIoD, CQRM
Managing Director of OSL Consulting Engineers
Chairman of OSL Risk Management LTD (UK)

INTRODUCTION

This introduction was written by Alastair Robertson, Managing Director of OSL Consulting Engineers and Chairman of OSL Risk Management. He has a BSc (Hons) in Chemical and Process Engineering from Heriot Watt University and became a chartered engineer in 1994. Since then he became a Fellow of the Institute of Chemical Engineers in 2001, a Fellow of the Energy Institute in 2019, Trustee of the Energy Institute, and CQRM in 2019. He has over 30 years of experience in the gas and oil processing industry. He has an in-depth knowledge of the gas production business, having worked as a consultant for most of the gas producing companies in the UKCS. Alastair uses his knowledge and experience to provide clients with implemented solutions to a variety of challenges in their businesses (feasibility studies, design, construction, engineering, commissioning, and decommissioning).

When offshore structures, such as oil and gas platforms and wind turbines, reach the end of their lifecycles, they need to be removed from service—decommissioned—with minimal risk to safety and the environment, organisational reputation, cost, and schedule. As the oil and gas industry, in particular, starts to reach its end of life, decommissioning is only becoming a larger industry on a worldwide scale. At the time of this book, there are approximately 170 installations, 10,000 km of pipeline, and 5,000 wells within the North Sea alone.

Decommissioning is not only a concern for the UK; it is also an activity that must be carried out by the rest of Europe, the USA, Latin America, Africa, and Asia. While such global activity implies large cash and liquidity commitments, decommissioning presents significant opportunities in a number of areas.. for example; operating cost reduction, reduction of liability for damages to people and the environment, decarbonisation, acquisition of transferable skills, new integrated energy projects, innovation, and a competitive advantage to those who undertake it most efficiently.

Decommissioning of an offshore oil and gas asset is a long and complex process that involves the safe disposal of the production equipment and support structure as well as the safe isolation of the hydrocarbons within the earth's surface. The ultimate goal of this final stage of a project's life cycle is to return the ocean and seabed floor back to its original, natural condition (Briggs et al., 1997).

Before introducing the risk management topics in its later chapters, the book begins by describing the various activities that make up a decommissioning project. It sets the scene of where to look for uncertainty within the process and lists the standard stages or macro-activities that map the scope of work. It goes on to describe the elements and techniques involved within project management, engineering planning, permitting, platform preparations, well plugging and abandonment, platform removal, materials disposal, and ongoing monitoring. The chapter includes a number of industry references and guidance notes that have already been developed for specific parts of decommissioning, most of which are from the Oil and Gas UK. These give the reader additional information on which to develop their project strategy, as well as technical options and methods involved in physically sealing, abandoning, and removing a platform's infrastructure and pipelines..

Chapter 2 looks at the high-level decommissioning challenges, including asset integrity; well plug and abandonment; information management; health, safety, and environment concerns; option awareness; and supply chain versus talent management. The authors point out that since no two projects will be the same, the impact of these challenges will be different in each case and, so, will need to be assessed carefully. In this chapter they describe the nature of the challenge and ways in which they may be overcome. Option awareness will be of particular interest because of the how the industry is evolving to find new and better ways to undertake different parts of a decommissioning project. Having an option selection process and the tools to make informed decisions allows the decision makers to take advantage of new technology on an informed basis (see in chapters 4, 5, and 6 for more details).

In any project, making decisions in a timely and effective manner is a key element of ensuring that the project achieves its objectives within the timescales and budgets that are set. Chapter 3 talks about the types of stakeholders and decision makers that are involved in a decommissioning project and the importance of their engagement throughout the lifecycle so that when a decision needs to be made quickly, it is done with the correct information and with the right level of authority. The chapter begins with internal stakeholders and the different levels of information they need and at what stage. It goes on to discuss the project leaders as well as the typical team makeup and how and where certain types of decision can be made. Then it lists all of the many external stakeholders that need to be informed throughout the process from initial planning to final implementation and ongoing monitoring, and describes their area of influence, as well as gives some guidance as to how they should be managed. Finally, the chapter concludes with some guidance and ideas on ways in which to engage with stakeholders; for example, planning activities, checklists, and some website references. This chapter is particularly helpful in providing a basis for the reader in developing a communication and managerial plan for their project.

Within the context of Chapter 4, the concept of risk, which can have a wide range of meanings to many people, is narrowed down to a small niche, namely, applied business risk modelling and analytics, including real options analysis, that can be used when planning decommissioning activities. The chapter focuses on the introduction of risk management in the sense of how to adequately apply the tools to identify, understand, quantify, and diversify risk such that it can be hedged and managed more effectively. With this in mind, the chapter includes a review of the basics of real options as a paradigm shift in the way of thinking about and evaluating emerging strategies around decommissioning projects. It goes on to explain why real options are important and attempts to demystify the concept of real options and how they can be applied in support of effective decision making. The final part of the chapter provides a number of case studies that document where industry leaders have adopted the use of real options. Such examples illustrate that, when real options are implemented, they provide value in reducing the impact of unfavorable outcomes or actions and improving the chances of achieving a successful outcome (i.e., similar to putting contingency plans in place).

Building on Chapter 4, Chapter 5 presents some decommissioning strategies and economic/financial aspects for managers and decision makers. It touches on topics such as accounting, auditing, taxes, project valuations, scenarios analysis, financial guidelines, strategic options, and hands-on risk modeling. The chapter not only covers the more conventional decommissioning options, it also presents emerging strategies that exist for late-life field extension that may be possible for the particular asset. Finally, Chapter 5 introduces the financial and economic perspectives of decommissioning, using an advanced decision analytics and risk management tool, centralized in the PEAT-DECOMM software.

Chapter 6 covers project risk management in decommissioning, describing in simple terms the use of the tools to identify and model the impact of uncertainty sources and risk factors on project schedule, cost, and safety. To increase the odds of completing a project safely, on time, and on budget, this chapter provides decision makers with two complementary decision-making procedures. Firstly, it discusses the need for decision makers, managers, and work teams to understand project networks, interrelations among activities, project flexibility, alternative strategies, contingencies plans, team integration and leadership, and the value of communication. Secondly, it talks about the tools available to carry out an analysis, which includes a reliance on Monte Carlo simulations, tornado analysis, sensitivity charts, and other advanced analytics to quantify and manage project risks. These techniques and methodologies al-low decision makers to analyse how fluctuations of relevant project variables (activities, costs drivers, schedule implications) might impact on the project schedule and cost. This information, in turn, allows the project team to target critical activities for both linear and complex paths with the aim of minimising the risk of overrunning or overspending, essential criteria for examining how well a project or well P&A activity is performing. The chapter concludes with how to use the outputs in support of the decommissioning decision making process. Where Chapter 5 presents the use of the PEAT-DECOMM software to support financial decisions in decommissioning; in Chapter 6, the project management (PM) version of this technology is implemented to demonstrate the dynamics of project risk management regarding cost and schedule.

The final chapter presents the use of Enterprise Risk Management tools in capturing organisational knowledge as part of an Integrated Risk Management approach to decommissioning. It discusses the ERM process, which mostly involves a qualitative assessment and risk register analysis. These risk registers preliminarily record and categorise different types of risk, which then allows the project team and managers to quickly quantify, analyse, and mitigate risk with more efficiency and efficacy. The chapter goes on to describe the quantitative methods used within ERM. Finally, it introduces the risk management solution called PEAT-DECOMM (ERM), which is used to implement an Integrated Risk Management approach in well P&A. This decision analytics tool has been developed specifically for quantitative risk management in decommissioning and well plugging and abandonment, but it can also be used for regular feasibility studies, project valuations, and project analysis on construction, engineering, procurement, and commissioning.

Lastly, the Appendix provides a sound explanation of the traditional project evaluation methods currently in use.

CHAPTER 1: DECOMMISSIONING IN A NUTSHELL

When offshore structures, such as oil and gas platforms and wind turbines, reach the end of their life cycles, they need to be removed from service—decommissioned—with minimal risk to cost, schedule, reputation, safety, and the environment. As the oil and gas industry, in particular, starts to reach its end of life, decommissioning is only becoming a larger industry on a worldwide scale. At the time of writing, there are approximately 170 installations, 10,000 km of pipeline, and 5,000 wells within the North Sea alone. It is estimated, for example, that between 2016 and 2021, 600 installations will have to be decommissioned globally due to approaching the end of their operational lives. The Offshore Decommissioning Study Report commissioned by the IHS Markit states that in 2015, spending on decommissioning projects was approximately $2.4 billion and will reach $13 billion per year by 2040. That is an increase of 540% in just 25 years. (For further information, trends, and insights, see the Oil and Gas UK's decommissioning reports [OGUK, 2018b, 2019].)

Generally a legal requirement (see, e.g., the UK's "Petroleum Act 1998" and see http://www.legislation.gov.uk/ukpga/1998/17/contents for more information), decommissioning is not only a concern for the UK; it is also an activity that must be carried out by the rest of Europe, the USA, Latin America, Africa, and Asia. And while such global activity implies large cash and liquidity commitments, decommissioning presents significant opportunities for operating cost reduction, reduction of liability for damages to people and the environment, decarbonisation, acquisition of transferable skills, new integrated energy projects, innovation, and a competitive advantage (Oil and Gas Authority, n.d.) to those who undertake it most efficiently. All oil and gas platforms are installed by their owners to extract the hydrocarbons from reservoirs below the earth's surface. The asset will have been designed to perform over a set period of time, believed to be long enough to extract the reserves within that given sector or block. As the reservoirs become depleted and less hydrocarbon product is being extracted, it becomes less cost efficient to continue to operate that asset, triggering its end of life process and, ultimately, final decommissioning.

Decommissioning of an offshore oil and gas asset is a long and complex process that involves the safe disposal of the production equipment platform as well as the safe isolation of the hydrocarbons within the earth's surface. Depending on the type of asset in question, there might also be other subsea equipment to remove, for example, pipelines and associated items, power cables, manifolds, mattresses, etc. The ultimate goal of this final stage of a project's life cycle is to return the ocean and seabed floor back to their original, or natural, pre-lease condition (Briggs et al., 1997).

PROCESS OF DECOMMISSIONING

Traditional decommissioning of an oil- or gas-well offshore asset typically starts with a standard list of stages or macro-activities to map the scope of work (i.e., project management, engineering planning, permitting, platform preparations, well plugging and abandonment, platform removal, and so forth). This section provides a general overview of these macro-activities. For further information, see the Oil and Gas UK's well decommissioning guidelines to support decision makers and well operators (OGUK, 2018a).

Project Management

Generally, the decommissioning process should start three to five years before the end of production of an asset, but this can be both shorter or longer to suit the schedule and depending on the size of the asset and the organisation's work team. A decommissioning programme needs to be created, which is the main document for a decommissioning project and the one sent to the regulators for review and approval. Other key decommissioning documents that should be completed and could assist in the construction of the decommissioning programme include but are not limited to:

- Decommissioning Roadmap
- Supply Chain Communication Flowchart and Policy
- Waste Management Plan
- PLANC (Permits, Licences, Authorisations, Notifications, and Consents) Report
- Active Waste Management Plan
- Comparative Pipeline Assessment
- Comparative Subsea Cable/Equipment Assessment
- Execution Cost Estimate
- Project Schedule
- Project Execution Plan
- Environmental and Decommissioning Approval Strategy

Other key activities to complete within this stage are any contractual obligations with leases that must be followed up for ending agreements, and the required regulatory bodies need to be informed via the correct procedures. An example of this sort of activity is the completion of a Cessation of Production (COP).

Given the size of a decommissioning project, financing needs to be organised in advance due to the large amount funds required. The finances should be planned as per the business procedure, either full release or stage release of funds, to suit the organisation's project management process.

Contracting firms should be engaged at this early stage due to the resources required in specialist trades and equipment to suit the decommissioning market.

Engineering and Planning

The engineering stage of the project is deemed the most important; if any element of decommissioning is engineered incorrectly, the risk when completing the work offshore could lead to catastrophic results to people, the plant, and the environment. All engineering needs to be completed up to construction "work packs" to suit each individual task throughout the decommissioning. The main documents prepared during this stage would be a full suite of construction work packs with construction work risk assessments, method statements, and job cards. Other key decommissioning documents that should be completed during this stage include but are not limited to:

- Offshore Surveys Reports
- Offshore Waste Sampling Reports
- Topside Removal Report
- Detailed Design Packs for All Works
- Jacket Heavy Lift and Transportation Study Report
- Well P&A Detailed Design with Proposed Montages
- Well Programmes for P&A
- Subsea Inspections Reports
- Baseline Survey Report
- Environmental Report

The schedule needs to be well planned out within this stage, as any delays or issues during construction will lead to the risk of overspending and schedule overruns. The project team should decide, via risk analysis models, how much risk to apply to the schedule, including weather risk. Given the nature and location of the decommissioning project, weather can have a significant impact on work to be performed. This risk assessment would be completed as per the organisation's scheduling and risk management process.

Permitting

A decommissioning project must adhere to numerous legal and regulatory factors, including multiple regulatory bodies all requiring different permitting or documentation to suit the work scope. In addition, different local laws will apply depending on the location of the asset. For example, assets in the North Sea (UK) are subject to the Petroleum Act of 1998. All permitting and legal and regulatory documentation should be included in the project's decommissioning programme document.

No work should be undertaken by an organisation without the correct permitting in place, or it risks having legal action taken against it, which will lead to further cost overspending, schedule overruns, reputational issues, and, in extreme cases, a project being shut down for a period of time. A critical note to remember is that many regulatory bodies require a review period of 6 months. Some may be able to turn around the review period more quickly, but this is not a given or the norm, so companies should factor the correct review/approval periods into their schedules.

Platform Preparation

Before any asset can be removed, it must be prepared for the heavy lift/removal activities. The main preparation activities include, but are not limited to, the following:

- Deep clean of all the topside equipment to remove any hydrocarbon that may still be left on the asset. This includes a flush clean (generally to 30 ppm oil in water is a more recent common limit used but not a legal standard) of all pipes, tanks, and other process equipment that will have seen hydrocarbons throughout the life of the asset. This cleaning would also assist the organisation in limiting its ongoing inspections and maintenance regime.

- Installation of lifting points and aids specifically designed to suit the asset. These can be lifting eyes for the rigging equipment to attach to and structural strengthening or reinforcement support beams if the platform requires them as per the structural analysis in the detailed design. These can also include reusing the existing lifting points if they are still available and accessible and pass the required inspections.

- Dismantling or disconnection of nonrequired equipment such as anything topside no longer needed for the end of life operations. Module splitting would fall into this category, as well as electrical and utilities disconnection provided that the equipment has been deep cleaned. Again, this element of the decommissioning work can assist the organisation in limiting its ongoing inspections and maintenance regimes on the modules or systems.

- Sea line preparations, including deep cleaning via pigging methods or flushing, especially if the pipeline is being left *in situ*, i.e., filled with treated sea water. The sea line should only be worked on if there is no further use for it to avoid contaminating it with hydrocarbons and having to complete the process again. If leaving pipelines *in situ*, the organisation must complete a pipeline assessment and apply for a permit to leave them on the seabed.

- Removal of loose items not required for the future use of the asset. Aging assets normally store a lot of loose items such paperwork, desks, computers, fridges, gym equipment, and so on. These need to be removed, affixed, or stored in a safe manner prior to heavy lifting as they will act like large marbles that could move around during final lifting, causing damage and possibly leading to the lift failing.

Depending on the type of asset, there could be other preparation tasks that could be completed before the arrival of a heavy-lift vessel. Every day the heavy-lift vessel sits beside the asset costs money. So, it is at this stage that completing as much preparation work as possible would be the most cost effective.

Well Plugging and Abandonment

Generally, well plugging and abandonment (P&A) is one of the highest risks in terms of safety, environment, cost, and schedule. Completing this stage is important for ensuring that no well fluids, including hydrocarbons, can resurface once the asset has been removed. The liability of abandoned wells stays with the operator of the field (see Chapter 5 for details on recognising decommissioning liabilities). This is the main element of any decommissioning project, and the traditional method for completing it is via a jack-up mobile offshore drilling unit (MODU). While there are other methods, such as rigless, to complete well P&A, the traditional method is seen as the most effective for the type of asset referenced within this publication.

A general vertical well P&A activity list is divided into four phases:

- Phase 1 – the preparation phase in which the well's operation is suspended. It consists of:
    - Retrieving the tubing hanger plugs/safety valve.
    - Installing a deep-set mechanical plug.

- Perforating the tubing.
- Circulating kill weight fluid through the tubing/annulus to remove any contaminated fluid.

- Phase 2 – the reservoir isolation or abandonment phase. It consists of:
  - Rigging up the drill rig with BOP (blowout preventers) and completing the required testing of this kit.
  - Removal of the tubing hanger and tubing.
  - Installing the primary barrier to the reservoir.
  - Installing a secondary barrier to the reservoir.

  The location of the barriers must be identified within the well P&A design, on the schematic. Note that in some instances, remedial cement work may be required behind the casing to meet OGA guidelines.

- Phase 3 – the final phase of the actual isolating/abandonment where upon completion the well is classified as fully isolated. This phase consists of:
  - Removing the casing strings.
  - Installing barriers to other potential flow zones. The location of these barriers must be identified within the well P&A design, on the schematic. There might be a number of these barriers depending on the number of flow zones, rock formations, and other factors.
  - Installing an environmental barrier, also known as a surface plug. This is the final plug. Note that in some instances, this plug may not be required but study work and approvals from the regulators would be needed to allow this barrier to be omitted.

- Phase 4 – the final recovery phase in which the remaining well infrastructure is recovered for disposal. It consists of:
  - Well head removal.
  - Conductor removal.

Figure 1.1 provides an example of an offshore production well before and after P&A, showing the rock zones, reservoir, main configuration, and different levels of cement and mechanical retaining plug. Note especially the primary and secondary barriers towards potential flow zones and reservoirs. Also note that all elements above the seabed levels need to be removed.

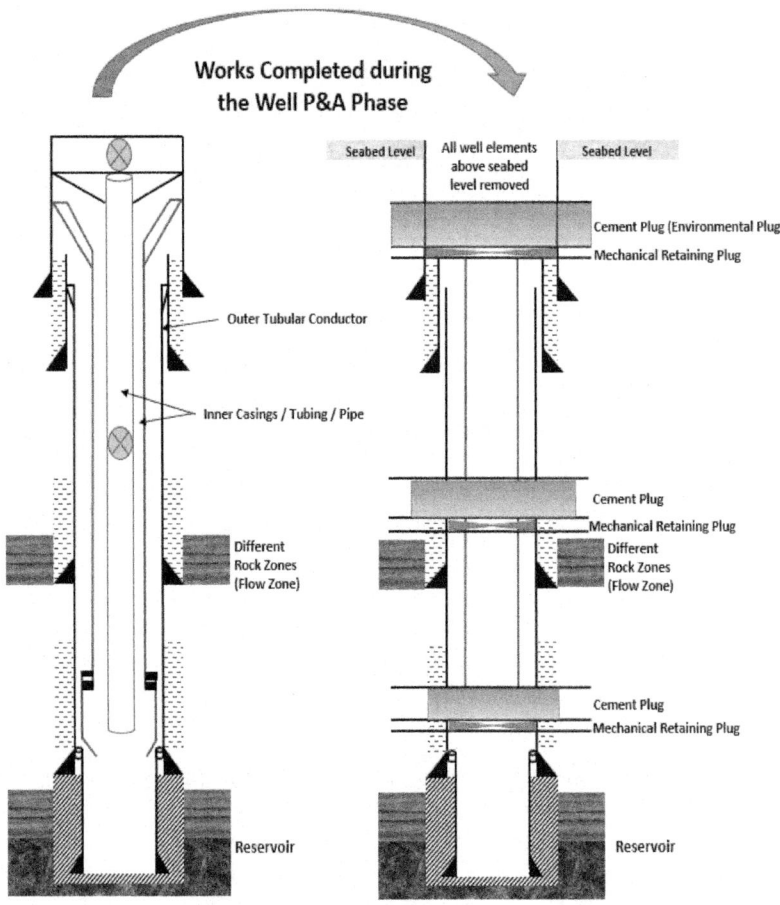

Figure 1.1: Simplified Offshore Well Before and After P&A (Adapted from Vrålstad et al., 2019)

Conductor Pipe Removal

The conductor pipe is the main structure of an oil or gas well between the asset and the seabed. This pipe and its associated casings must be removed to a minimum of 10 feet below the seabed level, as per the current OGA guidelines, unless consent is given from a local regulatory body to differ from this standard. (If applying for a consent, the operating company should allow for this review period in its schedule.) Such consent is not a given, though, and the norm is to remove 10 feet below the seabed level.

The main reason for completing this stage is to ensure that the casings do not interfere with marine activities and to meet the requirements of the license, which normally states that the seabed should be returned to its original condition, prior to any development work having taken place.

The traditional procedure is to sever the casings into 40-foot sections and remove them for disposal. Methods for severing the casing include but are not limited to:

- Explosives
- ID Cutters
- Diamond Wire Cutter
- Abrasives
- Hand Cutting (Hot or Cold)

Platform Removal

The method in which a platform is removed will be detailed in the decommissioning programme and will have gone through many checks during the engineering phase. A heavy-lift barge will have been chartered to suit the lift size and weights, plus a safety factor. With every asset being different in size, weight, and center of gravity, the lifting methods will differ accordingly.

The most common method, if possible, is reverse construction, where the modules are removed in the reverse order in which they were installed.

Smaller assets can be removed in a single lift given the advanced lifting barges within the current market. Needing fewer lifts generally saves time and cost due to a reduced heavy-lift barge hire period, while also reducing any risk to people, the plant, and the environment. Figure 1.2 illustrates the lifting process from a barge, which is a preprocess requiring controlling and monitoring environmental and ocean risks (wind, movements, tides, levels, water density differences, weather conditions, etc.).

Pipeline and Power Cable Removal

By completing a comparative risk assessment, an organisation can apply to local regulatory bodies to leave pipelines (with associated structures) and power cables in place that are generally not seen to pose an environmental hazard or to interfere with any sea traffic within the area. These items should be left in a safe and cleaned state as agreed to within the consent. It is now deemed in certain areas that removal of a pipeline could cause more damage to the seabed's micro-environment that could have formed over the years around the line. The assessment would clearly identify the pipeline's configuration on the seabed (Figure 1.3), as that would affect its removal method and amount of damage to the seabed according to corrosion, migration, inspection, and asset integrity information. OGUK (2013) offers generic information on pipeline configuration on the seabed.

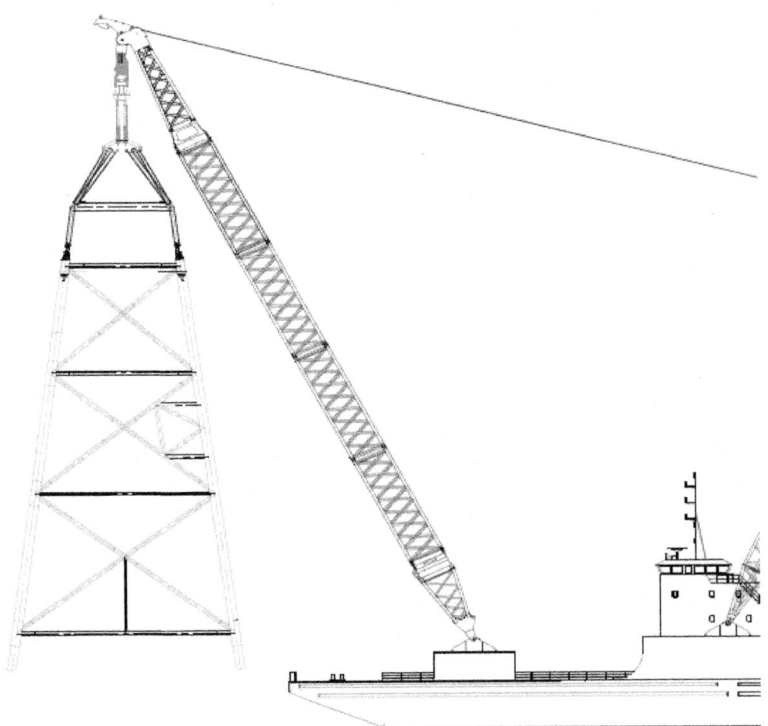

Figure 1.2: Heavy-Lift Vessel Lifting a Jacket Structure

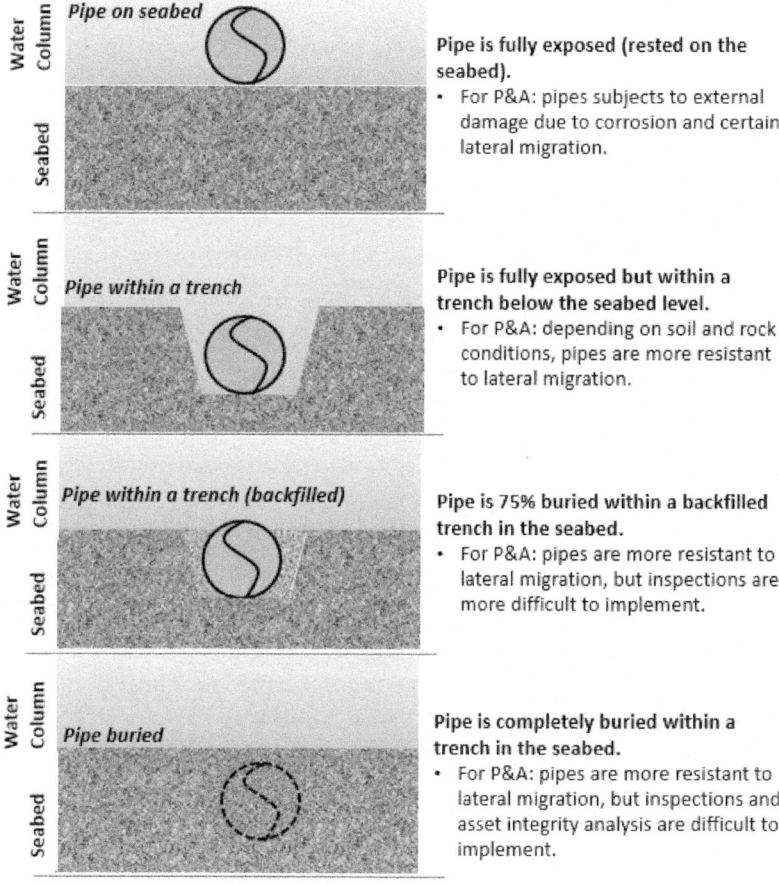

Figure 1.3: Seabed Pipeline Configurations
(Adapted from rom OGUK, 2013)

If an organisation does not have consent to leave in place, then these items must be removed as per the agreed method within the decommissioning programme. Methods of pipeline removal include but are not limited to:

- Reverse reeling of pipeline
- Reverse S-lay of pipeline
- Cut and lift of the pipeline in smaller sections

Materials Disposal and Site Clearance

Generally, all waste items from the asset, including the platform itself, will be transported to an agreed upon disposal site onshore. Once onshore, the asset will be lifted off any transport vessel and disposed of via recycling or waste, as per the active waste disposal plan within the decommissioning programme. Some assets might be reused in other areas of the world if they still hold some value or, if permission is given, they can be used as artificial reefs.

Some items might have a sell on value or scrap value. For example, old well heads might be able to be refurbished and sold on as spares as fewer of these aging components are available on the market due to technological advancements. Other package items such as instrument air packages, generators, and cranes can be sold on as a stand-alone package. Once all items are believed to have been removed, the site must be scanned using a survey vessel that will highlight any debris left on the seabed that must be removed. The area must be left in a natural state as per its pre-lease conditions.

Monitoring

If any items have been left in position, further monitoring may be required to ensure they do not cause a nuisance to sea traffic or an environmental hazard in the future. A general rule is that all pipelines left in position should be monitored for at least 10 years or for a period in which the operator can prove no change in its condition. If for any reason an issue arises with an item left in position, it remains the organisation's responsibility to correct the issue.

Final Considerations

Although the decommissioning strategy could start between three to five years before the end-life of an oil and gas asset, lessons learned from the nuclear industry indicate that it should initiate as the project concept, engineering, and construction start. Early planning and monitoring provide asset operators the ability to adapt to market changes quickly. For instance, strategically, they can take advantage of technological developments, business opportunities (e.g., reuse of assets), and regulatory environments.

Finally, agile asset's operators can better manage decommissioning risks (e.g., schedule, costs, health, safety), estimate financial and non-financial needs, evaluate potential lifting/cutting and mobilisation/demobilisation strategies, and engage in new options for site clearance and land remediation, among other activities described in the process of decommissioning.

REFERENCES

Briggs, M., Buck, S., & Smith, M. (1997). *Decommissioning, Mothballing, and Revamping*. IChemE Press.

OGUK. (2013). Decommissioning of Pipelines in the North Sea Region. Retrieved October 14, 2019, from https://oilandgasuk.co.uk/wp-content/uploads/2019/05/OGUK-Guidelines-on-Decommissioning-of-Pipelines-in-the-North-Sea-Region-Issue-1.pdf

OGUK. (2018a). Well Decommissioning Guidelines Issue 6. https://oilandgasuk.co.uk/product/well-decommissioning-guidelines/

OGUK. (2018b). Decommissioning Insights 2018. Retrieved November 14, 2019, from https://oilandgasuk.co.uk/wp-content/uploads/2019/05/OGUK-Guidelines-on-Decommissioning-of-Pipelines-in-the-North-Sea-Region-Issue-1.pdf

OGUK. (2019). Decommissioning Insights 2019. Retrieved November 14, 2019, from https://oilandgasuk.co.uk/wp-content/uploads/2019/05/OGUK-Guidelines-on-Decommissioning-of-Pipelines-in-the-North-Sea-Region-Issue-1.pdf

Oil and Gas Authority. (n.d.). Decommissioning. Retrieved from https://www.ogauthority.co.uk/decommissioning

Vrålstad, T., Saasen, A., Fjær, E., Øia, T., Ytrehus, J. D., & Khalifeh, M. (2019). Plug & abandonment of offshore wells: Ensuring long-term well integrity and cost-efficiency. *Journal of Petroleum Science and Engineering, 173*, 478–491.

CHAPTER 2: DECOMMISSIONING CHALLENGES

Large decommissioning projects of offshore assets come with many challenges that potentially carry a lot of risk in terms of safety, cost, schedule, the environment, and the organisation's reputation. One key challenge is that no two assets are the same, so each decommissioning task must be designed and engineered for the specific project. Given the complexity, age, and location of the assets, decommissioning them is time consuming and inherently hazardous. Because of various economic and environmental pressures, these large decommissioning projects are not only inevitable but essential, and therefore the challenges must be considered carefully. This chapter looks at some high-level decommissioning challenges.

It is worth noting, however, that not all decommissioning challenges are negative; some can be viewed as positive in affording opportunities for reducing costs and liability, acquiring transferable skills, fostering innovation, and providing a competitive advantage within the industry.

ASSET INTEGRITY

As these assets are reaching their end of life, some of them have been exposed to the elements at sea for nearly 30 years. This exposure can lead to higher than normal corrosion rates on the structural steelwork (Molnár et al., 2017) resulting in structural fatigue. In particular, the jackets that are predominately under water can pose a higher-level issue because the effect of corrosion is unknown, and the high level of marine growth adds an additional integrity factor.

The challenge with asset integrity is that the asset is now going to be lifted out of its standing position and transported for disposal. If the asset's integrity is compromised, making it unsafe for lifting, then the asset could fold in on itself when being lifted, causing several highly hazardous situations. The risk here involves all the key elements of a successful project: personnel and environmental safety issues, cost and schedule overruns, and global reputational damage.

To deal with the challenges concerning asset integrity, the following measures can be taken:

- Inspections – Inspection of the structure should be undertaken offshore as per the company's inspection maintenance routine. Pre-decommissioning, it is advisable to perform an inspection again to determine the corrosion rate losses and the remaining structural load capability. Inspections should be focused around the high stress points of the lift as well to ensure the base model is known. Based on these inspections, additional new structural steelwork/supports may need to be installed to strengthen the asset.

- Models – 3D models of an asset can be generated that can have structural data applied to them (see Figure 2.1 for an example). This model will allow the user to focus on key fatigue points from the lifts during a computer-based simulation.

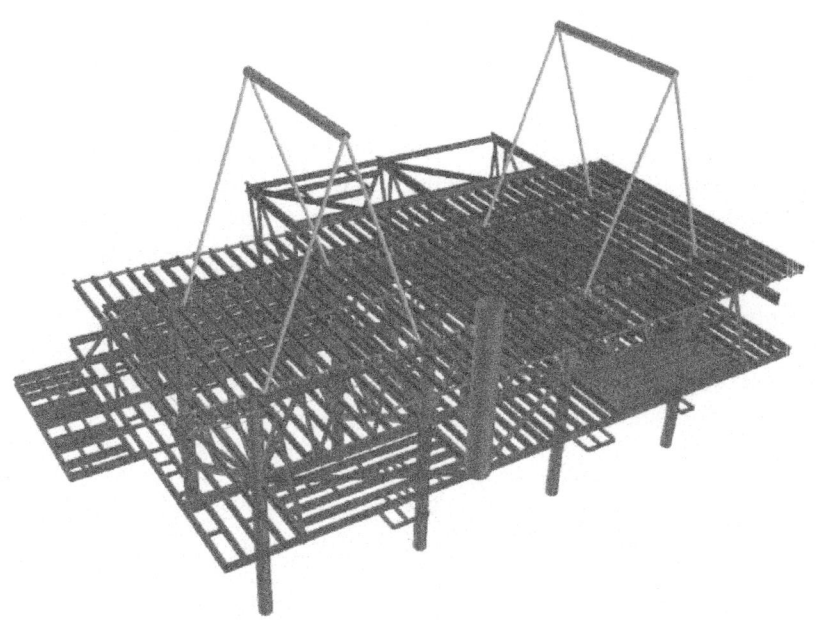

Figure 2.1: Example 3D Model Simulated Lift of a Topside

- Simulations – Depending on the contract being used to undertake the decommissioning, some decommissioning firms on the market run high-tech simulations on a large computer system. This way, the company can run various simulations to the point of failure, all in the safety of the office, to understand how the asset will act once lifted under certain conditions.

- Overapply operational risk – During heavy lifting there will be a safety factor or percentage added to the safe load of the lift and the main joints. A company can choose to increase the safety factor to a higher number to allow more fail space. This approach may lead to additional structural support being required but with less risk of it failing. This is a risk versus cost decision for the organisation to make.

WELL PLUGGING AND ABANDONMENT

It is generally believed that the well plugging and abandonment phase of a decommissioning project poses the highest risk and the most challenges primarily due to the nature of the equipment being worked on, the length of time needed to complete the work, and the daily cost involved. Also, information on aging assets that can be 30 plus years old since they were first drilled can be missing or inaccurate (see the following section on Information Management). Likewise, recent and current down well data runs are needed by the well's engineering team to more accurately complete the required work scope during the P&A campaign and to meet current regulatory and environmental standards. The risk for an operator of not knowing the well bore conditions could be a costly one as the daily hire of the equipment required is extremely high. This information issue also carries a large safety and environmental risk (Day & Gusmitta, 2016).

For example, a common issue is not knowing the cement conditions behind the casing. During detailed well P&A design, an organisation would have to decide on the best method to deal with this issue. Once the tubing has been recovered and the well bore cleaned out with fresh kill weight fluid, a logging run with a cement bond logging (CBL) tool would be performed to establish the condition of the cement behind the casing in the depth where the proposed primary reservoir abandonment plug is to be set. If it is deemed after analysis that there is sufficient cement present to satisfy the OGA guidelines, then the primary abandonment plug can be set. If, however, it is deemed that there is insufficient cement present behind the casing, then the operator will have to do some remedial cementation work to be able to isolate the reservoir to the correct standard.

There are several ways to accomplish this remedial work, including, but not limited to, section milling and, more recently, perf-and-wash cementing. Section milling involves running in hole (RIH) with a set of knives that will mill away the casing across a set depth range of 100 to 200 feet depending on the abandonment plug type, giving access to the formation behind the casing. The debris is continuously removed during the process, and the well is left with clean fluid for the cement plug to be pumped into. If required, a second set of knives can be RIH with a larger cutting arc to mill the window into a second larger casing before the cement plug is pumped.

Perf-and-wash cementing systems are a new technology in the market and have shown considerable time and cost savings over the traditional section milling approach detailed previously. The systems consist of a set of tubing-conveyed perforating (TCP) guns and a cement wash/spray system that enables the placement of the cement plug behind the casing. The system is RIH and the guns are fired across the desired setting depth for the plug. The guns are then dropped off the string (if enough space allows), and a bridge plug is set just below the bottom perforation. Kill weight fluid is then pumped down the string and washed across the perforated interval, cleaning that area, and removing any debris to the surface. Once clean fluid is observed at the surface, the cement plug is pumped and placed across the perforated interval, and the system is retrieved to the surface. Depending on the depth of the well and other factors, the perf-and-wash system can usually be deployed in around 24 hours, saving the operator a large amount of time and money in the project. There are, however, a few limitations to these systems; for example, if there are movable salts behind the casing, it is not advised to use these systems.

INFORMATION MANAGEMENT

A lot of assets within the North Sea were developed in the 1970s or 1980s, which means the raw data on these assets was compiled on a paper-based system and not the computerised systems known and used today. Also, over the years, many of these assets have been sold and bought between operators, which leads to these paper-based records going missing or not being passed on. Another issue within the oil and gas sector is that, as the assets have been modified over the years, accurate records have not followed, which leads to inaccurate data. All of these factors lead to misinformation being used within the decommissioning project, resulting in risk as elements are engineered incorrectly.

Therefore, to ensure that the data is up-to-date, surveys should be completed to get a more accurate as-built understanding of the asset. With technology moving forward, surveys can be done via a drone flown around the asset to pick up the images required. Also, 3D/point cloud models can be created to give a complete image of the asset. Traditional time-consuming hand surveys can be completed as well, which could be effective for hard-to-reach areas or key nodes that will be affected by the lifting.

HEALTH, SAFETY, AND THE ENVIRONMENT

Health, safety, and environmental (HSE) challenges within the offshore oil and gas industry are not new by any means but should remain a constant priority during any decommissioning project given the additional risk involved in certain standard offshore projects simply by the nature of the task being undertaken.

As decommissioning becomes more prevalent within the industry, the HSE side becomes more significant (Boothroyd et al., 2016). If decommissioning goes wrong, the outcome is generally catastrophic to people and the environment with possible long-term effects.

Quality assurance is a key matter within a decommissioning project (Oil and Gas Authority, 2017). The project should have a detailed Decommissioning Quality Assurance Plan in place to suit the project, clearly itemising the key elements that will have quality assurance applied against them and to what standard the assurance should be applied. It is recommended that external quality verification from accredited sources be obtained for the project.

OPTION AWARENESS

As the decommissioning market evolves, so does the number of options for completing the various tasks within the project. For example, within the well P&A element, a company can choose between rig and rigless to complete the abandonment. It would be easy to be drawn into the rigless option due to the cost savings of not having the drill rig on station but going rigless necessitates several requirements of the asset. For example, the deck space and capabilities of weight loadings increase, and accommodations are needed to house a full well P&A team on the platform. The draw on utilities and the need for a crane given these requirements when going rigless are apt to be more reliable on a drill rig than on an aging asset due to be decommissioned. However, the in-between option of using a jack-up barge to provide power, deck space, and accommodation when choosing the rigless method is generally cheaper than hiring a drill rig.

A company should understand its options in terms of cost, schedule impact, and risk, as these will be key business decisions for any decommissioning project. And while it is important to understand the options available to complete the task at hand, be aware that there is a fine line between knowing and overthinking that would result in delays and additional cost.

SUPPLY CHAIN MANAGEMENT VS. TALENT MANAGEMENT

Decommissioning requires an integrated supply chain management approach because it involves different contractors and service companies to deal with platform removal, heavy material, waste management, land restoration, safety management, and continued monitoring after closure (Ahmad et al., 2017). Decommissioning cost reduction involves complex actions, decisions, and risk scenarios for managing procurement, supply planning, logistics, scheduling, and storage, as well as people with different skills, experience, culture, and so forth.

Therefore, since decommissioning is relatively new to the energy industry, there currently is not a wide range of talents and understanding of the market to suit this element. The main challenge to an operator is to understand the talent requirements needed to undertake a decommissioning project and then decide whether to employ a team directly or to subcontract the project to one or multiple contracting firms.

As the decommissioning industry evolves, there are more companies in the market who can offer a full turnkey solution to decommissioning, which puts less stress on the operator to build such a capability in-house. Some people believe an operator should focus on operating its assets and let a decommissioning-focused business complete the decommissioning scope, which allows individuals to focus on their strengths and comparative advantages. It should also be noted that many current talents within the oil and gas industry are transferrable to decommissioning, mainly because of their knowledge of managing the assets or accumulated experience during their engineering, construction, and commissioning.

REFERENCES

Ahmad, N. K. W., de Brito, M. P., Rezaei, J., & Tavasszy, L. A. (2017). An integrative framework for sustainable supply chain management practices in the oil and gas industry. *Journal of Environmental Planning and Management*, *60*(4), 577–601.

Boothroyd, I. M., Almond, S., Qassim, S. M., Worrall, F., & Davies, R. J. (2016). Fugitive emissions of methane from abandoned, decommissioned oil and gas wells. *Science of the Total Environment*, *547*, 461–469.

Day, M. D., & Gusmitta, A. (2016). Decommissioning of offshore oil and gas installations. In *Environmental Technology in the Oil Industry*, Third Edition, S. Orszulik (Ed.), pp. 257–283. Springer Cham.

Molnár, V., Fedorko, G., Krešák, J., Peterka, P., & Fabianová, J. (2017). The influence of corrosion on the life of steel ropes and prediction of their decommissioning. *Engineering Failure Analysis*, *74*, 119–132.

Oil and Gas Authority (2017). UKCS Decommissioning - 2017 Cost Estimate Report. Retrieved December 14, 2019, from https://www.ogauthority.co.uk/media/4742/ukcs-decommissioning-cost-report-v2.pdf

CHAPTER 3: DECOMMISSIONING STAKEHOLDERS AND DECISION MAKERS

A shareholder is an individual or firm that owns shares in a publicly listed or private company. However, a stakeholder in decommissioning, is any person, company, or group who has an interest in or could be impacted by the activities undertaken within that decommissioning project.

Generally, stakeholders will have an interest in the overall success of that decommissioning project or a certain element of that project and can either be internal to the project or external to it. Regardless of whether they can have either a positive or negative influence on a decommissioning project, stakeholders require that decommissioning follows a transparent and consistent process based on scrutiny, best practices, and results (Gordon et al., 2019).

During the life span of a decommissioning project, many critical decisions will need to be made to cover various elements and set the project in the right direction. In any project there are many people, groups, or organisations who believe themselves to be experts or have an opinion on how to direct a specific element of the project, but not all of these will be useful or helpful regarding certain key decisions. When working on making a complex or critical decision, there will be much to be considered as the outcome could have positive or negative consequences for the project. A key element of ensuring that the correct decisions are made is ensuring that the correct stakeholders are involved.

Stakeholder management is the systematic identification of all stakeholders, the analysis of stakeholders, and the implementation of the key actions/communications designed to engage with stakeholders. Stakeholders within a decommissioning project should be treated like any other task within the project, by prioritising them based on their interest in the project and their level of power to influence decisions related to the project. A stakeholder management plan should be in place during the planning of a decommissioning project to ensure that all stakeholders and their engagement requirements are known and that an engagement/communication plan is in place. This plan should classify the stakeholders into separate tiers, according to level or importance, interaction, and influence/power.

Figure 3.1 exhibits a hierarchical structure of stakeholder and decision support; for example, Tier 1 highlights the main company representatives or stakeholders in decommissioning projects (assets' owners, directors, and top managers) influencing strategic decisions and project performance.

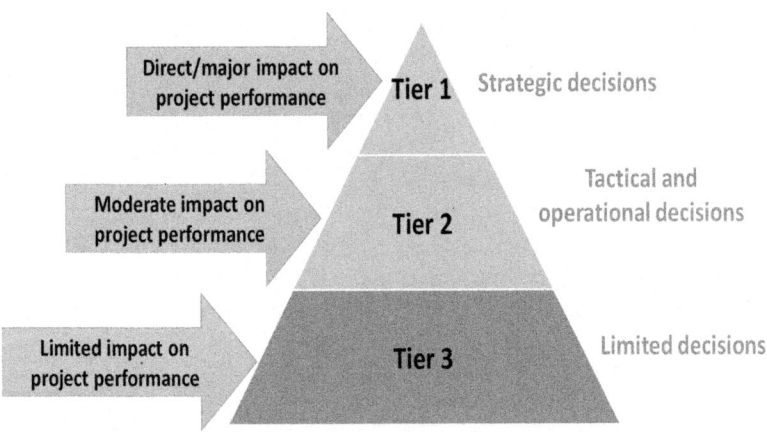

Figure 3.1: Stakeholders and Decision-Making Mapping

To fully understand which stakeholders should fall into what tier, they should be plotted onto a stakeholder engagement grid. For example, Figure 3.2 shows that the more influence and interest a stakeholder has in a decommissioning project, the more engagement is required. In other words, you must fully involve these stakeholders by making the greatest effort to engage and consult them.

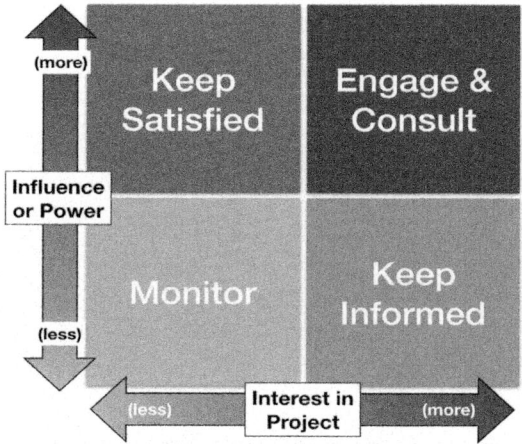

Figure 3.2: Stakeholder Engagement Matrix
(Based on Mendelow, 1981)

INTERNAL STAKEHOLDERS IN DECOMMISSIONING

Traditional decommissioning typically has a standard list of stakeholders associated with the project that are classed as internal stakeholders. Internal stakeholders are employees or teams within the operating company who have an interest in or are part of the decommissioning project. Examples of internal stakeholders within a decommissioning project include, but are not limited to, the following categories.

Senior Leadership Team (Directors/Board)

The board of directors or senior leadership team is responsible for the overall business, which, of course, includes the decommissioning project. Every business senior leadership team is set up differently, but it might have a project or decommissioning director within that leadership team. That person would be the main focal point for the decommissioning project outside of the actual project team who would provide key data and information to the rest of the leadership team.

The senior leadership team is normally where key decisions on funding releases and gate approvals are made, as and when the project team presents them for approval.

Project Team

The project team encompasses many different roles within the one team whose focus is to deliver the decommissioning project from concept stage to final close out stage. Some key roles within the project team are:

- Project Manager – The project manager has the overall responsibility to deliver the decommissioning project in terms of successful initiation, planning, design, execution, monitoring, controlling, and closure safely and while being on schedule and within budget. The project manager plays a key role in decision making throughout the project.

- Project Engineer – The project engineer generally reports to the project manager and plays a key role in preparing and coordinating the engineering tasks within the project. This individual will also monitor the compliance to standards, codes, and practices within the project. Much of the role is intertwined with that of the project manager, and the project engineer will provide data, knowledge, and key information to the project manager to assist in the decision-making process.

- Contract Manager – A contract manager will work closely with the project manager to manage and control the contracts in place within the decommissioning project, for example, the contract for a heavy-lift contractor brought in to undertake all major lifts on the project. The contract manager will construct the contract with the contracting firm and then monitor it throughout the project in terms of cost and to ensure no clauses are broken. This person will assist in the decision-making process with contracting firms from the tender point of view and through to nonconformances and payment as per the contract agreement.

- Financial Controller/Cost Manager – The cost engineer/manager or financial controller would manage all costs on the project along with the project manager. This individual would collect all the data and present it in a report at a desired interval (monthly/weekly) to suit the project manager's needs. The report would have such items on it as cost spend to date, committed cost, S-curve, and forecast spend, to name a few. This person would provide key financial data to the project manager to make financial decisions and would also advise given their knowledge related to the decisions.

- Communication Lead – Not all organisations would choose to have this role, but it could be important if the asset is located in a sensitive area in which the public is taking a greater than normal interest. The communication lead would generally run the communication plan and its contents according to the relevant stakeholders within the methods identified.

- HR Lead/Manager – As with any decommissioning project, several core crew will be working on the asset as it approaches final removal. Depending on the company, these core crew might have the opportunity to move to another asset/location internally. If not, they will need to go through a redundancy type of procedure that requires a lot of input from the HR team internally. As this activity could affect how the project runs if operatives decided to delay the final decision, it is a very important role within a decommissioning team.

- Operational Lead – Not every decommissioning team requires an operational lead, but this individual can bring a lot of benefits to a team, such as operation knowledge of the platform and general asset knowledge from the permit system to the asset layout. This knowledge can speed up process and work streams, as compared to using people new to the asset from a decommissioning contractor. A good operational lead would be a member of the existing core crew team from the asset.

- Logistics Lead – This person will lead and manage the logistics of the project, including helicopter movements, supply vessel movements, heavy-lift vessel movements, and any other movements of plant, labour, or other items associated with the project. If logistics are not managed correctly, they can cause expensive overages to the overall project, given the day rate of many of the items required (e.g., supply vessels and barges).

- Risk Manager – Agile asset' operators are incorporating risk management professionals into the decision-making process to communicate, analyse and identify uncertainty factors, policies and processes, and quantify their impacts on cost, schedule, financial performance, safety, among other key performance indicators. A risk manager should provide analytical support and hands-on applications and risk models combining business, market, credit, and operational risks to manage decommissioning projects effectively.

There are many other key team members within a decommissioning project team; the above are some who have some of the highest responsibility for and influence over the key decisions on a project. All team members within a decommissioning project team have an important part to play to ensure the overall success of a project.

EXTERNAL STAKEHOLDERS IN DECOMMISSIONING

In addition to internal stakeholders, decommissioning projects also include external stakeholders who are individuals, groups, or organisations outside the business or project but who have the ability or powers to affect the project's direction or outcome. Examples of external stakeholders within a decommissioning project include, but are not limited to, the following:

- Regulatory bodies, – including but not limited to the following examples in the UK:
    - Department for Business, Energy, and Industrial Strategy (BEIS) – for further information see www.gov.uk/government/organisations/department-for-business-energy-and-industrial-strategy
        - The department Offshore Petroleum Regulator for Environment and Decommissioning (OPRED), within BEIS, is responsible for offshore petroleum decommissioning activities within the UK. OPRED is also responsible for approving the decommissioning programme (DP) following consultation with other government and nongovernment agencies.
    - Oil and Gas Authority (OGA) – see www.ogauthority.co.uk
        - The OGA's role in decommissioning comprises three priorities:

            1. Cost certainty and cost reduction

            2. Decommissioning capability delivery

3. Decommissioning scope, guidance, and stakeholder engagement

While much of its work involves industry initiatives, it is important to consult with the OGA early in the development of the DP to ensure that all avenues of reuse have been explored.

- o Environment Agency – see www.gov.uk/government/organisations/environment-agency
    - The Environment Agency is responsible for enforcing waste management controls in England and Wales. It expects operators to comply with the following principles during decommissioning:

        1. Early engagement

        2. Active waste management plans

        3. Compliance with Waste Framework Directive

        4. Observe Duty of Care, the responsibility for all waste generated until its final disposal or treatment

        5. Inventory of offshore waste

- o Scottish Environment Protection Agency (SEPA) – see www.sepa.org.uk
    - Similar to the Environment Agency, SEPA is Scotland's principal environmental regulator, protecting and improving Scotland's environment. SEPA regulates activities that could lead to pollution or environmental damage, including decommissioning activities.

- o Offshore Safety Directive Regulator (OSDR)/Health and Safety Executive (HSE) – see www.hse.gov.uk/osdr/
    - The OSDR is part of the Health and Safety Executive (HSE) office, responsible for ensuring the safe dismantling, removal, and disposal of offshore installations and pipelines.

- - Joint Nature Conservation Committee (JNCC) – see www.gov.uk/government/organisations/joint-nature-conservation-committee and www.jncc.gov.uk
    - The JNCC is a primary point of contact for nature conservation advice on decommissioning plans outside 12 nautical miles and is a key stakeholder in determining the scope of the required EA.
  - Local Authority and Councils
    - Generally, a local Council is the local authority with responsibility where a pipeline meets the coastline.
- Organisations/groups
  - Greenpeace – see www.greenpeace.org.uk
- Fishing
  - There are several local fisheries' organisations who have specific interests along various coastlines.
- Marine
  - Crown Estate – see www.thecrownestate.co.uk
    - The Crown Estate owns around 55% of the foreshore and virtually the entire seabed out to 12 nautical miles. It also manages the area beyond 12 nautical miles in terms of leasing of the seabed for certain activities, which generally covers pipelines returning to the coastline.
  - Maritime and Coastguard Agency (MCA) – see www.gov.uk/government/organisations/maritime-and-coastguard-agency
    - The MCA is responsible for the safety of personnel on vessels in UK waters and the accuracy of hydrographic data on UK charts.
    - An executive agency, the MCA is sponsored by the Department for Transport. As such, it is a consultee to any application for the placing of

offshore installations and other works in tidal waters.

- Local Members of Parliament (MP)
    o Engagement with the local MP to inform them of the proposed DP is recommended because the general public may approach their MP with concerns regarding it.
- Local/linked operators/fields
    o Connections assets are those assets directly connected in the field or assets connected via a pipeline or cable. Also, other operators of local fields within the area are notified so they are aware of the activities.
- Nongovernmental organisations, including but not limited to:
    o Royal Yachting Association (RYA) – see www.rya.org.uk
    o Royal Society for Protection of Birds (RSPB) – see www.rspb.org.uk
    o World-Wide Fund for Nature (WWF) – see www.wwf.org.uk
    o Marine Conservation Society (MCS) – see www.mcsuk.org
    o Whale and Dolphin Conservation Society (WDCS) – see https://uk.whales.org/
- Trade associations
- Industry groups
    o General Lighthouse Authority – see www.trinityhouse.co.uk/general-lighthouse-authority-gla
- Local community stakeholders

ENGAGEMENT WITH STAKEHOLDERS IN DECOMMISSIONING

Stakeholders (communities, environmental representatives, fishing organisations, etc.) are identified within the stakeholder management plan, and a positive relationship with each stakeholder is required to ensure the project team meets their expectations as well as the objectives set within the project. As in life, a relationship is not a given and needs to be earned and nurtured by doing things correctly. The main key to building a good relationship and trust is through proactive communication. Therefore, it is essential that the project team understand different methods of communication, to suit each stakeholder, and which should be used in different circumstances. The various mechanisms of communication with these stakeholders will be identified within the stakeholder management plan and include but are not limited to:

- Early engagement letters/emails
- Face-to-face meetings
- Web-based portals
- Decommissioning website
- Video conference meetings
- Workshops
- Documentation/announcements published via website or web-based portal
- Telephone discussions
- Town halls
- Letter drops

As nations are increasing stakeholder involvement in decommissioning projects, it becomes more important to cultivate positive relationships and to avoid negative perceptions based on miscommunication of information (Fowler et al., 2014).

REFERENCES

Fowler, A. M., Macreadie, P. I., Jones, D. O. B., & Booth, D. J. (2014). A multi-criteria decision approach to decommissioning of offshore oil and gas infrastructure. *Ocean & Coastal Management*, *87*, 20–29.

Gordon, P. L., Poot, E. H., & O'Connor, G. S. (2019). Rigorous decommissioning decision making with strong stakeholder engagement using comparative assessment. *The APPEA Journal*, *59*(2), 591–595.

Mendelow, A. L. (1981, December). Environmental Scanning - The Impact of the Stakeholder Concept. In *ICIS 1981 Proceedings*, p. 20.

CHAPTER 4: RISK MANAGEMENT AND STRATEGIC OPTIONS

This chapter introduces concepts, tools, and methodologies to help decision makers analyse uncertainty, manage risk, and frame real options around decommissioning, including well plugging and abandonment (asset reuse, new projects, managerial flexibility, and so on). In general, risk is simply the inevitability of chance occurrence beyond the realm of human control. Although we may be able to predict the orbital paths of planets in our solar system with astounding accuracy or the escape velocity required to shoot a man from the Earth to the Moon, when it comes to predicting a firm's revenues the following year or the costs for the proposed decommissioning of an offshore asset, we are at a loss. Decommissioning managers are struggling with risk in every project, but through trial and error and the lessons learned, continually improving technologies and decision analytics, increased knowledge, and forward-looking thought, they have devised ways to describe, quantify, hedge, and take advantage of risk.

Risk management not only relies on understanding and quantifying how uncertainty impacts decisions, it also includes how managers take advantage of risk by creating related options. This chapter is concerned with only a small niche of risk, namely, *applied business risk modeling and analytics, including real options analysis, that can be used when planning decommissioning activities*. It focuses on the introduction of risk management in the sense of how to adequately apply the tools to identify, understand, quantify, and diversify risk such that it can be hedged and managed more effectively. Therefore, this chapter also explains why real options are important in mothballing activities in an attempt to demystify the concepts of real options. It starts by reviewing the basics of real options as a paradigm shift in the way of thinking about and evaluating emerging strategies around decommissioning projects and describes the various types of real options strategies and their execution. The chapter then presents examples of the use of real options in various industries and concludes with a summary of important considerations when using real options analytics and some final comments.

WHY IS RISK MPORTANT IN MAKING DECISIONS?

An assessment of risk should be an important part of the decision-making process in order to avoid bad decisions. For instance, suppose energy projects are chosen based simply on an evaluation of returns; clearly the highest-return project will be chosen over lower-return projects. In financial theory, projects with higher returns will in most cases bear higher risks. Therefore, instead of relying purely on bottom-line profits, a project should be evaluated based on its returns as well as its risks. Figures 4.1 and 4.2 illustrate the errors in judgment when risks are ignored.

> The concepts of risk and uncertainty are related but different. Uncertainty involves variables that are unknown and changing, but uncertainty will be become known and resolved through the passage of time, events, and action. Risk is something one bears and is the outcome of uncertainty. Sometimes, risk may remain constant while uncertainty increases over time.

Figure 4.1 lists three *mutually exclusive* projects with their respective costs to implement, expected net returns (net of the costs to implement), and risk levels (all in present values). Clearly, for the budget-constrained manager, the cheaper the project the better, resulting in the selection of Project X (Carbon Capture and Storage [CCS]). The returns-driven manager will choose Project Y (Gas-To-Wire) with the highest returns, assuming that budget is not an issue. Project Z (Hydrogen) will be chosen by the risk-averse manager as it provides the least amount of risk while delivering a positive net return. The upshot is that, with three different projects and three different managers, three different decisions will be made. Which manager is correct and why?

Why is Risk Important?

Name of Project	Cost	Returns	Risk
Project X	$50	$50	$25
Project Y	$250	$200	$200
Project Z	$100	$100	$10

Project X for the cost and budget-constrained manager
Project Y for the returns driven and nonresource-constrained manager
Project Z for the risk-adverse manager
Project Z for the smart manager

Figure 4.1: Deciding Among Different Projects

Figure 4.2 shows that Project Z should be chosen. For illustration purposes, suppose all three projects are independent and mutually exclusive, and that an unlimited number of projects from each category can be chosen but the budget is constrained at $1,000. Therefore, with this $1,000 budget, 20 Project Xs can be chosen, yielding $1,000 in net returns and $500 risks, and so forth. It is clear from Figure 4.2 that Project Z is the best project as for the same level of net returns ($1,000), the least amount of risk is undertaken ($100). Another way of viewing this selection is that for each $1 of returns obtained, only $0.1 amount of risk is involved on average, or that for each $1 of risk, $10 in returns are obtained on average. This example illustrates the concept of *bang for the buck* or getting the best value with the least amount of risk. An even more obvious example is if there are several different projects with identical single-point average net returns of $10 million each. Without risk analysis, a manager should, in theory, be indifferent in choosing any of the projects. However, with risk analysis, a better decision can be made—for instance, suppose the first project has a 10% chance of exceeding $10 million; the second, a 15% chance; and the third, a 55% chance. Clearly, the third project is the best bet.

This approach of *bang for the buck*, or returns to risk ratio, is the cornerstone of the Markowitz efficient frontier in modern portfolio theory. That is, if we constrained the total portfolio risk level and successively allowed it to increase over time, we will obtain several efficient portfolio allocations for different risk characteristics. Thus, different efficient portfolio allocations can be obtained for different individuals with different risk preferences.

At the bottom of Figure 4.2, we see a sample Markowitz efficient frontier to determine the optimal or best allocation of assets and investments or project selection within the context of a portfolio (maximising a certain objective such as profits or bang-for-the-buck Sharpe ratio subject to certain constraints such as time, budget, cost, risk, etc.). Briefly, in the chart in Figure 4.2, each dot represents a *portfolio* of multiple projects, projected in a two-dimensional plot of returns (y-axis) and risk (x-axis). If you compare portfolios A and B, a rational decision maker will choose portfolio A because it has a higher return with the same amount of risk as B. In addition, the same decision maker will choose portfolio A over portfolio C because for the same returns, A has a lower risk. For similar reasons, D will be chosen over C.

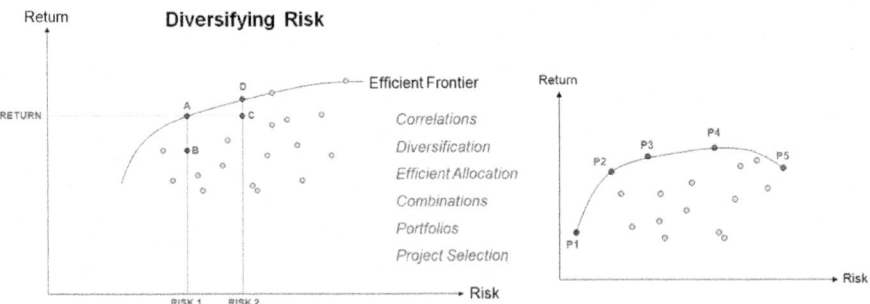

Figure 4.2: Adding an Element of Risk

In other words, there are multiple combinations of portfolios that can be developed, but there is an extreme set of portfolios that will yield the highest returns subject to the least amount of risk or the best *bang for the buck*, and these portfolios lie on the upper end of the curve, named the *efficient frontier*. We can obtain these portfolio points by running an optimisation. *Each point on this graph is an optimisation run, and the efficient frontier is simply multiple optimisation runs across different and changing constraints* (e.g., people, money, or technology). So, when presented with such an analysis, the decision maker can decide which portfolio to undertake, what the resources required will be, and what the projected returns and risks will be.

DEALING WITH RISK THE OLD-FASHIONED WAY

In most cases, energy and decommissioning managers have looked at the risks of a particular project, acknowledged their existence, and moved on. Little quantification was performed in the past. In fact, most decision makers look only to single-point estimates of a product's or project's profitability. Figure 4.3 shows an example of a single-point estimate, for example in well plugging and abandonment, net revenues related to recycled material, second-hand compressors, pipelines, and so forth. The estimated net revenue of $30 is simply that, a single point whose probability of occurrence is close to zero. Even in the simple model shown in Figure 4.3, the effects of interdependencies are ignored, and in traditional modeling jargon, we have the problem of *garbage-in, garbage-out* (GIGO). As an example of interdependencies, the units sold are probably negatively correlated to the price of the product, and positively correlated to the average variable cost; ignoring these effects in a single-point estimate will yield grossly incorrect results. For instance, if the unit sales variable becomes 11 instead of 10, the resulting revenue may not simply be $35. The net revenue may actually decrease due to an increase in variable cost per unit, while the sale price may actually be slightly lower to accommodate this increase in unit sales. Ignoring these interdependencies will reduce the accuracy of the model.

> A rational manager would choose projects based not only on returns but also on risks. The best projects tend to be those with the best bang for the buck, or the best returns subject to some specified risks.

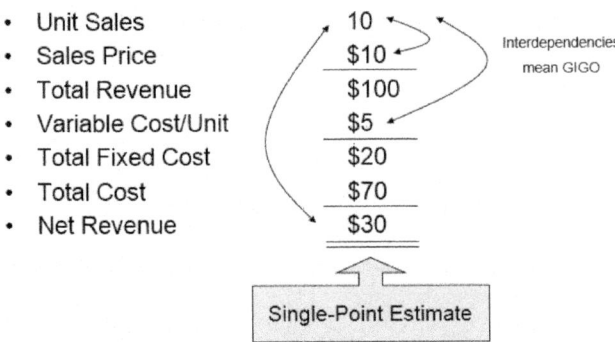

Figure 4.3: Single-Point Estimates

One approach used to deal with risk and uncertainty is the application of scenario analysis, as seen in Figure 4.4. Suppose the worst-case, nominal-case, and best-case scenarios are applied to the unit sales; the resulting three scenarios' net revenues are obtained. As earlier, the problems of interdependencies are not addressed. The net revenues obtained are simply too variable, ranging from $5 to $55. Not much can be determined from this analysis.

Scenario Analysis

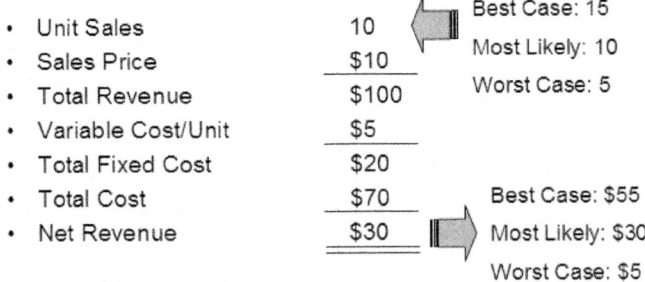

Outcomes are too variable–which will occur?

The best, most likely, and worst-case scenarios are usually simply wild guesses!

Figure 4.4: Scenario Analysis

A related approach is to perform *what-if* or *sensitivity* analysis as seen in Figure 4.5. Each variable is perturbed a prespecified amount and the resulting change in net revenues is captured. This approach is great for understanding which variables drive or impact the bottom line the most. Although these approaches are time consuming, to some extent they are still performed. Clearly, a better and more robust approach is required.

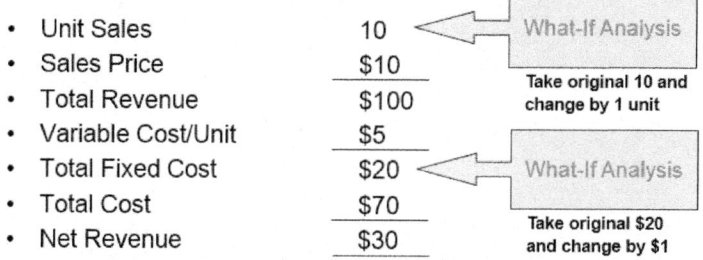

Figure 4.5: What-If Sensitivity Analysis

This is the point where simulation comes in. Figure 4.6 shows how simulation can be viewed as simply an extension of the traditional approaches of sensitivity and scenario testing. The critical success drivers or the variables that affect the bottom-line net-revenue variable the most, which at the same time are uncertain, are simulated. In simulation, the interdependencies are accounted for by using correlations. The uncertain variables are then simulated thousands of times to emulate all potential permutations and combinations of outcomes. The resulting net revenues from these simulated potential outcomes are tabulated and analysed. For example, Figure 4.7 shows that there is a 90% probability that the net revenues will fall between $20.15 and $39.85, with a 5% worst-case scenario of net revenues falling below $20.15.

Simulation Approach

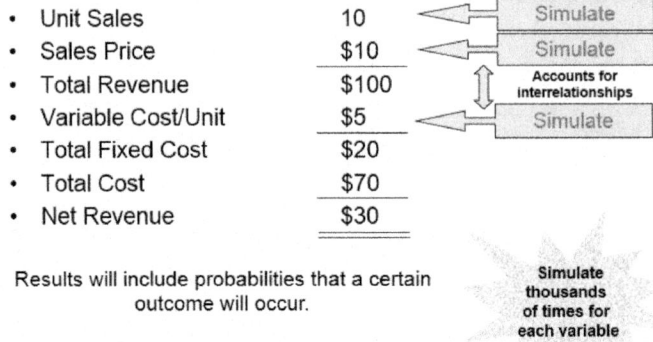

Figure 4.6: Monte Carlo Simulation Approach

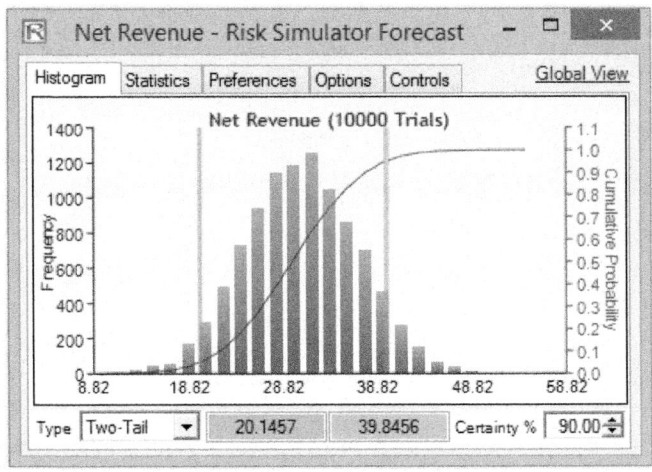

Figure 4.7: Simulation Results

Rather than having only three scenarios, simulation created 10,000 scenarios, or trials, where multiple variables are simulated and changing simultaneously (unit sales, sale price, and variable cost per unit), while their respective relationships or correlations are maintained. In essence, in its most basic form, simulation is simply an enhanced version of traditional approaches such as sensitivity and scenario analysis but automatically performed for thousands of times while accounting for all the dynamic interactions between the simulated variables. Therefore, the uncertainty analysis relies on *probability distributions functions* (*triangular, normal, lognormal, uniform*, etc.); experts' opinions or historical data, *seed values, correlations,* and *simulation trials* (e.g., 1,000 depending on the level of precision required).Consequently, the direct outcomes are *intervals of confidence* (e.g., 90%, 95%, 99%, and percentiles), *descriptive statistics* (mean, median, standard deviation, coefficient of variability, skew, kurtosis, etc.), *overlay results* (visualisation and comparison of risk profiles), and *dynamic sensitivity analysis* (rank correlation and percentages of fluctuations on the selected decision variable because of changes in all the selected projects' inputs, altogether).

As such, then, simulation is a relevant risk-based approach to value decommissioning projects (Chapter 5); analysing decommissioning projects on costs and schedule (Chapter 6); and quantify risk registers or governance-risk–compliance indicators in connection with dismantling activities (Chapter 7).

WHAT ARE STRATEGIC REAL OPTIONS?

In the past, corporate investment decisions were cut-and-dried. Buy a new machine that is more efficient, make more bulk materials costing a certain amount, hire a larger pool of engineering contractors, expand the current geographical area, integrate new business, delay decommissioning, and so forth, and if the benefits outweigh the costs, execute the investment. For instance, if the marginal increase in forecast sales revenues does not exceed the operational and maintenance costs, decision makers should start timing decommissioning or creating an integrated energy business. Need new gas compressors to augment gas flow rate? Show that the costs of implementation and commissioning can be recouped quickly and easily by the increase in revenues generated by the additional gas extraction and that profits and shareholder value will be enhanced, and the initiative is approved. However, real-life business conditions are a lot more complicated. Your firm decides to go with a carbon capture, utilisation, and storage (CCUS) strategy (platform adaptation, well integrity, regulatory approval, joint ventures, etc.), but multiple strategic paths exist. Which path do you choose? What are the options you have? If you choose the wrong path, how do you get back on the right track? How do you value and prioritise the paths that exist?

Real options are useful not only in valuing a firm through its strategic business options, but also as a strategic business tool in capital investment decisions with embedded decommissioning strategies or well plugging and abandonment. For instance, should a firm invest millions in a new facility expansion initiative (CCUS, hydrogen, geothermal, and the like) to postpone decommissioning? How does a firm choose among several seemingly cashless, costly, and unprofitable information-technology infrastructure projects? Should a firm indulge its billions in a risky research and development or decarbonisation initiative? The consequences of a wrong decision can be disastrous or even terminal for certain firms. In a traditional discounted cash flow or capital budgeting model, these questions cannot be answered with any certainty. In fact, some of the answers generated through the use of the traditional discounted cash flow model are flawed because the model assumes a static, one-time decision-making process whereas the real options approach takes into consideration the strategic managerial options that certain projects create under uncertainty and management's flexibility in exercising or abandoning these options at different points in time, when the level of uncertainty has decreased or has become known over time.

> Business conditions are fraught with uncertainty and risks. These uncertainties hold with them valuable information. When uncertainty becomes resolved through the passage of time, actions, and events, managers can make the appropriate midcourse corrections through a change in business decisions and strategies. Real options incorporate this learning model, whereas traditional analyses neglecting this managerial flexibility will grossly undervalue certain projects and strategies.

The real options approach incorporates a learning model into decommissioning (see Chapter 5 for further details), such that management makes better and more informed strategic decisions when some levels of uncertainty are resolved through the passage of time, actions, and events. Traditional discounted cash flow analysis, including for budgeting strategies, assumes a static investment or project decision and assumes that strategic decisions are made initially with no recourse to choose other pathways or options in the future. To create a good analogy of real options, visualise it as a strategic road map of long and winding roads with multiple perilous turns and branches along the way. Imagine the intrinsic and extrinsic value of having such a road map or global positioning system when navigating through unfamiliar territory, as well as having road signs at every turn to guide you in making the best and most informed driving decisions. Such a strategic map is the essence of real options.

The answer to evaluating projects and decommissioning strategies fraught with uncertainty lies in real options analysis, which has been used in a variety of industries, including pharmaceutical drug development, oil and gas exploration and production, manufacturing, start-up valuation, venture capital investment, information technology infrastructure, research and development, mergers and acquisitions, e-commerce and e-business, intellectual capital development, technology development, facility expansion, business project prioritisation, enterprise risk management, business unit capital budgeting, licenses, contracts, intangible asset valuation, and the like.

The Real Options Solution in a Nutshell

Simply defined, real options is a systematic approach and integrated solution using financial theory, project management, economic analysis, management science, decision sciences, statistics, and econometric modeling in applying options theory in valuing real physical assets and decommissioning strategies (such as decommissioning refineries, oil and gas wells, platforms, windfarms, engineering facilities, power plants, and so forth) in a dynamic and uncertain business environment where project decisions are flexible in the context of strategic capital investment decision making, valuing assets' reuse opportunities, and project capital expenditures. Real options analytics are crucial in:

- Identifying different corporate investment decision pathways or projects that management can navigate given highly uncertain business conditions (prices, production, competitions, regulations, demand, etc.).

- Valuing each of the strategic decision pathways and what it represents in terms of financial viability and feasibility, especially with regard to security, health, assurance, and environmental remediation

- Prioritising these pathways or projects based on a series of qualitative and quantitative metrics.

- Optimising the value of strategic investment decisions by evaluating different decision paths under certain conditions or using a different sequence of pathways that can lead to the optimal strategy.

- Timing the effective execution of investments and finding the optimal trigger values and cost or revenue drivers (e.g., early vs. late decommissioning [see Chapter 4]).

- Managing existing optionalities (e.g., asset sales, internal decommissioning, outsourcing) or developing new strategies (e.g., asset reuse or energy integration) and strategic decision pathways for future opportunities (e.g., combination of sequential or fully integrated renewables or clean energy strategies).

Issues to Consider

Strategic options do have significant intrinsic value, but this value is only realised when management decides to execute the strategies. Real options theory assumes that management is logical and competent, and that management acts in the best interests of the company and its shareholders through the maximisation of wealth and minimisation of risk of losses. For example, suppose an oil and gas firm owns the rights to 1,525 km of pipelines (for delivering blends of hydrogen and methane) that fluctuates dramatically in price because of markets conditions, similar operators, and optional secondary use. An analyst calculates the volatility of prices and recommends that management retain ownership for a specified time period, where within this period there is a good chance that the price of the piping system will triple. Therefore, management owns an *option to wait* and defer sale for a particular time period. The value of the asset is therefore higher than the value that is based on today's sale price. The difference is simply this option to wait. However, the value of the asset will not command the higher value if prices do triple but management decides not to execute the option to sell. In that case, the price of the piping system goes back to its original levels after the specified period, and then management finally relinquishes its rights.

Was the analyst right or wrong? What was the true value of the piping system? Should it have been valued at its explicit value on a deterministic case where you know what the asset price is right now, and therefore this is its value; or should it include some types of optionality where there is a good probability that the price of the piping system could triple in value, hence, the asset is truly worth more than it is now and should therefore be valued accordingly? The latter is the real options view. The additional strategic optionality value can only be obtained if the option is executed; otherwise, all the options in the world are worthless. This idea of *explicit* versus *implicit* value becomes highly significant when management's compensation is tied directly to the actual performance of particular projects or strategies.

To further illustrate this point, suppose the price of the piping system in the market is currently $100 million. Further suppose that the market is highly liquid and volatile and that the firm can easily sell off the asset at a moment's notice within the next 5 years, the same amount of time the firm owns the rights to the asset. If there is a 50% chance the price will increase to $150 million and a 50% chance it will decrease to $50 million within this time period, is the property worth an expected value of $100 million? If the price rises to $150 million, management should be competent and rational enough to execute the option and sell that asset immediately to capture the additional $50 million premium. However, if management acts inappropriately or decides to hold off selling in the hopes that prices will rise even further, the property value may eventually drop back down to $50 million.

Now, how much is this asset really worth? What if there happens to be an *abandonment option*? Suppose there is a perfect counterparty to this transaction, another gas operator with a fully diversified portfolio of projects (hydrogen, gas, and so on) who decides to enter into a contractual agreement whereby, for a contractual fee, the counterparty agrees to purchase the asset for $100 million within the next 5 years, especially if the firm wants to decommission this asset, regardless of the market price and executable at the whim of the firm that owns the asset. Effectively, a safety net has been created whereby the minimum floor value of the property has been set at $100 million (less the fee paid). That is, there is a limited downside but an unlimited upside, as the firm can always sell the piping system at market price if it exceeds the floor value. Hence, this strategic *abandonment option* has increased the value of the asset significantly. Logically, with this *abandonment option* in place, the value of the asset with the option is definitely worth more than $100 million. The asset price is stochastic and uncertain with some volatility (risk) and has some inherent probability distribution. The distribution's left tail is the downside risk and the right tail is upside value, and having an abandonment option (in this example, a price protection of $100 million) means that you take a really sharp knife and you slice off the distribution's left tail at $100 million because the firm will never have to deal with the situation of selling the asset at anything lower than $100 million. What happens is that the distribution's left-tail risk has been truncated and reduced, making the distribution now positively skewed; the expected return, or the average value, moves to the right. In other words, strategic real options in this case provided a *risk reduction and value enhancement strategy* to the firm.

Therefore, this option has value (e.g., insurance policies require a premium or price to obtain, and you can think of this abandonment option as a price protection insurance against any downside movements), and the idea is to determine what is the fair market value, whether the option is indeed worth it, the optimal timing to execute the option, and so forth. The real options approach seeks to value this additional inherent flexibility. Real options analysis, especially in projects with embedded decommissioning optionalities, allows the firm to determine how much this safety downside insurance or abandonment option is worth (i.e., what is the fair market value of the contractual fee to obtain the option?), the optimal trigger price (i.e., at what price will it be optimal to sell the asset?), and the optimal timing (i.e., what is the optimal amount of time to hold on to the asset?).

IMPLEMENTING REAL OPTIONS ANALYSIS

First, it is vital to understand that real options analysis is *not* a simple set of equations or models. It is an *entire decision-making process* that enhances the traditional decision analysis approaches. It takes what has been tried-and-true financial analytics and evolves it to the next step by pushing the envelope of analytical techniques. In addition, it is vital to understand that 50% of the value in real options analysis is simply thinking about it. Another 25% of the value comes from the number crunching activities, while the final 25% comes from the results interpretation and explanation to management. Several issues should be considered when attempting to implement real options analysis in energy projects and their decommissioning strategies:

- **Tools**—The correct tools are important. These tools must be more comprehensive than initially required because analysts will grow into them over time. Do not be restrictive in choosing the relevant tools. Always provide room for expansion. Advanced tools will relieve the analyst of detailed model building and let him or her focus instead on 75% of the value—thinking about the problem and interpreting the results. The Real Options Super Lattice Solver (SLS) software can solve complex and customised real options problems with great ease (Mun, 2016).

- **Resources**—The best tools in the world are useless without the relevant human resources to back them up. Tools do not eliminate the analyst but enhance the analyst's ability to effectively and efficiently execute the analysis. The right people with the right tools will go a long way. Because there are only a few true real options experts in the world who really understand the theoretical underpinnings of the models as well the practical applications, care should be taken in choosing the correct team. A team of real options experts, for example, engineers, plant managers, decommissioning specialists, project managers, experienced contractors, and service providers, is vital to the success of the initiative. A company should consider building a team of in-house experts to implement real options analysis and to maintain the ability for continuity, training, and knowledge transfer over time. Knowledge and experience in the theories, implementation, training, and consulting are the core requirements of this team of individuals. This is why training is vital. For instance, the Institute of Professional Education and Research's CQRM certification programme provides analysts and managers the opportunity to immerse themselves into the theoretical and real-life applications of simulation, forecasting, optimisation, and real options (for details about this programme, please see www.ipper.org).

- **Senior Management Buy-in**—The analysis buy-in has to be top-down where senior management drives the real options analysis initiative. A bottom-up approach where a few inexperienced junior analysts and engineers try to impress the powers that be will fail miserably.

TYPES OF REAL OPTIONS STRATEGIES

Abandonment Option

An *abandonment option* provides the holder the right, but not the obligation, to sell off and abandon some project, asset, or property that it owns, at a prespecified price and term. This option helps hedge downside risks and losses by being able to salvage some value of a failed project or asset that is out-of-the-money (e.g., sell intellectual property and assets, early decommissioning, abandon and walk away from a project, and execute buyback or sellback provisions). Other examples include *Exit and Salvage* (sale of assets and intellectual property to reduce losses); *Divestitures; Spin-offs; Contractual Buyback Provisions; Stop and Abandon* (stop before executing the next phase); *Termination for Convenience; Early Exit;* and *Guaranteed Buyback or Salvage Value*.

Barrier Option

A *barrier option* means that the option becomes live and available for execution and, consequently, the value of the strategic option depends on either breaching or not breaching an artificial barrier. Examples include *Protective Barriers* (options become live only if a project's net profits are above a certain level); *Price Protection* (a vendor contract that becomes null if market prices go above or below a certain threshold, integration of gas-to-wire options into offshore well platforms); and any other *Options-Embedded Contracts* that get *knocked in-the-money* or *out-of-the-money* if a certain benchmark is surpassed.

Chooser Option

A *chooser option* implies that management has the flexibility to choose among several strategies (e.g., CCUS, platform leasing, hydrogen, gas-to-wire, and so forth). Examples of chooser options include contractual obligations allowing the holder (i.e., asset operator) to *Choose One or Multiple Options* (to expand, abandon, switch, or contract, and combinations of other exotic options).

Contraction Option

A *contraction option* provides management the right and ability to contract its existing operations under the right conditions, thereby saving on operating expenses. The option provides a reduction in downside risk but still allows the firm to participate in reduced benefits. For instance, a counterparty takes over or joins in some activities to share profits and share risks (e.g., outsourcing or leasing offshore platforms instead of early decommissioning, unmanning plant operations), which helps reduce the firm's risk of failure or reduce severe losses in a risky but potentially profitable venture. Other examples include *Outsourcing, Alliances, Sub-Contractors, Leasing, Joint Venture, Foreign Partnerships, Co-Development,* and *Co-Marketing.*

Deferment Option (Optimal Timing, Option to Wait, Option to Execute)

A *deferment option* is also known as an *option to wait* or *option to execute*. This option allows decision makers and asset operators to buy additional time to wait for new information by pre-negotiating pricing and other contractual terms to obtain the option, but not the obligation, to purchase or execute something in the future should conditions warrant it (wait and see before executing).

Examples of options to wait and defer, in the context of decommissioning, include *Proof of Concept* (run a small-scale project first to better determine the costs, schedule, and market risks of a project versus jumping in right now and blindly taking the risk into blue or green hydrogen, for example); *Build, Buy, or Lease* (develop internally or use commercially available technology or products for lifting and cutting heavy platforms structures); *Multiple Contracts* (contracts in place that may or not be executed); *Market Research* (engage with the regulator and research centres to obtain valuable information before deciding on CCUS or hydrogen projects); *Venture Capital* (small seed investment with a right of first refusal before executing large-scale financing); *Contract Negotiations* (negotiate with vendors for competitive sustainment and strategic capability and availability); *Research & Development* (parallel implementation of alternatives while waiting on technical success of the main project, and no need to delay the project because of one bad component in the project); *Prototyping; Advanced Concept Technology Demonstration* (test before full-scale implementation); *Right of First Refusal Contracts; Value of Information* (wait and see to obtain better demand or cost inputs, capability, schedule, and other metrics); *Hedging* (Call- and Put-like options to execute something in the future with agreed upon terms now); and other wait-and-see options.

Expansion Option

An *expansion option* provides management the right and ability to expand into different markets, products, and strategies or to expand its current operations under the right conditions. This option allows companies and assets' operators to take advantage of upside opportunities by having existing platforms, structures, or technology that can be readily expanded (e.g., utility peaker plants, larger oil platforms, early/leapfrog technology development, larger capacity or technology-in-place for future expansion). Note that if an asset's operator can spend a little more money up front, having a prebuilt facility ready to be expanded is oftentimes cheaper in the long run than to restart any development in the future (e.g., a larger and flexible offshore platform is cheaper than re-initiating a secondary development in the future by engineering and building again in the middle of the ocean). Some additional examples of expansion options include *Platform Technologies; Mergers and Acquisitions; Pre-Built Expansion Capabilities;* and *Geographical, Technological, and Market Expansion;* as well as *Reusability and Scalability Options* (prebuilt into existing infrastructure).

Sequential Compound Option

A *sequential compound option* means that the execution and value of future strategic options depend on previous options in sequence of execution. Significant value exists if you can phase out investments over time, thereby reducing the risk of a one-time up-front investment (e.g., energy projects, pharmaceutical and high technology development and manufacturing that usually happens in phases or stages). Other examples include *Stage-Gate Implementation* (high-risk project development); *Prototyping; Low-Rate Initial Production; Technical Feasibility Tests; Market Research* (prior to launching a new product); *Technology Demonstration Competitions; Multiple Staged Contracts with Options to Abandon; Termination for Convenience; Built-in Flexibility* (ability to execute different courses of action at specific stages of development); *Milestones; Stage-Gate Research & Development; Phased Options;* and *Platform Technologies.*

Switching Option

A *switching option* provides the right and ability, but not the obligation, to switch among different sets of business operating conditions, including different technologies, markets, or products. This option provides the ability to choose among several options, thereby improving strategic flexibility to manoeuvre within the realm of uncertainty (maintain a foot in one door while exploring another to decide if it makes sense to switch or stay put). Examples include *Ability to Switch* among various integrated energy products (i.e., electricity, hydrogen, gas) when prices fluctuate significantly and the company needs to continue enhancing revenues; also, readiness and capability risk mitigation by switching services contractors (engineering, commissioning, decommissioning, etc.) through *Multiple Suppliers;* and *Switching Between Several Raw Materials* to cheaper inputs for the required industrial processes.

EXECUTION TYPES

For all of the preceding options, you can have different allowed execution times, including American, European, Bermudan, and Asian options (Mun, 2016; Hull, 2018). So, you can have an American Abandonment option or a European Abandonment option, and so forth. An American option allows you to execute at any time before and up to and including the expiration date. European options will allow you to execute only on a specific date, typically the expiration date itself. Bermudan options are a mix between European and American in that there is a blackout or vesting period when you cannot execute the option, but you can do so at any time after this blackout period up to and including expiration (e.g., an employee stock option usually has a 10-year maturity and a 4-year vesting period, where you cannot exercise the option within this first 4 years and you lose the option if you leave your job during this vesting period, but once this requisite service period has passed, the option is yours and you can exercise it at any time between year 4 and year 10). Finally, Asian options are look-back options, where specific conditions in the option are dependent on some factor in the future. For example, United Airlines buys some Airbus A380 planes where they sign the purchase order today for delivery of the planes in two years, and the price of the plane depends on the average market price between now and two years from when the purchase order was placed. Once the planes have been delivered, both parties can look back over the two-year period to determine the final sale price of the planes.

INDUSTRY LEADERS EMBRACING REAL OPTIONS

To provide more information to assets' operators, regulators, oil and gas specialists, energy consultants, and service contractors, among other specialists, on how to embrace real options, this section presents various industry case studies using real options as a tool for strategic decisions to enhance the companies' performance and decision makers' perspectives (Brach, 2003; Hernandez-Perdomo et al., 2017).

Automobile and Manufacturing Industry

In automobile and manufacturing, General Motors (GM) applied real options to create *switching option*s in producing its new series of autos. This option is essentially to use a cheaper resource over a given period of time. GM holds excess raw materials and has multiple global vendors for similar materials with excess contractual obligations above what it projects as necessary. The excess contractual cost is outweighed by the significant savings of switching vendors when a certain raw material becomes too expensive in a particular region of the world. By spending the additional money in contracting with vendors and meeting their minimum purchase requirements, GM has essentially paid the premium on purchasing an *option to switch*, which is important especially when the price of raw materials fluctuates significantly in different regions around the world. Having an option here provides the holder a hedging vehicle against pricing risks.

Switching options are highly recommended for valuing and assessing integrated energy projects (e.g., gas-to-wire, gas-to-hydrogen) because of price fluctuations, allowing firms to extend an asset's life or postpone decommissioning.

Computer Industry

In the computer industry, HP–Compaq used to forecast sales in foreign countries months in advance. It then configured, assembled, and shipped the highly specific configuration printers to these countries. However, given that demand changes rapidly and forecast figures are seldom correct. The preconfigured printers usually suffer the higher inventory holding cost or the cost of technological obsolescence. HP–Compaq created an *option to wait* and defer making any decisions too early through building assembly plants in these foreign countries. Parts can then be shipped and assembled in specific configurations when demand is known, possibly weeks in advance rather than months in advance. These parts can be shipped anywhere in the world and assembled in any configuration necessary, while excess parts are interchangeable across different countries. The premium paid on this option is building the assembly plants, and the upside potential is the savings in making incorrect demand forecasts.

The usage of *options to defer* enhances the valuation and analysis of postponing an asset's mothballing because of technological changes or future (short- or medium-term) cost-effectiveness strategies. For example, lifting and cutting processes, well cementing, or conductor removal.

Airline Industry

In the airline industry, Boeing spends billions of dollars and takes several years to decide if a certain aircraft model should even be built. Should the wrong model be tested in this elaborate strategy, Boeing's competitors may gain a competitive advantage relatively quickly. Because so many technical, engineering, market, and financial uncertainties are involved in the decision-making process, Boeing created an *option to choose* through parallel development of multiple plane designs simultaneously, knowing well the increased cost of developing multiple designs simultaneously with the sole purpose of eliminating all but one in the near future. The added cost is the premium paid on the option. However, Boeing would be able to decide which model to abandon or continue when the uncertainties and risks become known over time. Eventually, all the models will be eliminated save one. This way, the company can hedge itself against making the wrong initial decision and benefit from the knowledge gained through parallel development initiatives.

Options to choose are valuable for those operators wanting to time decommissioning (e.g., early or late decommissioning) during an asset's full lifecycle, for example, performing early decommissioning if the fluctuations of oil and gas prices are not improving profits, or performing late dismantling if the reuse value of the current asset allows deferring future decommissioning expenditures.

Oil and Gas Industry

In the oil and gas industry, companies spend millions of dollars to refurbish their refineries and add new technologies and, hence, created an *option to switch* their mix of outputs among heating oil, diesel, and other petrochemicals as a final product, using real options as a means of making capital and investment decisions. This option allows the refinery to switch its final output to one that is more profitable based on prevailing market prices, to capture the demand and price cyclicality in the market. (See in Chapter 5 for emerging strategies to time decommissioning, such as gas-to-wire, hydrogen, biomass, and CCUS, among other options.)

Telecommunications Industry

In the telecommunications industry, in the past, companies like Sprint and AT&T installed more fibre-optic cable and other telecommunications infrastructure than any other company in order to create a *growth option* in the future by providing a secure and extensive network and to create a high barrier to entry, providing a first-to-market advantage. Imagine having to justify to the board of directors the need to spend billions of dollars on infrastructure that will not be used for years to come. Without the use of real options, this decision would have been impossible to justify.

Growth options are becoming relevant for asset operators with significant decommissioning liabilities. They can allow operators to invest and develop new processes, systems, and technologies to manage costly decommissioning more efficiently. Furthermore, they can enhance future cross-selling or growth opportunities across other operators (e.g., licenses, patents, IP, consulting support, decommissioning outsourcing).

Real Estate Industry

In the real estate arena, leaving land undeveloped creates an option to develop at a later date at a more lucrative profit level. However, what is the *optimal wait time* or the *optimal trigger price* to maximise returns? In theory, one can wait for an infinite amount of time, but real options analysis provides the solution for the optimal timing and optimal price trigger value.

This type of option is highly relevant to decommissioning activities for determining optimal trigger time to sell or repurposing the oil and gas assets, either to maximize profits and savings or to minimize capital expenditures, or for the reuse value in recycling.

Utilities Industry

In the utilities industry, firms have created an *option to execute* and an *option to expand* by installing cheap-to-build inefficient energy generator *peaker* plants to be used only when electricity prices are high and to shut down when prices are low. The price of electricity tends to remain constant until it hits a certain capacity utilisation trigger level, when prices shoot up significantly. Although this occurs infrequently, the possibility still exists, and by having a cheap standby plant, the firm has created the option to turn on the expanded capacity generation whenever it becomes necessary, to capture this upside price fluctuation. Flexible platforms on gas-to-wire and power-to-gas are also relevant strategies to hedge gas and electricity fluctuations (*option to switch*).

Pharmaceutical Research and Development Industry

In pharmaceutical or other research and development initiatives, real options can be used to justify the large investments in what seems to be cashless and unprofitable under the discounted cash flow method but that actually creates *sequential compound options* in the future. Under the myopic lenses of a traditional discounted cash flow analysis, the high initial investment of, say, a billion dollars in research and development may return a highly uncertain projected few million dollars over the next few years. Management will conclude under a net present value analysis that the project is not financially feasible. However, a cursory look at the industry indicates that research and development is performed everywhere. Hence, management must see an intrinsic strategic value in research and development (Paxson, 2003; Mun, 2016). How is this intrinsic strategic value quantified? A real options approach would optimally time and spread the billion-dollar initial investment over a multiple-stage investment structure.

At each project stage, management has an *option to wait* and see what happens as well as the *option to abandon* or the *option to expand* into the subsequent stages. The ability to defer cost and proceed only if situations are permissible creates value for the investment, making these essential options for analysing emerging energy projects associated with hydrogen and carbon capture, utilization, and storage (CCUS) while asset operators are managing decommissioning liabilities

High-Tech and e-Business Industry

In e-business strategies, real options can be used to prioritise different e-commerce initiatives and to justify those large initial investments that have an uncertain future. Additionally, real options can be used in e-commerce to create incremental investment stages compared to a large one-time investment (invest a little now, wait and see before investing more), specifically, to create *options to abandon, options to expand,* and other future growth options in decommissioning projects (i.e., autonomous risk-based inspections, virtual reality, marine remote operated vehicle [ROV], and so on).

Mergers and Acquisitions (Takeover Strategies)

In valuing a firm or project for acquisition, especially with embedded decommissioning liabilities and land remediation, you should not only consider the revenues, mothballing expenditures, and cash flows generated from the firm's operations but also the strategic options that come with the firm. For instance, if the acquired firm does not operate up to expectations, an *abandonment option* can be executed where it can be sold for its intellectual property and other tangible assets. If the firm is highly successful, it can be spun off into other industries and verticals, or new products and services can eventually be developed through the execution of an *expansion option*. In fact, in mergers and acquisitions, several strategic options exist. For instance, a firm acquires other entities to enlarge its existing portfolio of products or geographic location, to obtain new technology (*expansion option*), or to divide the acquisition into many smaller pieces and sell them off as in the case of a corporate raider (*abandonment option*); or it merges to form a larger organisation due to certain synergies and immediately lays off many of its employees (*contraction option*). If the seller does not value its real options, it may be leaving money on the negotiation table. If the buyer does not value these strategic options, it is undervaluing a potentially highly lucrative acquisition target.

Integrated engineering, construction, commissioning, and decommissioning projects (including well plugging and abandonment) where the high cost of implementation and capital expenditures with no apparent payback in the near future makes the paths taken seem foolish and incomprehensible in the traditional discounted cash flow sense, are fully justified in the real options sense when taking into account the strategic options created for the future, the uncertainty of the future operating environment, and management's flexibility in making the right choices at the appropriate time.

The following three examples illustrate how managers, decision makers, and analysts can frame and perform real options valuations. The most substantial percentage of the value in real options analysis is simply thinking about and understanding optionalities, decision making flexibility, uncertainty sources, and project dimensions. The remaining value comes from quantitative information, real options models, and the interpretation and explanation of the results to management.

Expansion and Compound Options: The Case of an Asset Integrity System

You are the Chief Technology Officer of a large multinational oil and gas corporation, and you know that your firm's Asset Integrity Management (AIM) system is antiquated and requires an upgrade (e.g., to some new cloud-based online tool). You arrange a meeting with the CEO, letting him in on the situation. The CEO quips back immediately, saying that he will support your initiative if you can prove to him that the monetary benefits outweigh the costs of implementation—a simple and logical request. You immediately arrange for a demonstration of the new operating system, and the highly technical experts from the vendor (e.g., Microsoft, SAP, Oracle, IBM, AspenTech) provide you and your boss a marvellous presentation of the system's capabilities and value-added enhancements, for both current assets' operations and future decommissioning activities, that took in excess of a few million dollars and several years to develop. The system even fixes itself in times of dire circumstances and is overall more reliable and stable than its predecessors. You get more excited by the minute and have made up your mind to get the much-needed product upgrade. There is still one hurdle, the financial hurdle, to prove not only that the new system provides a better operating environment, but also that the plan of action is financially sound. The new system will not help your sales force sell more products and generate higher revenues because the firm looks state-of-the-art only if a customer questions what AIM operating system it is using—hardly an issue that will arise during a sales call.

You lose sleep over the next few days pondering the issue, and you finally decide to assemble a task force made up of some of your top IT personnel and operational engineers. The nine of you (five IT specialists and four engineers) sit in a room considering the same issues and trying to brainstorm a few really good arguments. You link up the value-added propositions provided in the vendor technician's presentation and come up with a series of potential cost reduction drivers. Principally, the self-preservation of operational and asset data, critical assets, and self-fixing functionality will mean less technical assistance and help-desk calls, freeing up resources to focus more on maximising production and developing clear maintenance programmes. Your mind races through some quick figures, you feel your heart pounding faster, and you see a light at the end of the tunnel. Finally, you will have your long-awaited AIM system, and all your headaches will go away. Wait, not only does it increase operational efficiency because engineers and technician will focus more on asset performance rather than spending lot of time on call or hold for technical assistance, which at the same, reduce the help-desk time.

Your team spends the next few days scouring through mountains of data on operational, reliability, risk, and maintenance problems, but also help-desk calls and issues—thank goodness for good record-keeping and relational databases. Looking for issues that could potentially become obsolete with the new system, you find that at least 40% of operational troubleshooting can be detected, and 20% of your help-desk calls could be eliminated by having the new system in place because it is more stable, is capable of self-fixing these critical issues, can troubleshoot internal hardware conflicts, and so forth. Besides, does not employee morale count? Satisfied with your analysis, you approach the CEO and show him your findings.

Impressed with your charts and analytical rigor in such a short time frame, he asks several quick questions and points out several key issues. The cost reduction in technical assistance and asset management is irrelevant because you need these people to install and configure the new system. The start-up cost and learning curve might be steep, and engineers and technicians may initially have a tough time adjusting to the new operating environment—help-desk calls may actually increase in the near future, albeit slowing down in time. But the firm's mission has always been to cultivate its employees and not to fire them needlessly. Besides, there are 10 people on staff at the help desk and the asset's monitoring department and a 20% reduction means one less full-time employee out of 2,000 in the entire firm—hardly a cost reduction strategy! You still have not sufficiently persuaded your boss on getting the new AIM system, and you are up a tree and out on a limb. Thoughts of going shopping for a camera haunt you for the rest of the day.

Sound familiar? Firms wrestle with similar decisions daily, and, to make their products more marketable, vendors have to first address such financial and strategic issues. Imagine you are the sales director for a software or hardware vendor. How do you close a sale like this?

Performing a series of simple traditional analyses using a discounted cash flow methodology or economic justification based on traditional analyses will fail miserably, as we have seen above. The quantifiable financial benefits do not exceed the high implementation costs. How do you justify and correctly value such seemingly cashless and cash-flow-draining projects? The answer lies in real options. Instead of being myopic and focusing on current savings, the implementation of a large-scale AIM system will generate future strategic options for the firm. That is, having the system in place provides you a springboard to a second-, third-, or fourth-phase IT implementation. Having a powerful connected system gives you the technical feasibility to pursue online collaboration and global data access for reliability, maintenance, availability, decommissioning, production, stress testing, digital signatures, encryption security, remote installations, document recovery, and the like, which would be impossible to do without it.

Hence, the value of upgrading to a new system provides the firm an *expansion option,* which is the right and ability, but not the obligation, to invest and pursue some of these value-added technologies. Some of these technologies, such as security enhancements and global data access, can be highly valuable to your organisation. You may further delineate certain features into groups of options to execute at the same time—that is, create a series of *sequential compound options* where the success of one group of initiatives depends on the success of another in sequence, similar to a stage-gate investment process. Notice that using an extrapolation of the traditional analytic approaches would be inappropriate here because all these implementation possibilities are simply options that a senior manager has, and are not guaranteed execution by any means. When you view the whole strategic picture, value is created and identified where there was none before, thereby making you able to clearly justify financially your plans for the upgrade. You would be well on your way to getting your new operating system installed.

Expansion and Switching Options: The Case of the Oil and Gas Exploration and Production

The oil and gas industry is fraught with strategic options problems because oil and gas exploration and production involves significant amounts of risk and uncertainty. For example, when drilling for oil, the reservoir properties, fluidic properties, trap size and geometry, porosity, seal containment, oil and gas in place, expulsion force, losses due to migration, development costs, and so forth are all unknowns. How then is a reservoir engineer going to recommend to management the value of a particular drill site? Let us explore some of the more frequent real options problems encountered in this industry.

You are hired by a second-tier independent oil and gas firm, and your first task is to value several primary and secondary reservoir recovery wells. You are called into your boss's office, and she requests that you do an independent financial analysis on a few production wells. You are given a stack of technical engineering documents to review. After spending a fortnight scouring through several books on wells and oil and gas management, you finally have some basic understanding of the intricacies of what a secondary recovery well is. Needing desperately to impress your superiors, you decide to investigate a little further into some modern analytics for solving these types of recovery-well problems.

Based on your incomplete understanding of the problem, you begin to explore all the possibilities and come to the conclusion that the best analytics to use may be the application of a Monte Carlo simulation and real options analysis. Instead of simply coming up with the value of the project, you decide to also identify where value can be added to the project by incorporating strategic real optionality. Suppose that the problem you are analysing is a primary drilling site that has its own natural energy source, complete with its gas cap on one side and a water drive on the other. These energy sources maintain a high upward pressure on the oil reservoir to increase the ease of drilling and, therefore, the site's productivity. However, knowing that the level of energy may not be sustainable for a long time and its efficacy is unknown currently, you recognise that one of the strategies is to create an *expansion option* to drill a secondary recovery well near the primary site. Instead of drilling, you can use this well to inject water or gas into the ground, thereby increasing the upward pressure and keeping the reservoir productive. Building this secondary well is an option and not an obligation for the next few years. Another option that is on the table is hydraulic fracturing or fracking, where a high-pressure mixture of water, sand, and chemicals is directed at the rock strata to release the oil and gas trapped beneath. The secondary well can also be drilled vertically or horizontally to the rock layer to create new pathways to release the trapped gas, or the pathways can be used to extend existing channels for the oil to flow.

The first recommendation seems to make sense given that the geological structure and reservoir size are difficult to estimate. Yet these are not the only important considerations; the price of oil in the market is also something that fluctuates dramatically and should be considered. Assuming that the price of oil is a major factor in management's decisions, your second recommendation includes separating the project into two stages. The first stage is to drill multiple wells in the primary reservoir, which will eventually maximise its productivity. At that time, a second phase can be implemented through smaller satellite reservoirs in the surrounding areas that are available for drilling but are separated from the primary reservoir by geological faults. This second stage is also an *expansion option* on the first: When the price of oil increases, the firm is then able to set up new rigs over the satellite reservoirs, drill, and complete these wells. Then, using the latest technology in subsurface robotics, the secondary wells can be tied back into the primary platform, thereby increasing and expanding the productivity of the primary well by some expansion factor. Obviously, although this is a strategic option that the firm has, the firm does not have the obligation to drill secondary wells unless the market price of oil is favourable enough. Using some basic intuition, you plug some numbers into your models and create the optimal oil price levels such that secondary drillings are profitable. However, given your brief conversation with your boss and your highly uncertain career future, you decide to dig into the strategy a little more.

Perhaps the company already has several producing wells at the reservoir. If that is so, the analysis should be tweaked such that instead of being an *expansion option* by drilling more wells, the firm can retrofit these existing wells in strategic locations from producers into injectors, creating a *switching option*. Instead of drilling more wells, the company can use the existing wells to inject gas, water, or chemical mixtures (i.e., perform fracking) into the surrounding geological areas in the hopes that this will increase the energy source, break through the rock strata, and force the trapped oil to surface at a higher rate. These secondary production wells should be switched into injectors when the recovery rate of the secondary wells is relatively low and the marginal benefits of the added productivity on primary wells far outstrip the retrofit costs. In addition, some of the deep-sea drilling platforms that are to be built in the near future can be made into *expansion options,* where slightly larger platforms are built at some additional cost (premium paid to create this option), such that if oil prices are optimally high, the flexible capacity inherent in this larger platform can be executed to boost production.

Finally, depending on the situation involved, you can also create a *sequential compound option* for the reservoir. That is, the firm can segregate its activities into different phases. Specifically, the strategic option can be separated into four phases. Phases I, II, and III are exploration wells, and Phase IV is a development well.

- Phase I: Start by performing seismic surveys to get information on the structures of subsurface reservoirs (the costs incurred include shooting the survey, processing data, mapping, etc.).

- Phase II: If large structures are found, drill exploration wells; if not, then abandon the project now.

- Phase III: If the exploration well succeeds industrially or commercially (evaluated on factors such as cost, water depth, oil price, and rock, reservoir, and fluid properties), drill more delineation or "step out" wells to define the reservoir.

- Phase IV: If the reservoir is productive enough, commit more money for full development (platform building, setting platform, drilling development wells).

Abandonment Options: The Case of the Manufacturer of Oil and Gas Vessels and Equipment

You work for a midsize hardware manufacturing firm located in the heartland of America. Having recently attended a corporate finance seminar on real options, you set out to determine whether you can put some of your newfound knowledge to good use within the company. Currently, your firm purchases powerful laser-guided robotic fabrication equipment for state-of-the-art 3D additive printing technology, photopolymerisation, fused deposition modeling, and selective laser sintering. Your main clients include companies like BP, Shell, Petrofac, Petrobras, Saudi Aramco, Schlumberger, and Honeywell. Each of these pieces of equipment run in the tens of millions of dollars and has to be specially ordered more than a year in advance, due to its unique and advanced specifications. These tools break down easily, and if any one of the main machines that your firm owns breaks down, it can be disastrous because part of the manufacturing division may have to be shut down temporarily for a period exceeding a year. So, is it always desirable to have at least one fabrication tool under order at all times, just as a precaution? A major problem arises when the newly ordered tool arrives, but the remaining ones are fully functional and require no replacement. The firm has simply lost millions of dollars. In retrospect, certainly having a backup machine sitting idle (that costs millions of dollars) is not optimal. However, millions can also be lost if, indeed, a tool breaks down and a replacement is a year away. The question is what do you do, and how can real options be used in this case, both as a strategic decision-making tool and a valuation model?

Using traditional analysis, you come to a dead end, as the tool's breakdown has never been consistent and the ordered parts never arrive on schedule. Turning to real options, you decide to create a strategic option with the vendor. Instead of having to wait more than a year before a new machine arrives, while during that time not knowing when your existing machines will break down, you decide to create a mutually agreeable contract. Your firm decides to put up a certain amount of money and enter into a contractual agreement whereby the vendor will put you on its preferred list. In addition, your firm spends some development funds to retrofit your manufacturing equipment to an open architecture and modular configuration, allowing quickly replaceable and interchangeable parts. This cuts down delivery time from one year to two months. If your firm does not require the equipment, you will have to pay a penalty exit fee equivalent to a certain percentage of the machine's dollar value amount, within a specified period, on a ratcheted scale, with different exit penalties at different exit periods.

In essence, you have created an *abandonment option* where your firm has the right not to purchase the equipment should circumstances force your hand, but hedging yourself to obtain the machine at a moment's notice should there be a need. The price of the option's premium is the contractual price paid for such an arrangement. The savings come in the form of not having to close down part of your plant, losing potential revenues, incurring higher costs, and having a bad reputation. By incorporating real options insights into the problem, the firm saves tens of millions of dollars, ends up with the optimal decision, reduces the amount of potential downtime, and upgrades its equipment with modular open architecture configurations suitable for future growth and inclusion of any new disruptive technology.

CONSIDERATIONS WHEN IMPLEMENTING REAL OPTIONS VALUATIONS

Before embarking on real options analysis, a number of things need to be considered. To begin with, according to Mun (2016), the following five requirements need to be satisfied before a real options analysis can be run:

- *A financial model must exist.* Real options analysis requires the use of an existing discounted cash flow model, as real options build on the existing tried-and-true approaches of current financial modeling techniques. If a model does not exist, it means that strategic decisions have already been made and no financial justifications are required, and, hence, there is no need for financial modeling or real options analysis.

- *Uncertainties must exist.* Without uncertainties, the option value is worthless. If everything is known for certain in advance, then a discounted cash flow model is sufficient. In fact, when volatility (a measure of risk and uncertainty) is zero, everything is certain, the real options value is zero, and the total strategic value of the project or asset reverts to the net present value in a discounted cash flow model.

- *Uncertainties must affect decisions* when the firm is actively managing the project, and these uncertainties must affect the results of the financial model. These uncertainties will then become risks, and real options can be used to hedge the downside risk and take advantage of the upside uncertainties.

- *Management must have strategic flexibility or options* to make mid-course corrections when actively managing the projects. Otherwise, do not apply real options analysis when there are no options or management flexibility to value. If options do not exist, then the option value is zero, but if they do exist, neglecting their valuation will grossly and significantly underestimate the project's or asset's value.

- *Management must be smart enough and credible enough to execute the options when it becomes optimal to do so.* Otherwise, all the options in the world are useless unless they are executed appropriately, at the right time, and under the right conditions.

FINAL COMMENTS

Risk management requires understanding and quantifying how uncertainty impacts decisions and includes how managers take advantage of risk by utilizing real options analysis. Furthermore, when working with multidisciplinary decommissioning teams (engineers, project managers, health and safety professionals, asset operators, risk analysts, real options experts, among others), relevant analytical tools (Monte Carlo simulations, scenarios, optimizations, capital budgeting analysis, forecasting, etc.) can be adequately applied to identify, understand, quantify, and diversify risk to support the decision making process.

Although it was true in the past that real options analysis was merely academic, many corporations have begun to embrace and apply its pragmatic concepts real options. With the use of the Real Options Super Lattice Solver software (Mun, 2016), even challenging problems can be easily solved. Mun's book and software have helped bring the theoretical a lot closer to practice. Firms are using the software and universities are teaching it. It is only a matter of time before real options analysis be-comes part of standard financial analysis.

Because decommissioning projects are highly risky (cash usage, liquidity constraints, capital expenditures, health and safety considerations) and have high volatility (budget, schedule, mobilisations and demobilisations costs, etc.), real options analysis becomes more important. In fact, if a project is strategic but is risky, then you better incorporate, create, integrate, or obtain strategic real options to reduce and hedge the downside risk and take advantage of the upside uncertainties and managerial flexibility.

And with all that has been said, the authors believe that 50% (rounded, of course) of the challenge and value of real options analysis, not only in decommissioning but also across engineering projects, is simply *thinking about it*. Understanding that you have options or obtaining options to hedge the risks and take advantage of the upside, and to think in terms of strategic options, is half the battle. Another 25% of the value comes from actually running the analysis and obtaining the results. The final 25% of the value comes from being able to explain the analysis to management, to your clients, and to yourself, such that the results become actionable intelligence that can be capitalised and acted upon, and not merely another set of numbers or risk management outputs.

REFERENCES

Brach, M. A. (2003). *Real Options in Practice*. John Wiley & Sons.

Hernandez-Perdomo, E. A., Mun, J., & Rocco, C. M. (2017). Active management in state-owned energy companies: Integrating a real options approach into multicriteria analysis to make companies sustainable. *Applied Energy, 195,* 487–502.

Hull, J. (2018). *Options, Futures, and Other Derivatives*, Tenth Edition. Pearson Education India.

Mun, J. (2016). *Real Options Analysis: Tools and Techniques for Valuing Strategic Investments and Decisions with Integrated Risk Management and Advanced Quantitative Decision Analytics,* Third Edition. ROV Press.

Paxson, D. A. (2003). *Real R&D Options*. Elsevier Science Ltd.

CHAPTER 5: RISK-BASED STRATEGIC DECISIONS IN DECOMMISSIONING

Energy companies—including oil and gas, mining, utilities, chemicals, and telecommunications—are exposed to significant financial and nonfinancial risks in the decommissioning of large operational fixed assets, which includes safe dismantling and removal of the facilities and production equipment, plugging oil and gas wells, and restoring the environment as close to pre-operational conditions as possible. However, active decision makers begin thinking early about the removal of property, plant, and equipment (PP&E) during the initial conceptual and feasibility studies. From the financial perspective, companies start accounting for decommissioning liabilities and future expenditures when an asset starts producing despite the uncertainties around future costs, regulations, safety, and so forth.

This chapter presents some decommissioning strategies and economic/financial aspects for managers and decision makers. It touches on topics such as accounting, auditing, taxes, project valuations, scenarios analysis, financial guidelines, strategic options, and hands-on risk modeling. These topics include important skills that financial and engineering professionals need to manage risk-based decommissioning timing and scenarios while at the same time considering requirements from assets owners, operators, regulators, contractors, and the supply chain.

DECOMMISSIONING STRATEGIES

Asset decommissioning, especially well plugging and abandonment (P&A), involves a significant amount of capital expenditure, planning (cost and time), due diligence, and nonfinancial resources (i.e., people and equipment). Decommissioning is not a money-generating activity; it follows a strict evaluation order: safety (first), cost effectiveness (second), and land restoration (third). Because of market fluctuations (i.e., prices and demand), decommissioning decisions can be greatly influenced by low profits or the availability of the financial resources needed to fulfil obligations. Hence, the timing of decommissioning (early or later) is key in any mothballing strategy.

In addition to finances, consistent decommissioning strategies also require understanding regulatory aspects, compliance, similarities among assets across companies, and economies of scale. For example, in the UK, decommissioning has important support from the government. The Oil and Gas Authority (2019) states that decommissioning is a matter of public policy interest, not only because of tax reliefs but also because of counterparty risk. As a last resort, when oil and gas firms cannot afford decommissioning themselves, the decommissioning liability falls on the taxpayers.

As a result, it does not matter whether the assets are in the final stage of their operational life cycle or are in the production phase, decommissioning strategies need to be constantly in the minds of decision makers (investors, shareholders, managers, regulators, etc.) either to time decommissioning or to evaluate alternative strategies (conventional or emerging).

Timing in Decommissioning Strategies

The decision to trigger the decommissioning option, early or late, relies on economic and market fluctuations, infrastructure obsolescence, technical challenges, regulatory pressure, and, especially, on cash management. In general, regulators (including the government) and companies need to find the balance between decommissioning costs and new investments to generate more income that would provide more taxes and revenues and even finance future decommissioning expenditures. Hence, decommissioning not only requires considering many uncertainty factors related to cash flows but also involves complex decisions based on an asset's condition, residual value, business models, supply chain, safety, and so forth, all of which influence the timing of the decommissioning.

- **Late Decommissioning**

Late decommissioning happens when an asset is in the late stage (i.e., cold stacked, no production, but decision makers want to postpone its decommissioning). Therefore, it requires active engagement among managers, regulators, and stakeholders, for example, to evaluate the following questions:

  o Can the current asset under management continue generating ongoing residual or new income to companies and taxes to the government?

  o Is it feasible to delay decommissioning for firms keeping marginal reserves in wells, if there are any?

  o Can companies generate extra revenues around diversification or new business (e.g., CCUS, hydrogen, gas-to-wire, infrastructure reuse) while delaying decommissioning?

  o What are the expected costs and schedule for decommissioning?

  o What are the operational and maintenance (O&M) costs of the facilities, job support, and the asset's conditions (health, safety, and assurance)?

- **Early Decommissioning**

This option applies when an asset's owners want to accelerate decommissioning (well plugging and facilities abandonment, for instance) of an asset not in its final stage of its life cycle (marginal fields, low flow-rates or production levels), but alternative projects and money-making options around transferring and hedging decommissioning risks are available.

Early decommissioning is a strategy that depends on market fluctuations (prices, supply, demand, etc.), the operational asset's condition (maintenance, direct and indirect expenses), economic and regulatory pressures (decarbonisation policies and taxes), asset integrity management (obsolescence and mechanical stress), and the likelihood of ceasing production. Consequently, these factors not only impact business performance (low operating profits, economic breakeven, cash constraints, etc.) but can also speed up decommissioning or asset sales.

Conventional Decommissioning Strategies

Conventional strategies are identified around asset sales or full decommissioning. They primarily depend on the ongoing value of a company's resources and production levels, which allows generating revenues to support current business and new opportunities (e.g., running late-life assets) or, ultimately, overseeing the full decommission process with its associated responsibilities and risks (project management, security, technologies available, technical capabilities, etc.).

Among conventional strategies, the first decision involves what to do with the assets (keeping or selling them), which equates to whether the decommissioning liability will be retained or transferred, and if the transferal is provisional (i.e., UK law only) whereby if the new owner cannot carry out the obligations, the asset goes back to the original proprietor. What are the pros and cons of maintaining or transferring the decommissioning liabilities? What other options can help to time decommissioning, enhance cost saving, and maximise cash usage? Figure 5.1 illustrates a strategic decision tree mapping conventional decommissioning options considering timing (early or late decommissioning) that are described as follows:

- **Traditional Asset Sales (Divesting Strategy)**

This option implies a transfer of ownership (production assets and decommissioning liabilities, including site restorations). It works when the buyer detects important synergies in the transaction (e.g., financial performance, salvage value, and technical skills and expertise on or from the decommissioning). For asset sales, the seller mostly receives cash to finance its other projects (shares or mixed payments can also be used), while the buyer maximises the economic value on assets that are not at the end of their life cycle.

Note that in the UK tax system this approach has been constrained, mainly because decommissioning costs can be deducted up to 50% of tax liabilities. If decommissioning costs exceed the tax liabilities, look-back adjustments are applied. As a result, the government finances the remaining proportion of decommissioning costs through tax reliefs. Also note that the buyer needs to have either a long UK tax history for the look-back analysis or relevant future profits on assets purchased to prove that it can fulfill its decommissioning obligations (counterparty risk).

To enhance value through divestitures, both buyers and sellers need to value the assets and synergies, precisely estimate decommissioning costs and liabilities, and analyse the tax impacts and counterparty risks on asset sales.

- **Economic Value and Liquidity Maximisers (Postponing Decommissioning)**

Generally, this strategy works when assets still have economic value, but owners have cash constraints or other investment opportunities (new high-value projects). They require liquidity but maintain the decommissioning liabilities while the buyer looks to optimise the economic value of the underlying assets. Usually, the value negotiated is higher than the full asset sale (divestiture) because the decommissioning liability remains on the seller's balance sheet.

To maximise the ownership value of this strategy, the seller needs to create strong decommissioning cost-reduction capabilities and look for better usage of the asset to be dismantled (e.g., recycling, CO_2 carbon capture, electrification, or new emerging options), which helps to buy more time to decommissioning and to take advantage of more mature technologies and efficient processes to reduce costs.

- **In-house Ownership (Internal Decommissioning Strategy)**

Owners maintain both assets and decommissioning liabilities. They require managing operational conditions to maximise recovery value, enhance revenues, and develop in-house decommissioning capabilities. Therefore, contractors, consultants, suppliers, and service companies help companies to execute on budget and on time, and to implement a safe and responsible decommissioning process.

Some of the biggest challenges associated with this option are project management risk (see Chapter 6 for further information); asset integrity management; permits; health, safety, and environmental issues; labour and engineering capabilities; and cash management during project execution (see Chapter 7 for some details on these risks).

Sophisticated managers are creating alternative approaches around internal decommissioning to optimise salvage values (compressors sales, spare parts, etc.), cost-efficiency project scenarios, HR and contractors management, information legacy, consultancy and expertise, and participation in other decommissioning projects to create new business opportunities (know-how, engineering outsourcing, resource reallocations, etc.). These opportunities require advance scenario and risk analysis, especially regarding timing the decommissioning according to the asset's life cycle.

- **Subcontracting Operations and Decommissioning (Outsourcing Strategy)**

Outsourcing decommissioning can provide significant flexibility for assets' owners to generate liquidity and manage cash opportunities. To enhance value by subcontracting operations and decommissioning, companies need to deal with well-known and efficient asset operators in overseeing the assets efficiently, including decommissioning activities.

Although companies can transfer risks on asset operations to third parties, this option comes with many caveats and requires due diligence, monitoring, governance, and business targets because of the counterparty risk (operators not fulfilling their obligations). Therefore, sophisticated managers use risk (market, operational, and business) and scenario analysis, asset integrity information, and project management approaches to minimise disruptions and plug and abandonment activities as they become more focused on the remaining assets not outsourced.

Note that outsourcing strategies are mostly cost- or NPV- (net present value) driven decisions. However, they can be "value-enhanced" if managers and decisions makers evaluate and quantify them using emerging decommissioning strategies (e.g., secondary usage of the facilities or new integrated business to delay decommissioning) and real options analysis (Mun, 2016).

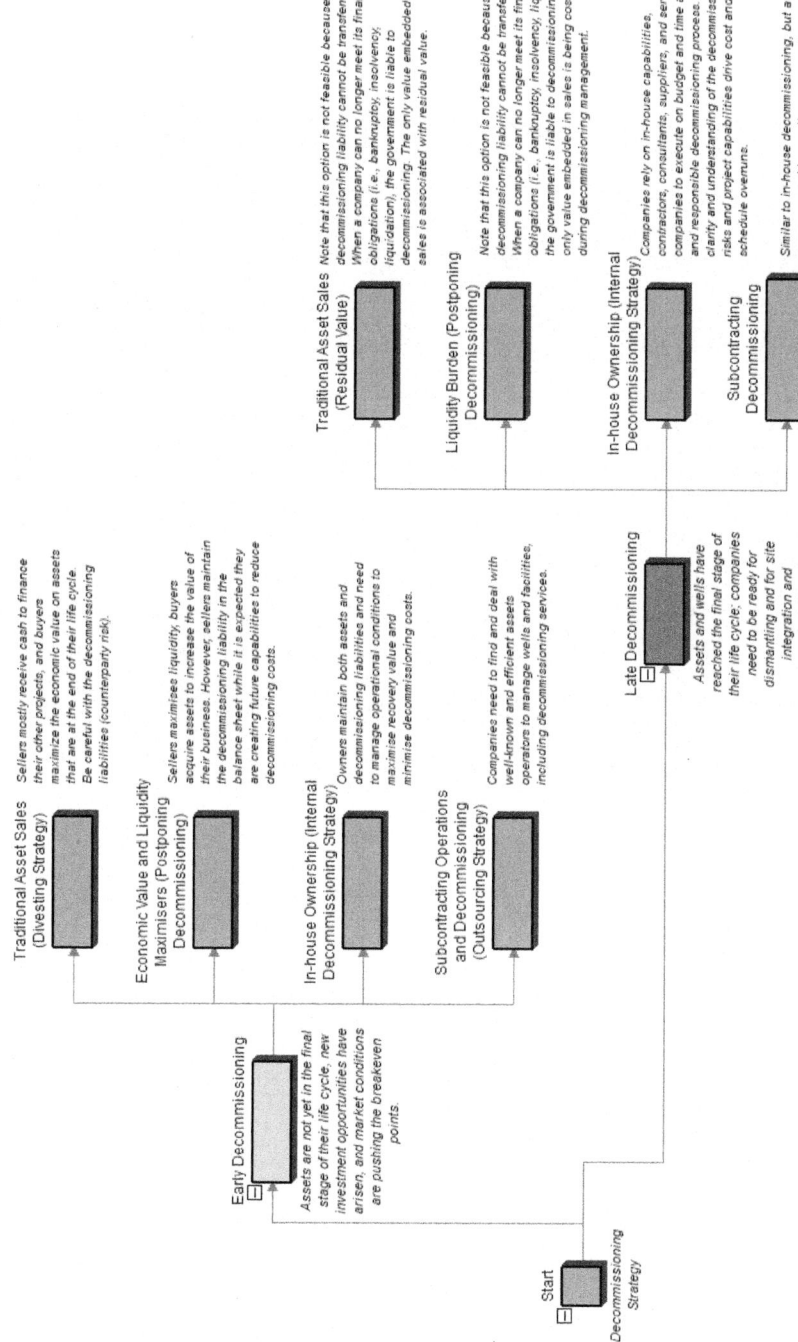

Figure 5.1: Conventional Decommissioning Strategies

Emerging Decommissioning Strategies

Emerging strategies for dealing with decommissioning of assets encompass alternatives to the outright disassembly and removal of an asset as well as ways to maintain a balance between decommissioning timing and managing business performance (i.e., savings, profits). Therefore, there are questions arising from managers wanting to utilise emerging strategies, in particular, to delay decommissioning, reduce expenditures, and enhance performance. For example:

- Can companies reuse end-life assets for other purposes (e.g., CCUS, hydrogen production, electrification)?

- Can companies integrate their assets into other economic strategies (e.g., decarbonisation, renewable energy)?

- Can companies move their assets to other locations?

- Can companies integrate the rigs into the current site to enhance environmental restoration?

- Can the decommissioning process create new business options (e.g., technologies, business, IP, expertise, patents)?

Although most of the strategies listed in the following paragraphs have been developed for offshore oil and gas assets, the approach to create and analyse emerging strategies can be extrapolated to other industries (wind farms, onshore facilities, utilities, mining, nuclear). Regardless of their application, all such strategies must be compliant with regulations and health, safety, environment, and quality (HSEQ) requirements. For example, in offshore wells plugging and abandonment, it is unquestionably essential to ensure that the wells do not leak and have long-term integrity (Vrålstad et al., 2019) by including extreme safety evaluations of casing strings, wellheads, and conductors.

- **Asset Infrastructure Reuse by Windfarm Operators (Windfarm Intervention)**

This option is considered when the platforms have stopped burning gas. Asset operators or owners can lease the infrastructure to wind farms or substations to generate electricity. These new business lines allow generating cash through either joint ventures (partnerships) or renting and leasing the facilities (outsourcing). The viability of the option relies on the history of maintenance, integrity of the facilities (e.g., material conditions, safety, weighting support), and fault and reliability analysis (technical risks) to improve both voltage (HVDC vs. AC power) and frequency stability, which help the lessee to assure their usage and lessor delay decommissioning.

Flexible infrastructure reuse can be considered a real options approach, in particular, when offshore projects are at the conceptual or feasibility stage when options such as to *delay* (decommissioning), *contract* (savings in CO_2 per year, pollution taxes), and *expand* (maximise economic value through electricity production) are being thought about, and can contribute to the decarbonisation targets. Additionally, to unlock funding and investment for flexible infrastructure reuse projects, risk drivers such as the required wind speed at the location for potential wind farm development, the life cycle and depreciation of the assets, project management risks on costs and time, legislation, economic feasibility, technical challenges, and HSEQ, among others, need to be quantified, which can be done using real options risk analysis.

- **Gas-to-Wire (GTW)**

This emerging option can help operators defer decommissioning and maximise the assets' economic value on both mature and marginal fields. It involves the generation of electricity at source on the offshore platform using the gas from the reservoir before transmitting to shore through subsea cable systems (potential to share this infrastructure with windfarms if based near the asset, mainly). Firms can hedge the associated revenue volatility by managing gas production and power generation simultaneously. Engineering capabilities (e.g., bidirectional cable systems) can help to manage electricity either from offshore wind power (nearby facilities) or from the onshore grid depending on the fluctuation of the demand.

Note that the investment opportunities with GTW depend on the feasibility study (fit-for-purpose) and capabilities to combine gas and electricity (technical risks), ageing of the platforms, wells' performance, project management risk on costs and time, legislation, HSEQ, and the economic analysis of managing gas-to-power, power-to-gas, or both, depending on the level of gas demand and competition in the power generation market. However, GTW is quite feasible for marginal gas fields or companies in breakeven net profits because the recovery value can help them to finance GTW projects and postpone decommissioning.

In terms of real options analysis, as well as in infrastructure reuse, options to *delay, expand,* and *contract* are also embedded in GTW strategies. Furthermore, companies can also value the option to *switch* because all gas generated would be converted (fully or partially) to power, depending on the supply and demand fluctuations. In other words, both outputs can be produced and commercialised using the same offshore platform.

- **Carbon Capture, Utilisation, and Storage (CCUS)**

CCUS has become part of the UK and EU strategy for decarbonisation (Paris Climate Agreement targets), opening a potential opportunity to manage late decommissioning. Oil and gas assets targeted for dismantling can be used for CCUS. The biggest risk involved is policy timing, and the assets should not be decommissioned before the CCUS project implementation. Otherwise, the feasibility of CCUS (high CAPEX) is reduced.

CCUS requires capturing CO_2 at its emissions sources and separating it from other gases (i.e., nitrogen and oxygen). Oil and gas platforms can store millions of tons of CO_2 in those wells to be plugged and abandoned. Consequently, the gas is transported to a storage location using pipelines, including repurposed gas pipelines, and stored, for example, within ground formations. It is important to review degradation and asset integrity (e.g., internal/external corrosion, internal erosion, flow assurance problems) and develop robust cement systems more resistant to CO_2 levels (Vrålstad et al., 2019).

When offshore oil and gas projects are connected to onshore projects, and are at the conceptual or feasibility stage, CCUS is a significant real option (option to *expand* and *grow*) for the assets' operators that can be managed by phase (feasibility, FEED [front-end engineering design], engineering, procurement, construction, integration, and commissioning *sequential options*). Using CCUS, companies can increase firm value and reduce future expenditures on well P&A. At the same time, CCUS projects can be integrated into dismantling, easing taxpayers' burden on decommissioning liabilities. Note that the option to *contract*, in terms of CCUS, disappears if the oil and gas infrastructure starts being decommissioned before CCUS approval, because wells and facilities utilisation are important drivers to reduce initial CAPEX on CCUS projects.

- **Alternative Projects (Biomass, Hydrogen, Geothermal)**

Alternative projects centered around biomass, hydrogen, and geothermal production are other emerging strategies that can create shareholder value while managers are delaying the P&A of wells. Some of such projects might consider partial or complete platform removal. For example, *fish biomass* production (option to *expand*) becomes a possibility only when there is a partial platform removal. Although partial platform removal results in certain losses in fish biomass and production, this value can be enhanced by using rock boulders (habitat enrichment material), for example. The value of fish biomass projects, including operational expenses and breakeven points, needs to be compared against the intangible value of fauna located in the deeper dwelling. Notably, further environmental inspection, a biodiversity survey, and habitat development are required to align asset operators' and regulators' incentives on this type of project.

Similarly, conversion from electricity to *hydrogen* via electrolysis is another emerging strategy to help with decarbonisation. Existing oil and gas pipelines to be decommissioned can be used as an efficient way to transport hydrogen; however, this activity requires due diligence and initial investment to make the facilities, equipment, and pipelines fit-for-purpose (e.g., most compressors are originally designed for gas). Technical risks and engineering capabilities analyses (R&D, FEED, asset integrity, equipment integration, construction, etc.) are required for minimising capital expenditures and increasing the feasibility of hydrogen projects, especially around the pipeline systems and platform conditions. In projects at the conceptual phase, real options analysis helps to value an option to *expand*, which maximises the utilisation pipelines (hydrogen and gas) in other industries (petrochemicals, transportation, power generation, etc.).

Finally, some oil and gas wells are also appropriate for producing *geothermal* energy, by pumping up hot water and enhancing electricity production, heating/cooling, and industrial applications. The feasibility for this usage depends on how much heat can be transferred from the oil and gas wells, considering working fluids, water reservoirs, casing and tubing, flow rates, wellbore architecture, and operational parameters (circulation rate, inlet temperature, permeability, etc.) (Sui et al., 2019). Therefore, environmental risks associated with the mobilisation of contaminants (from rocks) leading to pollution of aquifers by geothermal fluids are important to quantify. As a result, regular inspections and maintenance programmes of geothermal wells should be carried out to increase the safety and feasibility of these type of projects.

- **New Business in Decarbonisation (Technologies and Services)**

Companies wanting to create a competitive edge in decommissioning are also engaging in other joint ventures (option to *expand* and *contract*), especially in new technologies for cutting, lifting, and transporting services, which all impact the supply chain and cost reduction. Examples may include platform expansion (reliability), removal, and transportation methods; agile ports; and harbor management. In addition, lasers and drones are improving planning and strengthening strategies for environmental remediation as well.

In addition, companies creating internal decommissioning capabilities are also detecting opportunities, especially as regards transferable skills (mechanical, electrical, civil, process, procurement, risk management, project management, etc.), to outsource their human resources to other industries (wind farms, nuclear, chemicals). These resources are required to develop new projects as well. In other words, decommissioning represents a real opportunity for companies and people to drive change, create efficiency, and bring innovation into the energy industry.

- **Recycling, Relocation, and Site Integration**

Recycling, relocation, or site integration imply that residual value enhances cash inflows during decommissioning. These activities are considered as traditional asset sales, which allow balancing decommissioning costs. For instance, during the dismantling of offshore oil and gas installations, engines, compressors, and pipelines can be reused or relocated, and metals, PVC, copper, and iron can be recycled. Note that transparency, compliance, and the asset's due diligence, risk management, and regulation are important aspects to understand for infrastructure clearance and material recycling.

Although end-of-life facilities pose distinctive heavy lifting and transport challenges, when their buildings and components are prudently managed and reinforced during the decommissioning process, they can be transported and redeployed to other sites for alternative usage (wind farms, electrification stations, etc.).

Finally, site integration, including remediation, requires all the practices necessary to reduce the environmental and human health risks. This is a cost-driven approach where remedial actions are considered. Note that further surveys (seismic, site specifications, geological boundaries, and faults), testing (hydrostatic, gas, pressure, asset integrity, etc.), HSEQ acceptance, and waste management assurance are required for the site integration strategy.

Emerging Decommissioning Strategies and Real Options

Emerging alternatives for decommissioning require a significant amount of due diligence and real options analysis to understand the flexibility and uncertainty management related to decommissioning. They enhance firm value while decision makers are managing the asset's life cycle (performance vs. obsolescence) and hedging cash flow fluctuations because of volatility of commodity prices (oil, gas, electricity, etc.).

The value enhancement from real options (e.g., *expansion, contraction, deferral*, and so on) creates both a relevant appetite for M&As, joint ventures (electrification, GTW, CCUS, renewables, etc.), and a framework to time decommissioning. Their implementation requires not only framing strategic options from managers and regulators, but also using data analytics to evaluate decommissioning risks while enhancing shareholder value. Figure 5.2 provides a general structure of a decision tree to frame conventional and emerging strategies in decommissioning projects.

It is important to emphasise that framing decommissioning strategies requires taking into account managerial flexibility in adapting to ever-changing options and corporate, economic, and financial environments over time, as well as the fact that in the real business world, opportunities and uncertainty exist and are dynamic in nature. Real options help to identify, justify, time, prioritise, value, and manage corporate investment strategies under uncertainty in the context of timing decommissioning.

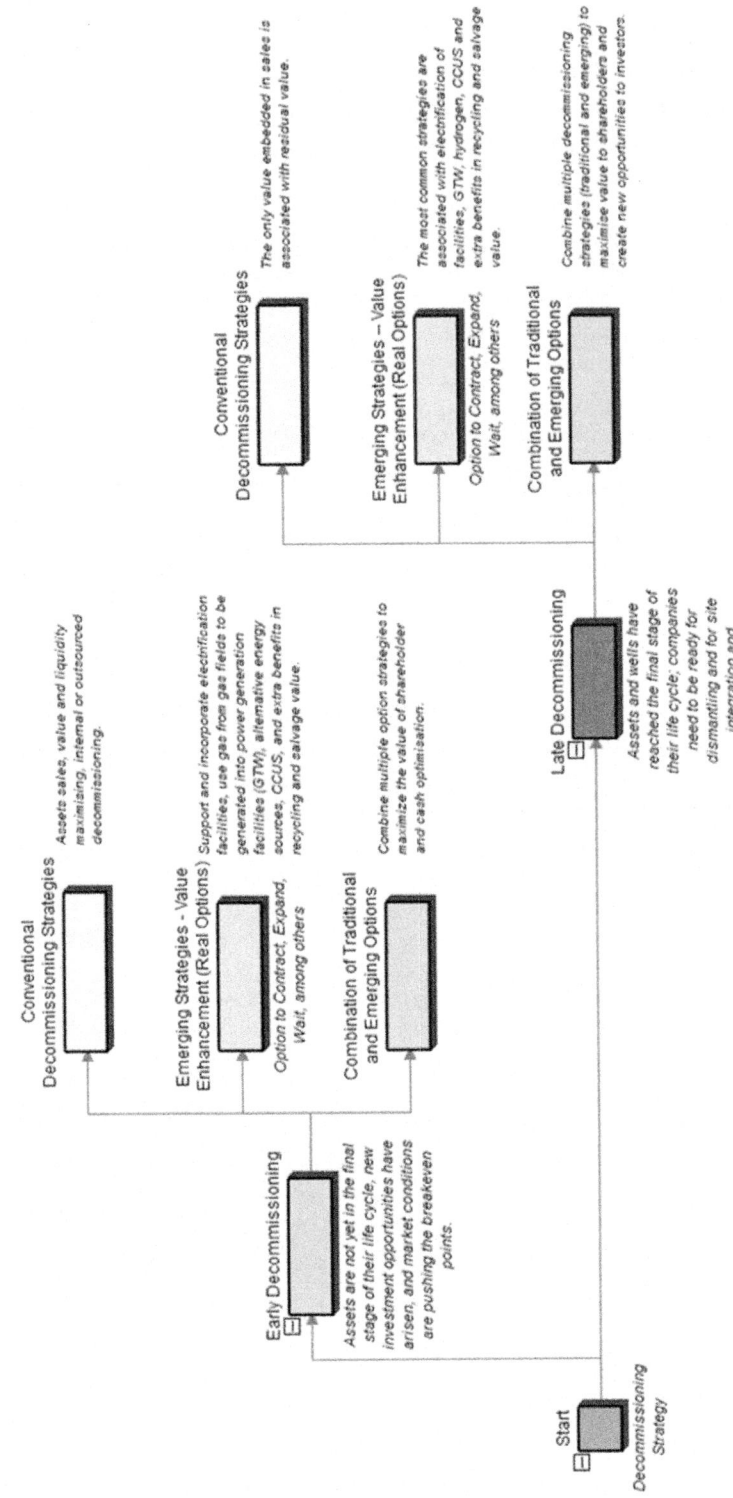

Figure 5.2: Conventional and Emerging Decommissioning Strategies (Framing the Real Options)

ACCOUNTING AND AUDITING IN DECOMMISSIONING

Responsive companies need to take a comprehensive risk management approach to quantify and reduce decommissioning risks (cost, schedule, cash flows, and dismantling strategies), which are common issues in any asset-intensive industry (e.g., energy, mining, metal processing, chemicals, oil and gas, nuclear, agroindustry, and so forth).

This section is intended to help managers and decision makers understand some accounting and auditing issues related to analysing and measuring decommissioning risks (e.g., provisions, depreciation, residual value, and auditing, among other aspects). Dealing with these issues can reveal significant information about an asset's operations and life cycle, financial value and performance, expected capital expenditures and salvage values, discount and inflation factors, major asset integrity updates, and so on.

Measuring and Recognising Decommissioning Provisions

Having an overview of the provisions (liabilities) connected with decommissioning provides an insight into how a company's expenses are allocated to plug and abandon assets, and, therefore, how it balances provision expenses as they arise. The following paragraphs briefly summarise nonfinancial guidelines on decommissioning provisions from the International Financial Reporting Standards (IFRS). The U.S. Generally Accepted Accounting Principles [GAAP] applies in an analogous approach to decommissioning provisions, known as Asset Retirement Obligation [ARO]. Managers should ask their company's financial specialists for more information on accounting standards, valuations, obligations, assumptions on assets' performance, and related expenses and adjustments.

Note that IAS 37 (International Accounting Standards), "Provisions, Contingent Liabilities and Contingent Assets," states that companies need to recognise a provision when there is a liability (IAS, 2019). In oil and gas, for example, the responsibility (liability) arises after the asset's construction and when removal at the end of its lifespan is required, including site restoration. Particularly, IAS 16,

"Property, Plant and Equipment (PP&E)," requires computing decommissioning costs and site restoration.

Also note that companies cannot recognise mothballing provisions in the income statement (profit or loss); they are part of the balance statement (PP&E in Assets). IFRIC 1 (International Financial Reporting Interpretations Committee), "Changes in Existing Decommissioning, Restoration and Similar Liabilities," also helps with decommissioning provision and recognition of its changes (IFRIC, 2019).

- **Measuring Decommissioning Provision**

Measuring decommissioning provision, especially in connection with well plugging and abandonment (P&A), is challenging because of the many uncertainties, mainly those associated with forecasting asset expenses (e.g., production process, operational and maintenance), lifespan, and dismantling costs and schedule, as well as the impact of inflation and discount factors. This measuring process requires using information from technical experts (operations, mechanical, electrical, structural, etc.); checking assumptions from prices (nominal and real), inflation trends, and discount rates (cost of capital, interest rates); and creating scenarios based on technology disruptions (current vs. unavailable technologies) and alternative strategies for decommissioning (decarbonisation projects) and environmental remediation.

A good practice to measure provision and model decommissioning risks is separating construction and operation obligations. The latter needs to contain information about rectifying environmental damages caused by an asset's operation. In terms of managerial accounting, a provision to rectify damages is caused by operation of an asset, not during its construction.

Regarding discount rates, IAS 37 requires selecting a pre-tax rate representing the current market assessment (time value of money [TVM]) and specific risks of liability. For example, using the WACC (weighted average cost of capital) is a common approach but it depends on how the company plans to finance the decommissioning (capital structure, cost of debt, and cost of equity), extrapolating the government bonds or risk-free interest rates, and timing the decommissioning process.

- **Recognising Decommissioning Provision**

IAS 16 requires recognising initial estimation of decommissioning expenses to the cost of an asset (Debit PP&E [IAS 16], and Credit Provision [IAS 37], for instance). In practical terms, a provision is created when a past event creates a present obligation. For example, when a firm builds an oil or gas platform and must remove it at the end of its life cycle, the liability or provision for removal is recognised at the time of construction (historical cost), in addition to site recovery and restoration costs. The further along the construction, the larger the liability.

Subsequent to the liability recognition, depreciation charges and finance cost adjustments are required in the computations. Therefore, at the end of the accounting or fiscal period, firms need to revise the provision and recognise those changes, if there are any, according to IFRIC 1 standards.

Summarising, decision makers should review the recognition aspects of decommissioning provision. Note that under the cost model, a firm recognises provision changes as historical costs; and under the revaluation model (fair value), it recognises provision changes in the asset's revaluation surplus or deficit, supported by market valuations. In decommissioning strategies, fair value can be problematic due to the many uncertainty factors in determining fair asset value and decommissioning costs.

- **A General Example of Decommissioning Provision**

After an asset is built and operation starts, companies immediately need to disclose and account for decommissioning expenditures and liabilities (requires technical and operational information), while they need to compare the liabilities against historical costs. Therefore, financial specialists should update decommissioning provisions according to changes in discounts rates, inflation estimations, and other assumptions.

For example, a company in 1997 commissioned a gas platform (life cycle 25 years, 7,000 tons of weight, and 6 operating wells). The estimated well P&A costs are about £30 million (distributed between 2019 to 2022 as shown in Table 5.1). In 2019 the company needed to know the decommissioning costs and provision values. Note that the historic decommission costs need to be adjusted by inflation to get the costs in current prices across the well's P&A as follows:

$Costs \times (1 + Inflation)^{\wedge}(Asset\ Life + t)$

..., current values are adjusted according to the *time value* ... using an appropriate discounted factor (government bonds, ...oor rate, WACC estimations, among others). Present value (PV) can be obtained as follows:

$Current\ Prices / (1 + Discount\ Rate)^{\wedge}(Asset\ Life + t)$

The total present value of the decommissioning costs is £35.08 million (see Table 5.1 for further details).

Table 5.1: Accounting Decommissioning Provisions

Average Inflation rate (Inflation)	2.50%
Discount rate (Yearly)	1.90%
Commissioning Date	1997
Platform Operation (AssetLife)	25

Description	2019	2020	2021	2022
Years to Decommissioning (t)	0	1	2	3
Decommissioning Expenses (Historical Costs*)	£0.50	£14.50	£10.00	£5.00
Decommissioning Expenses (Current Prices*)	£0.93	£27.55	£19.48	£9.98
Present Value (PV*)	£0.58	£16.89	£11.72	£5.89
Total PV (Decommissioning)	**£35.08**			

Monetary units in £ million

Of course, in terms of going concern (proven business continuity, long-term viability, production levels, assets integrity, and financial performance), the company is generating economic benefits and must recognise the decommissioning provisions as well as depreciation expenses. Otherwise, the rig needs to be prepared for decommissioning or be considered as "warm stacked". The provision recognition process can be described as follows:

a) Initial Provision Recognition

The provision recognised in 2019 is £35.08 million (total present value of the estimated decommissioning costs), indicating a journal entry as follows for the gas platform (Debit PP&E [IAS 16] and a Credit in provision for decommissioning [IAS 37]):

- *Debit (PP&E of £35.08 million) = Credit (Decommissioning Provision of £35.08 million)*

Assume that the platform is depreciated based on the unit of production over the proven gas reserves (i.e., 40 million cubic meters with a yearly production of 5 million) using the formula:

(Total PV / Reserves) × Yearly Production

The following journal entry for the given asset results:

- *Debit (Depreciation Expenses of £4.39 million) = Credit (Accumulated Depreciation of £4.39 million)*

b) Subsequent Provision Recognition

If there are no changes in inflation and discount factors in the subsequent reporting period (Year 2020), the company needs to unwind the discounted amounts using the IFRIC 1 standard, *Total PV × Discount Rate*. It indicates a journal entry as follows:

- *Debit P&L (Financial Costs of £0.67 million) = Credit (Provision for Decommissioning of £0.67 million)*

If there are changes in inflation and discount factors in the subsequent period (Year 2021 and Year 2022) or updates in decommissioning costs and schedule, the company needs to recalculate the decommissioning provision, asset depreciation, and changes in profits and losses (P&L) under IFRIC 1. Finally, when the company starts well decommissioning and site restoration, all expenses are charged against the created provision account (Debit Provision for Decommissioning and Credit Cash and Cash Equivalents).

As a final point, active decision makers and managers need to understand that accounting for decommissioning involves uncertainty analysis on inflation and discount factors impacting liabilities and cost estimations. Therefore, cost estimations require information from technical experts, asset integrity surveys, and market trends (e.g., availability of cost-efficient technologies, supply chain engagement, economies of scale).

Depreciation Analysis and Residual Value

Apart from managing the accounting aspects of depreciation (tangible assets) and amortisation (intangible assets) from the GAAP or IFRS principles and standards, agile decision makers need to understand how depreciations and investment costs (e.g., CAPEX) of long-lived tangible assets are allocated over their useful life. They need to consider not only original costs and residual value, but also the distinction between the estimated service (useful) life versus physical life. For instance, the depreciable amount equals the original cost minus residual value over the estimated asset life.

Among the most common depreciation approaches you can find are activity-based (units of use or production-based), straight-line (time-based), accelerated (declining balance or sum of the years' digits [SoYD]), and other special cases (e.g., hybrids methods). Note that the GAAP or IFRS accounting frameworks state the need for consistency among the usage of depreciation methods. Depreciation should reflect the expected future economic benefits to be consumed over the asset's useful life.

In addition, some companies decide—according to the information available, the asset's nature and integrity conditions, likely economic benefits, and other aspects—as to whether an asset is depreciated or amortised in full or has a salvage or residual value. The decision can be reviewed each financial year or when assets are expected to be decommissioned. However, if expectations change from previous figures, depreciation estimates need to be adjusted, and if any sales at the end of the asset's useful life are considered, they need to be accrued (including likely taxes) in the P&L statements. In fact, changes will be made in the current and future periods according to the asset life and total depreciable amount remaining after the change.

- **Asset Depreciation in Oil and Gas Companies**

Financial and accounting specialists in multinational companies mostly compute oil and gas assets in accordance with IAS 8, "Accounting Policies, Changes in Accounting Estimates and Errors." In upstream assets, accumulated exploration and evaluation (E&E) and development costs are amortised over the expected total production life (using the activity-based method corresponding to the economics of the reserves' pattern). Those assets consumed over the passage of time can be depreciated using a straight-line approach. However, managers should ask whether there are adjustments needed in the depreciation estimates because of proven, undeveloped, or probable reserves, and also current or future development costs.

Downstream assets such as refineries, gas treatment installations, chemical plants, distribution networks, and other facilities and infrastructure are often depreciated on a straight-line basis. Alternatively, for pipelines used for transportation, depreciation can be calculated based on units transported during their lifetime (unit-of-throughput basis), which is a proportion of the expected throughput over the pipeline's life.

- **Residual Value and Scenario Analysis**

Residual value has become an important approach in decommissioning strategies to buffer expenditures, create synergies among contractors and suppliers, and enhance value through sales in the secondary market (operational and reliability data, materials, MCS [management control systems], pipes, valves, pumps, meters, storage tanks, heater equipment, compressors, metal construction, copper from removal of wiring, concrete, plastic or PVC, parts and spares, hardware, sensors, and other miscellaneous equipment).

To improve residual value estimations on energy and oil and gas assets, sophisticated decision makers gather and analyse information on AIM, or asset integrity management (reliability, inspections, maintenance, repairs, etc.); cost-benefit analysis on recycling, reuse, and disposal; social and industry acceptance of recycled materials in other processes and companies; transparency on the level of scrutiny placed on AIM, risk identification, and compliance; regulatory process in terms of radiological protection, hazards, quality, and unrestricted release of materials; infrastructure cleared and available for material recycling and scrap metals; time to achieve the outcomes (regulatory analysis, environmental surveys, safety and quality assessments, administrative activities, etc.); degree of stakeholder involvement (supply chain, HSEQ, communities, and regulators); and other aspects.

- **Common Depreciation Approaches (Examples)**

When making assumptions for asset depreciation and salvage value, note that the matching principle (accrual accounting concept) expects that a firm recognises the expenses in the same period as the related revenues are earned. Here are some generic examples to illustrate depreciation methods considering salvage values:

a) Activity-based Approach

MAXY Gas installed a gas processing plant costing £140 million with an estimated production capacity of 60 million barrels of oil equivalent during its entire life. Production during the first year (Y1) of operation is 8 million barrels of oil equivalent a year. The expected residual value of the gas plant is £4 million.

The depreciation charge for year one (Y1) is calculated as:

Depreciation Expense = (£140 − £4) × (8/60) = £18.13 million

The activity-based (production-based) approach might be suitable when there is a high correlation between the asset's production and its physical usage. This method can be problematic when, for example, an asset remains idle or has a decreased earning potential because of its useful life stage, technological obsolescence, or market conditions.

b) Straight-line Depreciation

MAXY Gas bought and installed a gas compressor to increase gas flow rate at a cost of £15 million. MAXY estimates a salvage value of £1 million and a useful life of 10 years.

The annual depreciation is calculated as:

Depreciation Expense = (£15 − £1)/10 years = £1.4 million per year

This results in a depreciation percentage of 10% (£1.4 /£14).

Straight-line depreciation is a simple and widely used method, being a function of time only. Note that depreciation expenses run each year until an asset reaches its residual value.

c) Accelerated Depreciation

MAXY Gas designed and fabricated a three-phase heated separator device for the efficient separation of mixed crude oil and waste resources at a cost of £2 million, with a salvage value of £0.5 million and a useful life of 3 years. The depreciation approach used accounts for more expenses in the early years of the asset's life (asset's productivity is greater in the early days). Among the methods we have:

(1) SoYD, Sum of the Years' Digits

Computing the *SoYD* (3 + 2 + 1 = 6), we can determine a ratio (depreciation fraction) of the number of years left in the asset's useful life as follows: Y1 = 3/6, Y2 = 2/6, and Y3 = 1/6. Each fraction is multiplied by the depreciable amount (acquisition cost or construction including any successive CAPEX, less the residual or scrap value). In other words, annual depreciation progressively declines as the asset ages. Depreciation expense can be computed as:

Y1 = (2 − 0.5) × (3/6) = £0.75 million

Y2 = (2 − 0.5) × (2/6) = £0.5 million

Y3 = (2 − 0.5) × (1/6) = £0.25 million

(2) Declining Balance

A declining balance maintains a constant depreciation rate starting from the asset's historical cost (book value), which is generally 1.5 or 2 times the straight-line rate. Using the above example, the straight-line yearly depreciation is £0.5 million (33.3%). Thus, the double-declining balance (DDB) method uses a yearly rate that is twice the straight-line depreciation percentage (66.6%) until the asset is above its salvage value. For further information, review GAAP and IFRS principles and standards, including those pertaining to tax implications.

Capital Allowances, Taxes, and Decommissioning Reliefs

When organisations are dealing with decommissioning, especially in the UK, capital allowances rules (tax depreciation) help them to get some tax relief on capital expenditure to enhance investments, which also create an expense against the annual pre-tax income.

Mostly, tax reliefs are available when decommissioning expenditures are incurred (advanced regulatory or governmental approval might be required), so the defined percentage becomes available to close or dismantle all or part of the oil-gas fields and facilities. For instance, in the UK, tax allowances (100% for offshore and 25% for onshore assets) are offered for dismantling strategies. For further information, the UK's National Audit Office (2019) and HM Revenue & Customs (HMRC) can provide consultation on this matter. Note that while decommissioning tax relief impacts the government's finances, by recovering some of their costs through these instruments, oil and gas operators can plan and estimate future well P&A and other dismantling costs. Tax reliefs are not subsidies or new costs to taxpayers; they can be considered a refund to operators who have paid taxes on revenues in previous years. Thus, the government can help operators to buffer decommissioning expenditures by reducing taxable profits and considering tax reliefs based on the large sums of tax companies have paid historically. Those reliefs offset dismantling expenses against revenues, reducing the tax amount to pay on profits.

- **Tax Regimes and Decommissioning**

Although tax relief principles might change because of changing governmental views, active decision makers need to understand and manage the risks pertaining to tax regimes and decommissioning (Choudhury et al., 2016). They need to understand who has the responsibility for decommissioning (government, license holder, or both) and who pays for decommissioning (government or license holder, or as per an agreed to fraction or amount by the license holder).

Among the three most common tax deduction choices (direct expenditures, accrual, fund contributions), managers should know when each is applicable. A direct expenditures deduction can be taken when cash is expended in decommissioning (e.g., Australia, Denmark, Canada, Chile, USA, UK). When decommissioning is accrued (e.g., Netherlands, USA by election), an accrual deduction applies, and the fund contributions provide a tax deduction when decommissioning is pre-funded (e.g., Ghana, India, Mozambique, South Africa). Note that payments for security (e.g., letters of credit) are considered part of tax reliefs.

Observe that in tax deduction upon expenditure (cash basis), the government needs to ensure funds availability for decommissioning. The assumption is that the government will receive all taxes/receipts from the resource's extraction. In tax deduction upon accrual, dismantling expenses are accounted in the P&L statements; otherwise, provisions need to be created. Therefore, taxpayers can better deploy capital, and the government needs to monitor and control the provisions and decommissioning costs. Finally, in tax deduction upon pre-funding, companies can contribute, with government support, to decommissioning funds out of which the liability is settled. Although it provides cash flows advantages for governments, pre-funding raises concerns for companies on the timing of the deduction and taxation (surplus and deficits within the fund).

- **General Examples of Tax Reliefs**

This section provides some simplified examples of how business accounts for tax reliefs regarding tax deductions, credits, and exclusions. It is, of course, recommended to obtain more information from tax specialists, the government, and the tax administration (e.g., HMRC, Audit Offices, IRS) to determine how a company should manage tax reliefs, decommissioning regulation, and estimations of costs to be incurred in the future.

a) Tax Deductions

This approach to tax relief allows reducing the taxable income of a taxpayer, for example, by the amount of decommissioning (100%). To illustrate this approach, suppose MAXY Oil and Gas's taxable income is £45 million at the time the 1-year decommissioning project has started. Given a corporate tax of 25%, the tax payable is £11.5 (£45 × 25%) million. However, it qualifies for an £8 million tax deduction (decommissioning costs) and thus will be taxed on £45 − £8 = £37 million, not £45 million. MAXY ends up paying less in taxes to the government.

b) Tax Credit

A tax credit provides tax savings to companies by reducing the tax bill and not the income subject to taxes (tax deduction). For example, MAXY Oil and Gas has made significant tax payments to the government on profits from production and commercialisation of oil and gas. During the year of the decommissioning process, MAXY computes £15 million in tax payables. However, the company has a tax credit (rebate) of £8 million for decommissioning, which is applied to the tax owed. MAXY will have to pay £7 million after the tax relief is applied.

c) Tax Exclusion

Although this approach is uncommon in the literature of tax reliefs across upstream and downstream oil and gas business, tax exclusion remains an option for managing decommissioning trust funds (Rogers, 1992). A tax exclusion classifies a certain type of income as tax-free or tax relief, mostly because some types of income are either challenging to measure or persuading taxpayers to engage in certain economic activities (health, government, education). For example, an expatriate earning income abroad can be excluded from taxation.

Auditing Decommissioning Costs

Although a traditional auditing process relies on examining estimations, assumptions, and measurements of decommissioning costs, asset depreciation, and potential residual values, it also includes analysing provisions, funds, adjustment factors (interest and inflation rates), tax regimes, and type of decommissioning strategies (partial and full dismantling), as well as reviewing compliance frameworks imposed by regulators, among other aspects. To enhance this traditional process, the authors proposed a risk-based auditing approach, not only to scrutinise decommissioning assumptions and measurement, but also to analyse the uncertainty factors impacting decommissioning costs and strategic decisions.

Risk-Based Auditing

- Because inappropriate assumptions can undermine both the initial decommissioning costs and potential liabilities, agile decision makers must use Monte Carlo risk simulations and scenarios analysis to validate expected costs, asset life cycles, decommissioning schedule, and discount factors to calculate the present value of the expected costs.

- Although the effect of discounting has a significant impact on decommissioning provisions, IAS 37 recommends selecting an interest rate adjusted by market trends (time value of money) and risk-specific to provision (US government bonds can be used as a benchmark). Interest rates used for discounting cash flows should be reviewed regularly (at least annually) using forecasting analysis (e.g., yield curves) and simulations tools. Decommission provision is unwound each year to increase its present value. If it has not increased, this could indicate that management has changed some assumptions (e.g., using a higher interest rate).

- Decommissioning costs represent a significant burden for a company's cash and liquidity. Auditors recommend reviewing them annually according to the market changes. However, managers also need to use cost models, scenarios, and sensitivity analysis to determine the effects of law and regulations adjustments, including the impact of climate change and decarbonisation, usage of new technologies (e.g., cutting, lifting, waste disposal, well P&A), and changes in stakeholder expectations.

Compliance, Process, and Evidence

- IAS 37 requires companies to disclose and describe, in the financial statement notes, the nature of future obligations and outflows of economic benefits, including timing and uncertainties, numerical disclosure, and provision movements, among other material information.

- Managers need to be sure auditors obtain enough and appropriate evidence to assess risks of material misstatements on decommissioning costs, including agreements and licenses issued by regulators to confirm any liabilities of dismantling (ISA, 2009).

- Decommissioning calculations need to be reviewed based on assumptions provided by the company, including estimation methods and provisions measurement.

To summarise, accounting and auditing in decommissioning are not trivial activities; they require understanding substantial uncertainty factors, financial approaches, tax regimens, and estimation methods. However, this activity is not a matter only for financial and tax specialists. It requires significant technical and engineering expertise. Oil and gas companies, including energy, mining, chemicals, renewables, and so on, need to consider and quantify engineering assumptions, including multidisciplinary industry information, to achieve consistent and reasonable recommendations to decommissioning.

RISK-BASED ANALYSIS IN DECOMMISSIONING

Cost estimations in decommissioning projects require information from the assets' operators, contractors, regulators, engineers, financial specialists, managers, and so forth. A common approach in cost modeling is accounting for this information and adding up the costs to obtain a formal base-case estimation. However, this approach is purely deterministic even though companies use a percentage (%) of contingency (e.g., 10%, 20%, 30%, and so on) to manage deviations around the base case to support and plan the expenditures.

Nevertheless, there are factors and uncertainty sources that affect the variability of estimations and increase risk in decommissioning forecasts. These can include project management scope (cost, schedule, safety), assets' specifications (size, history, weights), inflation, asset integrity, inspections, surveys, compliance, public concerns on waste materials, environmental remediation, taxations and subventions, contractual obligations (fixed costs vs. reimbursable costs), technical feasibility, health standards, and so on. Because of these influences, decisions can be misled without the usage of simulations and scenarios (i.e., Monte Carlo simulation and applied analytics), which also include expert information, historical data, assumptions, and so forth.

The following examples illustrate why simulation is important in estimating decommissioning costs and residual value (stand-alone risk modeling). Note that this proposed approach can be used for any of the decision-making aspects of decommissioning such as project management cost and schedule (Chapter 6), risk identification and quantification (Chapter 7), quote and tender management, budgeting, liability estimations, project finance, and conventional and emerging options valuations. We used the Risk Simulator (RS) and PEAT software applications, where extended trial copies can be downloaded from www.oslriskmamagement.com or www.realoptionsvaluation.com (see the Appendix). Information on running Monte Carlo simulation and PEAT can be obtained from the user manual and online RS videos.

Decommissioning Costs

Understanding risks in connection with decommissioning costs is important for active managers dealing with provisions, budgets, critical activities, and other estimations that might change during the decision-making process due to variations in prices, completion times, technologies available, labour and material costs, currency changes, contractors experience, standards (HSEQ), tenders' assumptions, change management, and so on.

Table 5.2 shows an activity-based cost approach in decommissioning with a base case of £43.98M. A traditional way of managing uncertainty is considering the percentage of contingencies (e.g., ±25%), which also implies that the given project might overrun £10.9M. However, with the Monte Carlo simulations and uncertainty analysis around the project inputs (Figure 5.3 shows the risk forecast and statistics), it can be observed that the expected value is £48.6M with the following information: 90% confidence it will fall between £40.2M and £55.6M, with high chances of having values above the most likely (negative skew = –0.28), and a probabilistic contingency (+25%) of £51.9M. As good practice, it is important to disclose any cost assumptions based on current or future technologies; in other words, account for any technical innovation or assume today's technologies. Therefore, it is imperative to sort the expenses by categories and contractors, related wells to be plugged, platform removals, and environmental rectification.

Table 5.2: Generic Decommissioning Costs (Activity-Based)

Task	Task Name	Total Cost	Uncertainty Sources
Activity 1	Scope Work (Feed study)	£500.00	
Activity 2	P&A Design	£250,000.00	
Activity 3	Engineering Planning	£600,000.00	Time driven activity (cost x duration)
Activity 4	Procurement	£250,000.00	Inflation and lead times
Activity 5	Decommissioning Permits & Compliance	£99,999.96	
Activity 6	Drilling Rig Arrival	£180,000.00	Multiples tenders and bids
Activity 7	Platform Preparation	£5,518,947.37	Multiple contractors values
Activity 8	Wells P&A	£10,347,500.00	Time driven activity (cost x duration)
Activity 9	Conductor Removal	£600,000.00	Multiple contractors values
Activity 10	Heavy Lift Vessel Arrival	£150,000.00	Time driven activity (cost x duration)
Activity 11	Platform Removal	£23,687,000.00	Time driven activity (cost x duration)
Activity 12	Disposal & Site Clearance	£1,900,000.00	Based on multiple logistics costs
Activity 13	Handover	£300,000.00	
Activity 14	Project Completion	£100,000.00	
	Total Cost	£43,983,947.33	
	-20% Contingencies	£32,987,960.50	Deterministic Scenarios
	+20% Contingencies	£54,979,934.16	Deterministic Scenarios

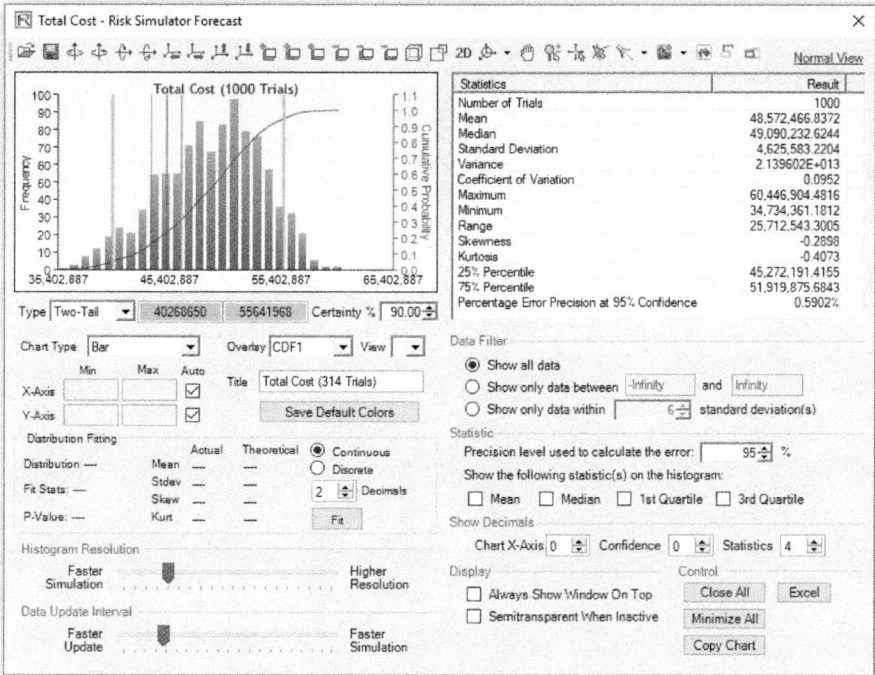

Figure 5.3: Simulations Results on Decommissioning Costs

Residual Value

According to the operational information (technical experts, engineering details, asset integrity surveys) and secondary market for sales (e.g., materials, equipment, and spare parts), there can be some monetary value around the dismantling process to buffer expenditures. Instead of managing static scenarios, risk simulations can help determine the profile of the remaining assets' value, either to generate some savings around the decommissioning expenditures or monetising certain synergies (e.g., offset of cost in certain activities) among contractors and suppliers.

Table 5.3 lists some common items (including prices, quantities, and total values) that secondary markets, including other assets' operators, have shown interest in buying, using, or selling. In terms of estimating the profile of the salvage value, running Monte Carlo simulations (Figure 5.4) helps to inform decision makers that there is an intrinsic value between £3.5M and £5.1M at the 90% confidence interval in residual value of the well decommissioning process. This enhances the savings or synergistic value on materials, spare parts, and recycling in the secondary market.

Table 5.3: Generic Residual Value in Decommissioning

Items	Description	Quantity	Price	Total Value
Item 1	Air Compressor Unit	1	£100,000.00	£100,000.00
Item 2	Diesel Power Generator	2	£260,000.00	£520,000.00
Item 3	Well Head XMas Trees	6	£350,000.00	£2,100,000.00
Item 4	Cranes	4	£25,000.00	£100,000.00
Item 5	Platform fixed generators	2	£460,000.00	£920,000.00
Item 6	Stell @ Tons	6200	£60.00	£372,000.00
Item 7	Copper & Nickel @ Kg	1400	£2.30	£3,220.00
Item 8	Reliability and operational data			£25,000.00
Item 9	Valves, pumps and meters			£95,000.00
Item 10	Storage tanks	2	£4,600.00	£9,200.00
Item 11	High-density polyethylene (HDPE) pipes			£30,000.00
Item 12	Reinforced thermoplastic pipe (RTP)			£15,000.00
Item 13	Bundle of parts and spares			£60,000.00
Item 14	Bundle of hardware, sensors, reelers, and miscellaneous			£45,000.00
Total	*Residual Value (in pounds)*			*£4,394,420.00*

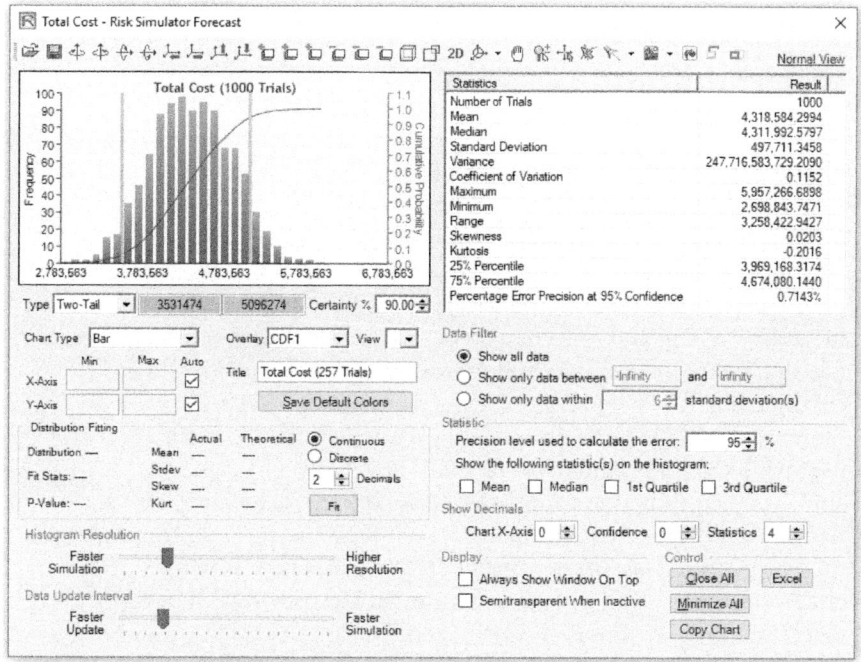

Figure 5.4: Simulations Results on Residual Value

Risk-based analysis using Monte Carlo simulations is a powerful approach to understanding uncertainty and quantifying decommissioning risks. It essentially allows hundreds of thousands of scenarios and contingency analyses to be performed that provide probabilistic risk profiles associated with costs and residual values, among other performance indicators. Of course, in addition to simulation analysis, other considerations such as correlations among costs, activities, and contractors, type of distributional functions, dynamic sensitivity analysis, and precision and errors control, also enhance the process of interpreting the results and risk statistics (Mun, 2015).

HANDS-ON PEAT-DECOMM FOR PROJECT VALUATIONS

Companies without additional opportunities to continue extracting resources (coal, metal, oil and gas, etc.) need to exercise their option of decommissioning. However, active decision makers in the oil and gas industry start assessing and evaluating alternative options for enhancing performance (e.g., other interrelated projects) while managing a decommissioning strategy (e.g., postponing or accelerating). Alternative options, projects, programmes, and engagements need to be integrated into commercial and operational strategies to enhance financial performance, capital budgeting, and investment requirements. To help them make the best decisions, agile managers use risk-based economic and financial analysis such as Monte Carlo simulations, predictive forecasting, portfolio management, and scenario and sensitivity analysis on well-known performance measurements: net present value (NPV), internal rate of return (IRR), modified internal rate of return (MIRR), payback period (PB), discounted payback period (DPP), profitability index (PI), return on investment (ROI), and so forth. This assessment goes beyond the analysis of warm-staked options (e.g., platform lights on, engines running, and a small crew aboard).

The Project Economics Analysis Tool (PEAT-DECOMM) software (Figure 5.5) was created not only to analyse various project economics and financial outcomes but also to integrate and evaluate current and potential strategies (conventional and emerging) around decommissioning, namely, to select the most important projects, detect critical risk-factor-driven decisions, and determine project risk profiles based on cash flow, cost of capital, CAPEX, OPEX requirements, and decommissioning costs and salvage values, for instance.

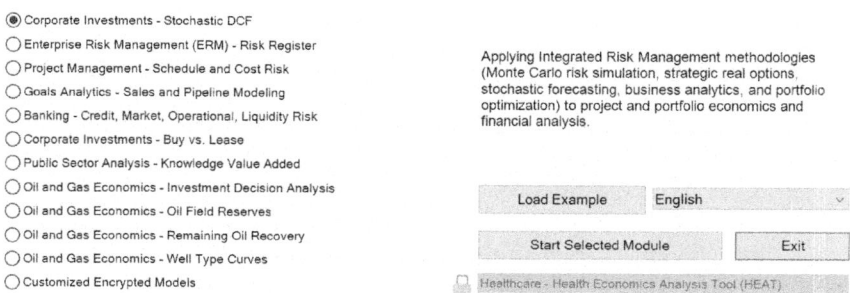

Figure 5.5: PEAT–DECOMM Expert Solution Software

Quick Interpretation of Some Economic Measures

Most corporate financial decisions rely on normal key performance indicators to guide option valuations (Berk et al., 2013; Mun, 2018), for example:

- The *net present value* (NPV) is a decision criterion that discounts cash flows at the cost of capital, for example, equity, debt, or a combination (weighted average cost of capital [WACC]). The NPV helps to justify whether or not a project goes ahead by looking at its financial and monetary profit levels (i.e., the project is accepted if NPV is positive).

- The *internal rate of return* (IRR), simple or modified, is a measurement of project profitability and investor or shareholder expectations. It is expected to be larger than the cost of capital.

- The *payback period* (PB), regular or discounted, is an indicator of the number of years required to recover the investment. It is a proxy for the project's short-term risk and liquidity.

- The *profitability index* (PI) is a relative measure of profitability considering benefits (present value) divided by costs (initial investments and CAPEX).

Although, for some projects, certain indicators mean more to decision makers than others, sophisticated managers mostly tend to consider as many indicators as possible to both analyse multiple angles of project valuations and justify the final decisions. Additional interpretations and formulas can be found in the PEAT-DECOMM's software help materials.

Navigating PEAT-DECOMM Software for Project Valuations

PEAT-DECOMM embeds several decision analytics in an expert system allowing sophisticated managers to conduct advanced risk-based project valuations. During this process, they can determine influential risk factors, assess multiple economic and financial indicators, and determine in real-time how risk changes when project assumptions and inputs vary.

- **Project Inputs, Assumptions, and Outputs**

Although PEAT-DECOMM has been developed to evaluate any type of project, it has been customised for projects that embed decommissioning, operational performance, and commercial expectations. Usually, decommissioning project evaluations are made after the plant construction at a later stage of the business. Consequently, because the project is already running, CAPEX and project expenses already incurred are considered sunk costs and part of the depreciation's expenses.

For example, Figure 5.6 shows a generic example of a stand-alone company project (i.e., wells and platform performance with 15 years of future operations remaining). For illustration purposes, the authors provide the financial variables and assumptions at the aggregated levels (OPEX, CAPEX, depreciation, residual values, decommission, overheads, and professional services). Note that the tab PEAT-DECOMM | *Forecast Prediction* can be used to forecast project inputs, if necessary.

PEAT-DECOMM allows contemplating any other desegregation of financial and economic variables, including balance sheet and capital structure data to compute other relevant financial ratios (e.g., EBIT, net income, net cash flows). Therefore, this software also helps to evaluate other versions of the underlying project and potential projects (portfolio analysis), for example, conventional or emerging options.

With a clear picture of the project assumptions, decision makers need to analyse multiple economic indicators (Figure 5.7). PEAT-DECOMM provides a tab for *Economic Results* (NPV, MIRR, PB, among other indicators). Note that this project is in a later stage (no initial investment); consequently, variables like PI, ROI, PB, and so on are not computed.

This project or current business provides a *present value* (PV) of £297M in terms of company profitability. Therefore, the *Net Income* is becoming critical at the end of the life of the project, mainly determined by commercial risk (prices, production, market conditions, etc.) and likely decommissioning expenditures as well.

- **Decision Analytics**

PEAT-DECOMM also provides different *Applied Analytics* to run static analysis on performance indicators for every project (one or two variables at once). For instance, *Tornado Analysis* provides static approaches to get the most influential risk factors by examining one variable at a time, while *Scenario Analysis* allows determining the impact on the main economic criteria of variations of one or two variables at once.

Figure 5.8 shows the *Tornado Analysis* on the NPV (stand-alone project) using PEAT-DECOMM. This type of static analysis verifies that revenues, OPEX, and decommissioning are critical for company performance. If there are further desegregations of these inputs by type of OPEX and decommissioning expenses, PEAT-DECOMM provides detailed analysis on which ones are the most impactful.

Figure 5.9 shows the settings of *Scenario Analysis* based on both variations, revenues and decommissioning expenses, and their impact on NPV. Figure 5.10 presents the NPV results in matrix form, emphasising the ranges where revenue and decommission changes impact NPV above or below certain expectations.

- **Risk Simulations**

Monte Carlo risk simulations comprise hundreds of thousands of scenarios and trials to help managers analyse how uncertainty on projects' inputs impact key economic indicators and their risk profiles, probabilities, charts, and statistics, and to thus make better decisions.

PEAT-DECOMM allows running simulations using *probability distributions functions* (triangular, normal, lognormal, uniform, etc.), experts' opinions or historical data, *seed values, correlations,* and *simulation trials* (e.g., 1,000 depending on the level of precision required). Therefore, the direct outcomes are *confidence intervals* (e.g., 90%, 95%, 99%, and percentiles), *descriptive statistics* (mean, median, standard deviation, coefficient of variability, skew, kurtosis, etc.), *overlay results* (visualisation and comparison of risk profiles), and *dynamic sensitivity analysis* (rank correlation and percentages of fluctuations on the key indicators because of changes in all the selected project inputs, altogether).

Figure 5.11 highlights that there is 90% confidence in the project's NPV (Stand-alone project) varying between £281.9M and £295.6M. However, the positive skew indicates higher chances that the NPV reaches values below the expected (£288.6M) when the selected inputs fluctuate simultaneously. In addition, Figure 5.12 shows this information in a sensitivity chart; note that the discount rate and decommissioning costs undermine NPV (negative nonlinear rank correlation). Therefore, revenues and discount rates contribute the most to the variability of the NPV (contribution to variance). These analytics can be implemented for single or multiple projects.

- **Portfolio Analysis**

PEAT-DECOMM allows not only analysing multiple projects (i.e., current and potential), business lines, market strategies, and so forth, but also integrating decommission strategies (early and late stage, conventional, and emerging). These strategies, for example, can embed carbon capture, utilisation, and storage (CCUS), reuse of offshore oil and gas assets (windfarm intervention, gas-to-wire), and decarbonisation projects (biomass, geothermal, wind farms, and electrification, among other alternative renewables projects).

Figure 5.6 presents five different emerging projects— infrastructure reuse, gas-to-wire, CCUS, hydrogen, and biomass—around well P&A to illustrate a portfolio for timing decommissioning. Figure 5.13 provides a static comparison among all these projects across the main economic and financial indicators (NPV, PI, and MIRR). For instance, note that embedding feasible options to extend the asset's life and postpone decommissioning enhances company profitability, reduces liquidity risk, and allows creating better strategies for managing project dismantling risks.

As shown for the "Standalone Company" project, PEAT-DECOMM automatically allows for new plans and projects, assessing uncertainties in their inputs, applying decision analytics and risk simulations, and obtaining risk profiles and statistics measurement to make wide-ranging comparisons and decisions. Decision makers can also select the best combination of projects that maximises a firm's key indicators regarding financial and nonfinancial constraints, shareholders' and investors' preferences, market conditions, and regulatory frameworks, among other aspects. For additional modeling and optimisation, see PEAT-DECOMM | *Portfolio Optimisation*.

- **Strategic Options**

In the energy industry, especially oil and gas firms, active managers are not only timing decommissioning with conventional or emerging strategies to protect the business, but they are also beginning to analyse new projects starting at the conceptual phase. In other words, decision makers are creating new projects with flexible strategic real options (expansion, contraction, abandon, wait and defer, etc.), simultaneously enhancing firm performance, risk management (e.g., financial, operational, regulatory), asset integrity, and decommissioning timing.

Real options provide a significant value enhancement to projects while decision makers simultaneously manage risks and flexibility. Thus, after visualising and modeling strategic options, managers can quantify the real options value. For example, gas-to-wire (GTW) is an emerging option that can be integrated with gas and offshore wind to help companies expand while hedging gas and electricity price fluctuations and energy transitions as well.

To illustrate project economics value, the authors used some preliminary financial and operational estimations for different projects. Figure 5.13 (*Portfolio Analysis*) shows that GTW enhances the traditional NPV because companies can continue maximising recovery value (marginal value of resources) while switching gas to electricity. Therefore, GTW is quite feasible given the current conditions of many oil and gas wells and facilities (asset integrity, fit-for-purpose, CAPEX, OPEX, decommissioning postponement, etc.). "GasToWire" (NPV = £465M) only allows timing decommissioning (early-stage), and "GTW Real Options" (NPV = £473M) embeds options to *expand* and *switch* gas production and electricity generation during project concept, feasibility, design, engineering, construction, and commissioning planning. It extends project life, enhances performance and shareholder value, and manages the decommission risks effectively. Of course, this approach can be used for other options (CCUS, electrification, hydrogen, biomass, etc.).

In addition to the portfolio outlook in PEAT-DECOMM, after simulations, Figure 5.14 shows *Overlay Results* (relative spread, location, dispersion, skewness of the economic results, statistics dominance, etc.) among projects, and Figure 5.15 exhibits the *Analysis of Alternatives* (comparisons of risk statistics, value-at-risk or VaR) among projects or implementation options.

Finally, Figure 5.16 presents a standard real options valuation associated with a "GTW Real Options" project. As an illustration, note that if offshore well platforms embed operational and technical conditions that fit-for-purpose on flexible GTW projects (e.g., an expansion factor of 1.2 or 20% growth), the difference between the valuation enhanced by real options and the value without them is how much flexibility and uncertainty management adds to the valuation (£647M – £582M = £64M).

In practical terms, using the PEAT-DECOMM software enables the application of this risk-based analysis to any project type (current, conventional, emerging, and potential). Sophisticated managers can also apply risk simulations, applied analytics, portfolio optimisation, predictive modeling, and other risk methodologies around real options and traditional economic and financial indicators to improve project valuations and business, and actively manage decommissioning timing.

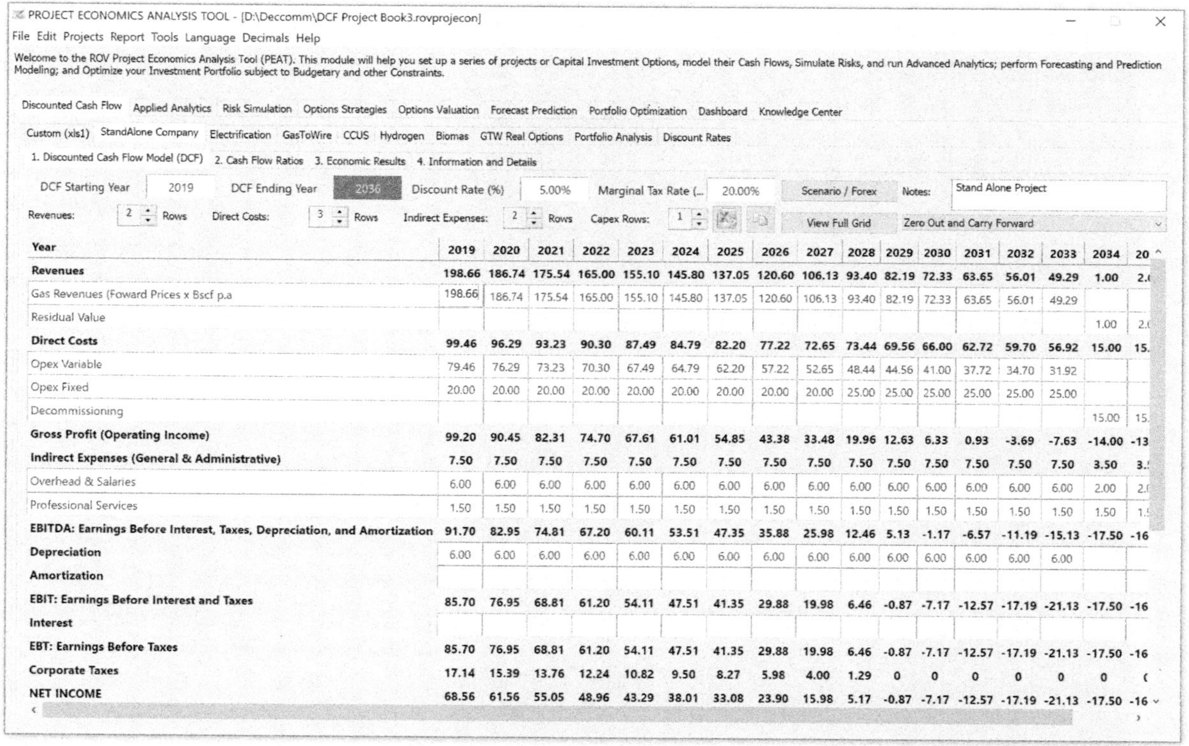

Year	2019	2020	2021	2022	2023	2024	2025	2026	2027	2028	2029	2030	2031	2032	2033	2034	20
Revenues	**198.66**	**186.74**	**175.54**	**165.00**	**155.10**	**145.80**	**137.05**	**120.60**	**106.13**	**93.40**	**82.19**	**72.33**	**63.65**	**56.01**	**49.29**	**1.00**	**2.(**
Gas Revenues (Foward Prices x Bscf p.a	198.66	186.74	175.54	165.00	155.10	145.80	137.05	120.60	106.13	93.40	82.19	72.33	63.65	56.01	49.29		
Residual Value																1.00	2.(
Direct Costs	**99.46**	**96.29**	**93.23**	**90.30**	**87.49**	**84.79**	**82.20**	**77.22**	**72.65**	**73.44**	**69.56**	**66.00**	**62.72**	**59.70**	**56.92**	**15.00**	**15.**
Opex Variable	79.46	76.29	73.23	70.30	67.49	64.79	62.20	57.22	52.65	48.44	44.56	41.00	37.72	34.70	31.92		
Opex Fixed	20.00	20.00	20.00	20.00	20.00	20.00	20.00	20.00	20.00	25.00	25.00	25.00	25.00	25.00	25.00		
Decommissioning																15.00	15.
Gross Profit (Operating Income)	**99.20**	**90.45**	**82.31**	**74.70**	**67.61**	**61.01**	**54.85**	**43.38**	**33.48**	**19.96**	**12.63**	**6.33**	**0.93**	**-3.69**	**-7.63**	**-14.00**	**-13**
Indirect Expenses (General & Administrative)	**7.50**	**7.50**	**7.50**	**7.50**	**7.50**	**7.50**	**7.50**	**7.50**	**7.50**	**7.50**	**7.50**	**7.50**	**7.50**	**7.50**	**7.50**	**3.50**	**3.!**
Overhead & Salaries	6.00	6.00	6.00	6.00	6.00	6.00	6.00	6.00	6.00	6.00	6.00	6.00	6.00	6.00	6.00	2.00	2.(
Professional Services	1.50	1.50	1.50	1.50	1.50	1.50	1.50	1.50	1.50	1.50	1.50	1.50	1.50	1.50	1.50	1.50	1.!
EBITDA: Earnings Before Interest, Taxes, Depreciation, and Amortization	**91.70**	**82.95**	**74.81**	**67.20**	**60.11**	**53.51**	**47.35**	**35.88**	**25.98**	**12.46**	**5.13**	**-1.17**	**-6.57**	**-11.19**	**-15.13**	**-17.50**	**-16**
Depreciation	6.00	6.00	6.00	6.00	6.00	6.00	6.00	6.00	6.00	6.00	6.00	6.00	6.00	6.00	6.00		
Amortization																	
EBIT: Earnings Before Interest and Taxes	**85.70**	**76.95**	**68.81**	**61.20**	**54.11**	**47.51**	**41.35**	**29.88**	**19.98**	**6.46**	**-0.87**	**-7.17**	**-12.57**	**-17.19**	**-21.13**	**-17.50**	**-16**
Interest																	
EBT: Earnings Before Taxes	**85.70**	**76.95**	**68.81**	**61.20**	**54.11**	**47.51**	**41.35**	**29.88**	**19.98**	**6.46**	**-0.87**	**-7.17**	**-12.57**	**-17.19**	**-21.13**	**-17.50**	**-16**
Corporate Taxes	**17.14**	**15.39**	**13.76**	**12.24**	**10.82**	**9.50**	**8.27**	**5.98**	**4.00**	**1.29**	**0**	**0**	**0**	**0**	**0**	**0**	**(**
NET INCOME	**68.56**	**61.56**	**55.05**	**48.96**	**43.29**	**38.01**	**33.08**	**23.90**	**15.98**	**5.17**	**-0.87**	**-7.17**	**-12.57**	**-17.19**	**-21.13**	**-17.50**	**-16**

Figure 5.6: DCF Model – Project Inputs and Assumptions (Stand-alone Project)

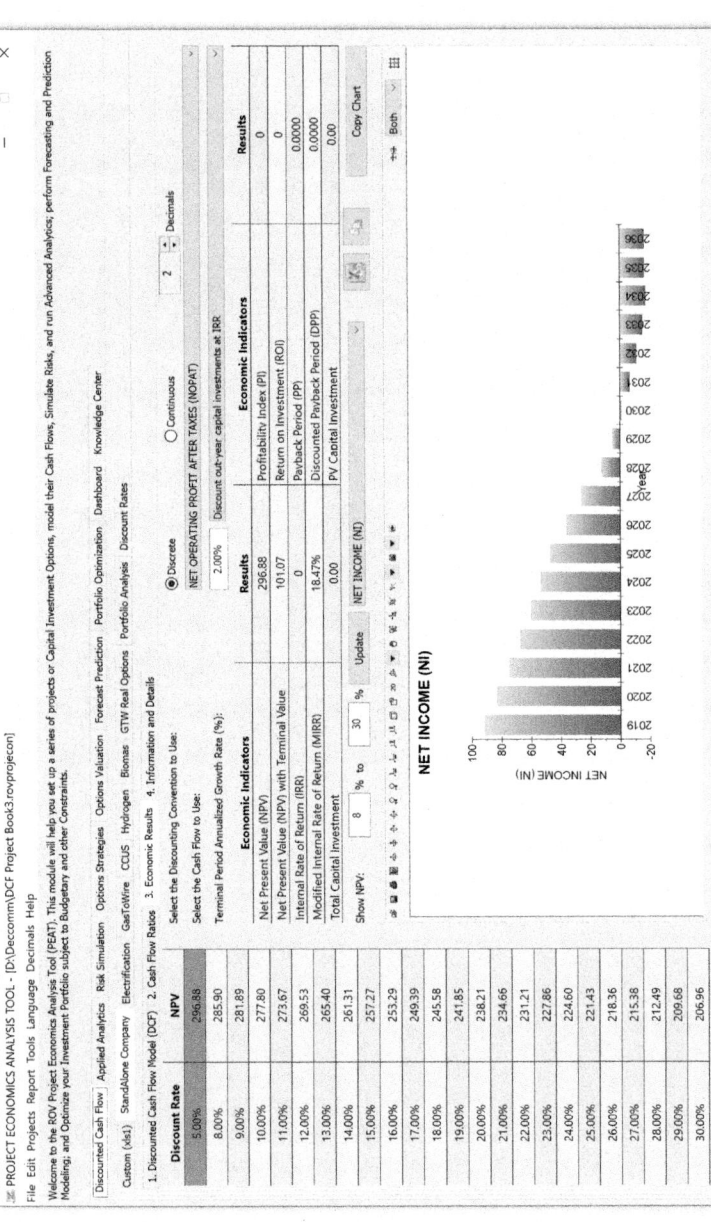

Figure 5.7: DCF Model – Project Results (Stand-alone Project)

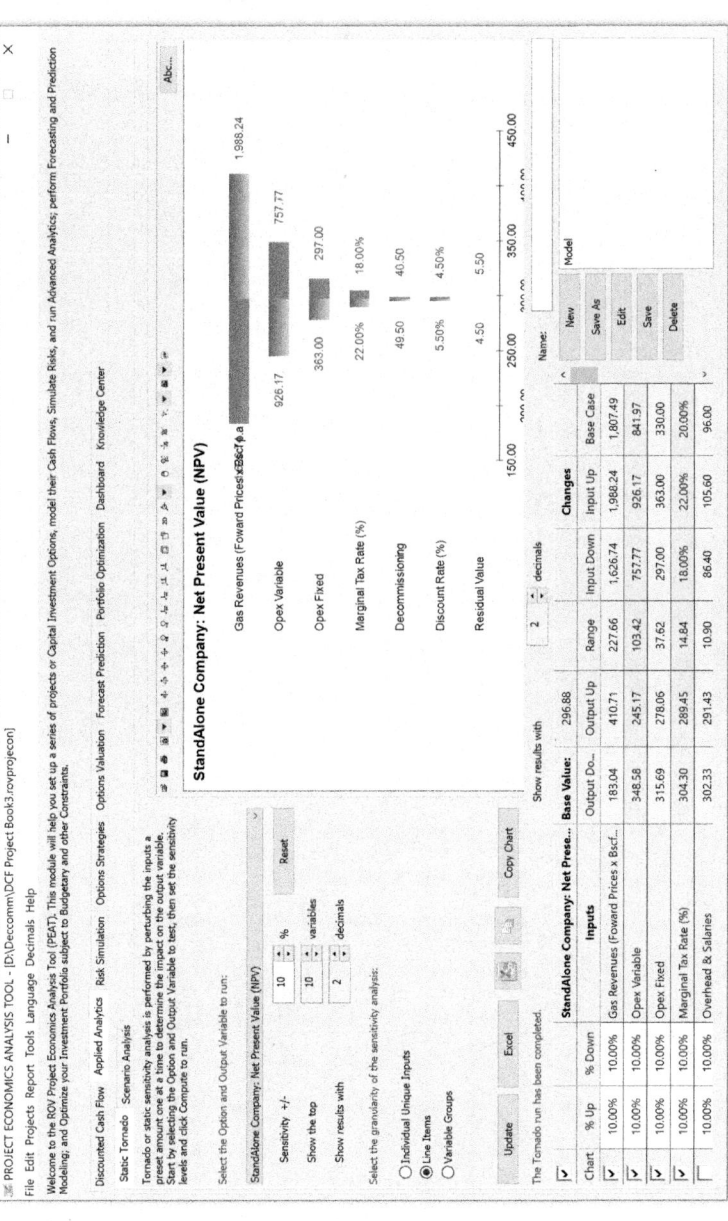

Figure 5.8: Tornado Analysis on Economic Indicators (NPV)

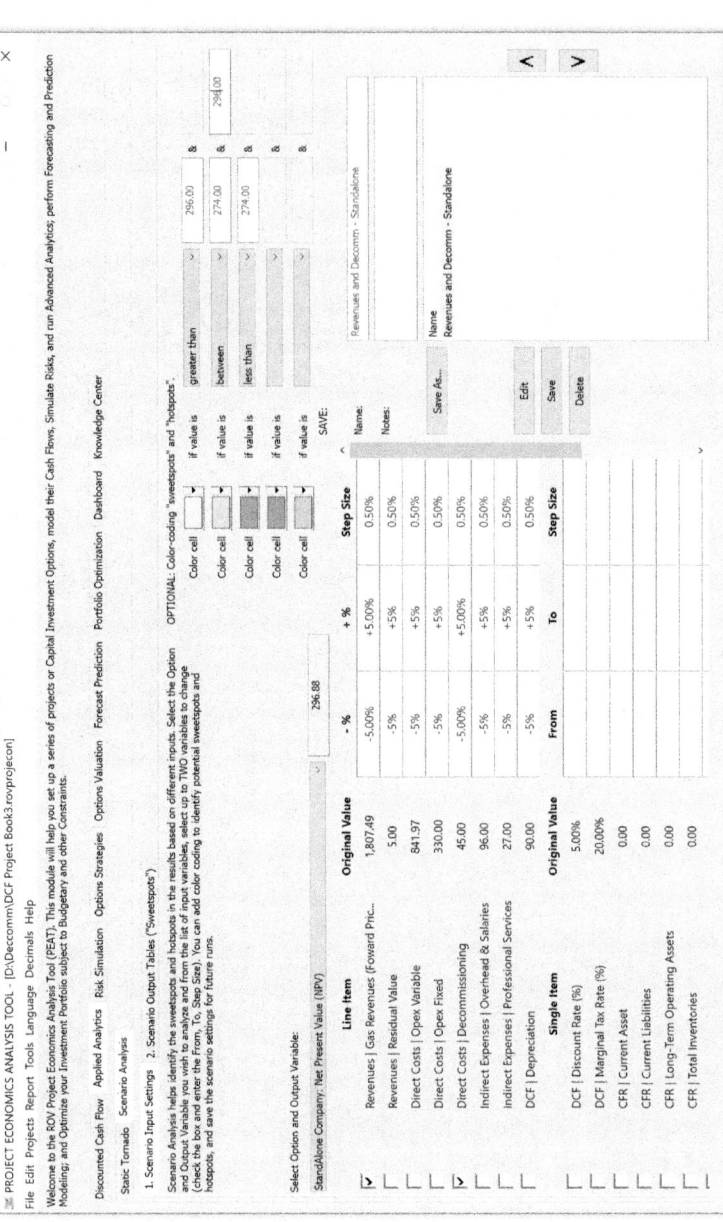

Figure 5.9: Scenario Analysis Settings

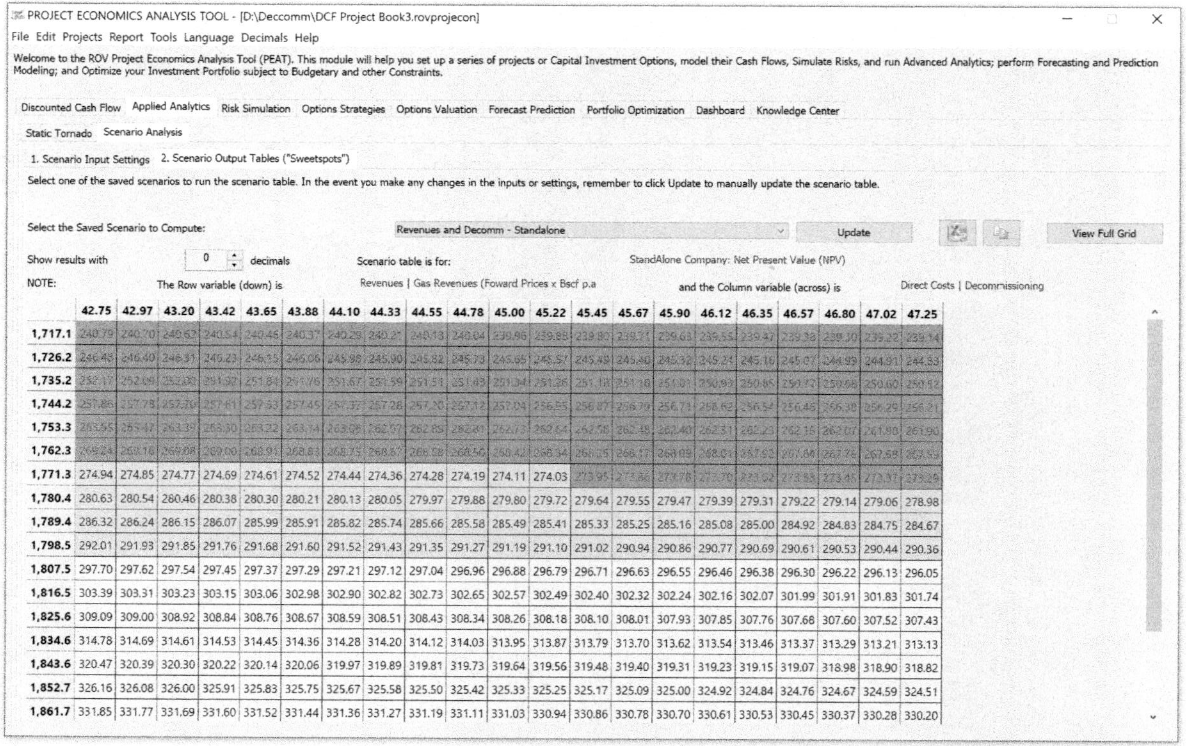

	42.75	42.97	43.20	43.42	43.65	43.88	44.10	44.33	44.55	44.78	45.00	45.22	45.45	45.67	45.90	46.12	46.35	46.57	46.80	47.02	47.25
1,717.1	240.79	240.70	240.62	240.54	240.46	240.37	240.29	240.21	240.13	240.04	239.96	239.88	239.80	239.71	239.63	239.55	239.47	239.38	239.30	239.22	239.14
1,726.2	246.48	246.40	246.31	246.23	246.15	246.06	245.98	245.90	245.82	245.73	245.65	245.57	245.49	245.40	245.32	345.24	245.16	245.07	244.99	244.91	244.83
1,735.2	252.17	252.09	252.00	251.92	251.84	251.76	251.67	251.59	251.51	251.43	251.34	251.26	251.18	251.10	251.01	250.93	250.85	250.77	250.68	250.60	250.52
1,744.2	257.86	257.78	257.70	257.61	257.53	257.45	257.37	257.28	257.20	257.12	257.04	256.95	256.87	256.79	256.71	256.62	256.54	256.46	256.38	256.29	256.21
1,753.3	263.55	263.47	263.39	263.30	263.22	263.14	263.06	262.97	262.89	262.81	262.73	262.64	262.56	262.48	262.40	262.31	262.23	262.15	262.07	261.98	261.90
1,762.3	269.24	269.16	269.08	269.00	268.91	268.83	268.75	268.67	268.58	268.50	268.42	268.34	268.25	268.17	268.09	268.01	267.92	267.84	267.76	267.68	267.59
1,771.3	274.94	274.85	274.77	274.69	274.61	274.52	274.44	274.36	274.28	274.19	274.11	274.03	273.95	273.86	273.78	273.70	273.62	273.53	273.45	273.37	273.29
1,780.4	280.63	280.54	280.46	280.38	280.30	280.21	280.13	280.05	279.97	279.88	279.80	279.72	279.64	279.55	279.47	279.39	279.31	279.22	279.14	279.06	278.98
1,789.4	286.32	286.24	286.15	286.07	285.99	285.91	285.82	285.74	285.66	285.58	285.49	285.41	285.33	285.25	285.16	285.08	285.00	284.92	284.83	284.75	284.67
1,798.5	292.01	291.93	291.85	291.76	291.68	291.60	291.52	291.43	291.35	291.27	291.19	291.10	291.02	290.94	290.86	290.77	290.69	290.61	290.53	290.44	290.36
1,807.5	297.70	297.62	297.54	297.45	297.37	297.29	297.21	297.12	297.04	296.96	296.88	296.79	296.71	296.63	296.55	296.46	296.38	296.30	296.22	296.13	296.05
1,816.5	303.39	303.31	303.23	303.15	303.06	302.98	302.90	302.82	302.73	302.65	302.57	302.49	302.40	302.32	302.24	302.16	302.07	301.99	301.91	301.83	301.74
1,825.6	309.09	309.00	308.92	308.84	308.76	308.67	308.59	308.51	308.43	308.34	308.26	308.18	308.10	308.01	307.93	307.85	307.76	307.68	307.60	307.52	307.43
1,834.6	314.78	314.69	314.61	314.53	314.45	314.36	314.28	314.20	314.12	314.03	313.95	313.87	313.79	313.70	313.62	313.54	313.46	313.37	313.29	313.21	313.13
1,843.6	320.47	320.39	320.30	320.22	320.14	320.06	319.97	319.89	319.81	319.73	319.64	319.56	319.48	319.40	319.31	319.23	319.15	319.07	318.98	318.90	318.82
1,852.7	326.16	326.08	326.00	325.91	325.83	325.75	325.67	325.58	325.50	325.42	325.33	325.25	325.17	325.09	325.00	324.92	324.84	324.76	324.67	324.59	324.51
1,861.7	331.85	331.77	331.69	331.60	331.52	331.44	331.36	331.27	331.19	331.11	331.03	330.94	330.86	330.78	330.70	330.61	330.53	330.45	330.37	330.28	330.20

Figure 5.10: Scenario Analysis Results

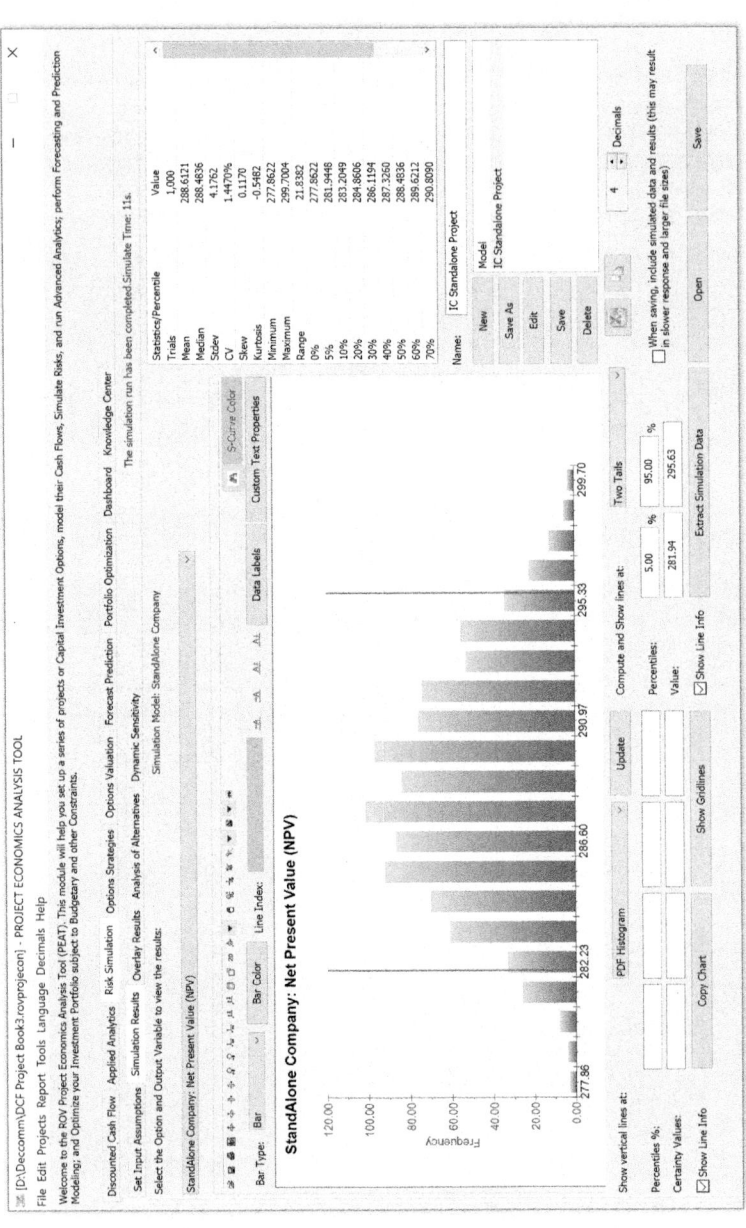

Figure 5.11: Simulation Results (Risk Profile on NPV)

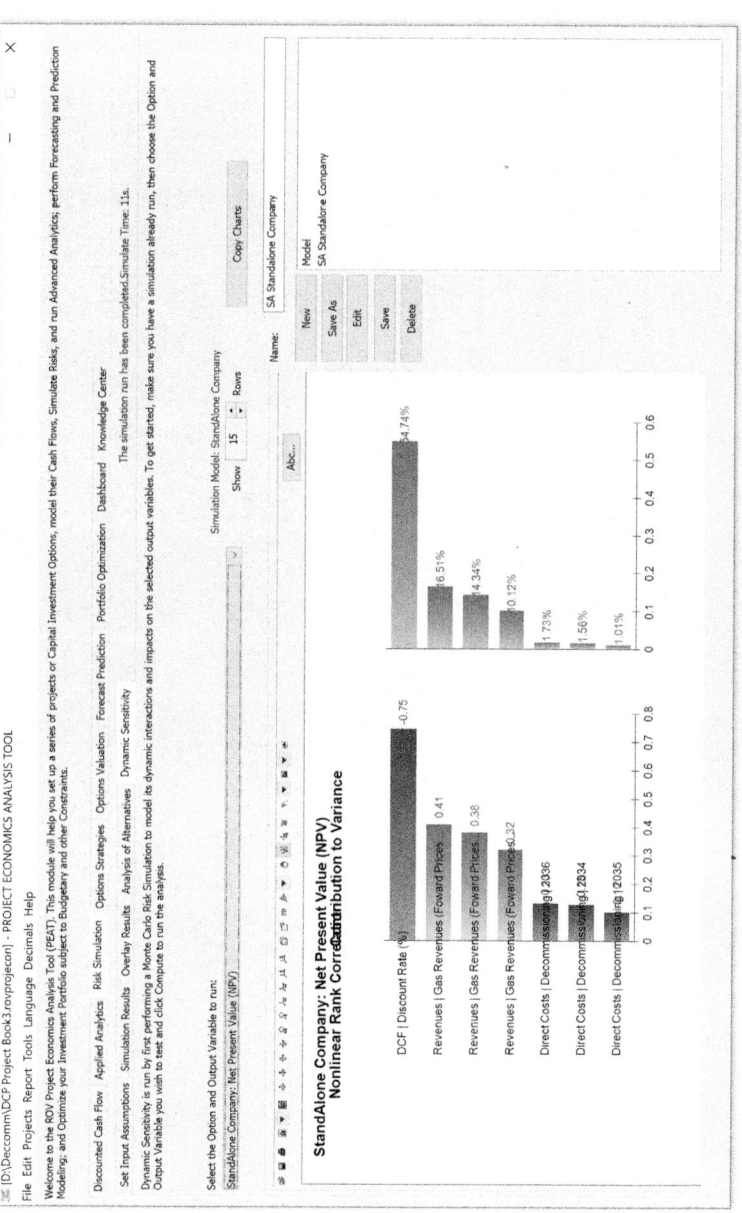

Figure 5.12: Dynamic Sensitivity Analysis on NPV

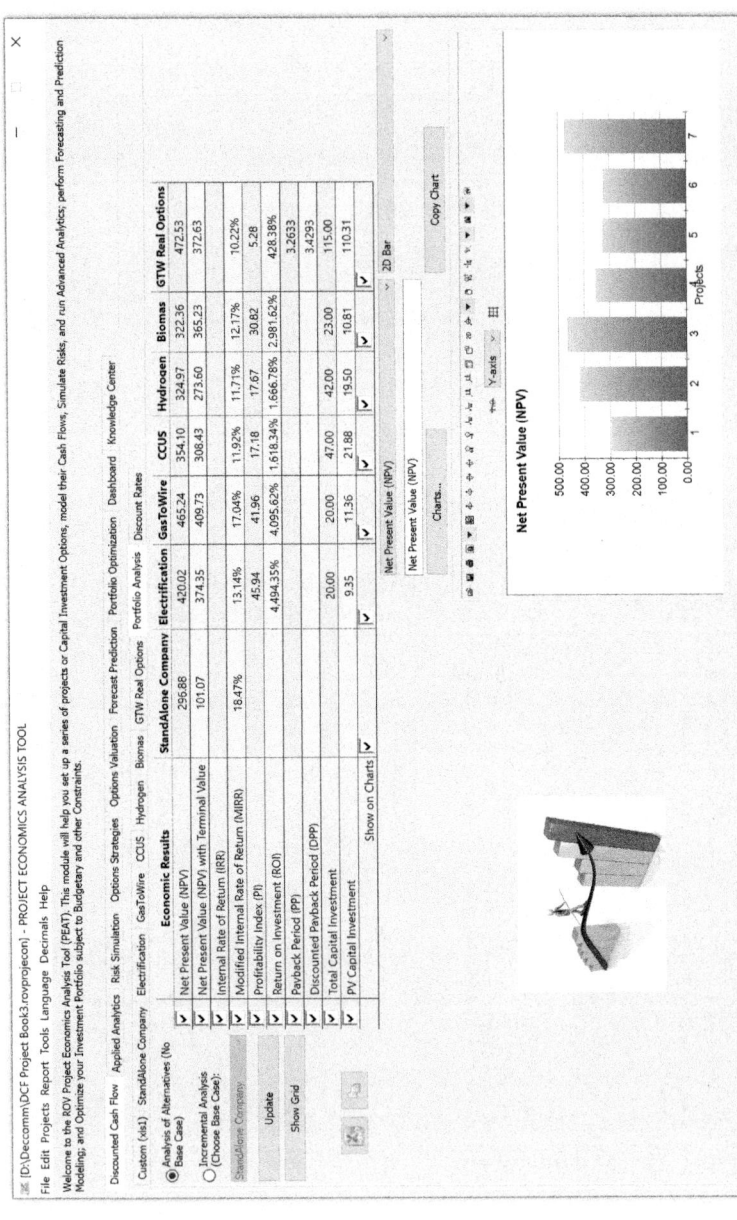

Figure 5.13: Scenario Analysis (Heat Map on Schedule and Total Cost)

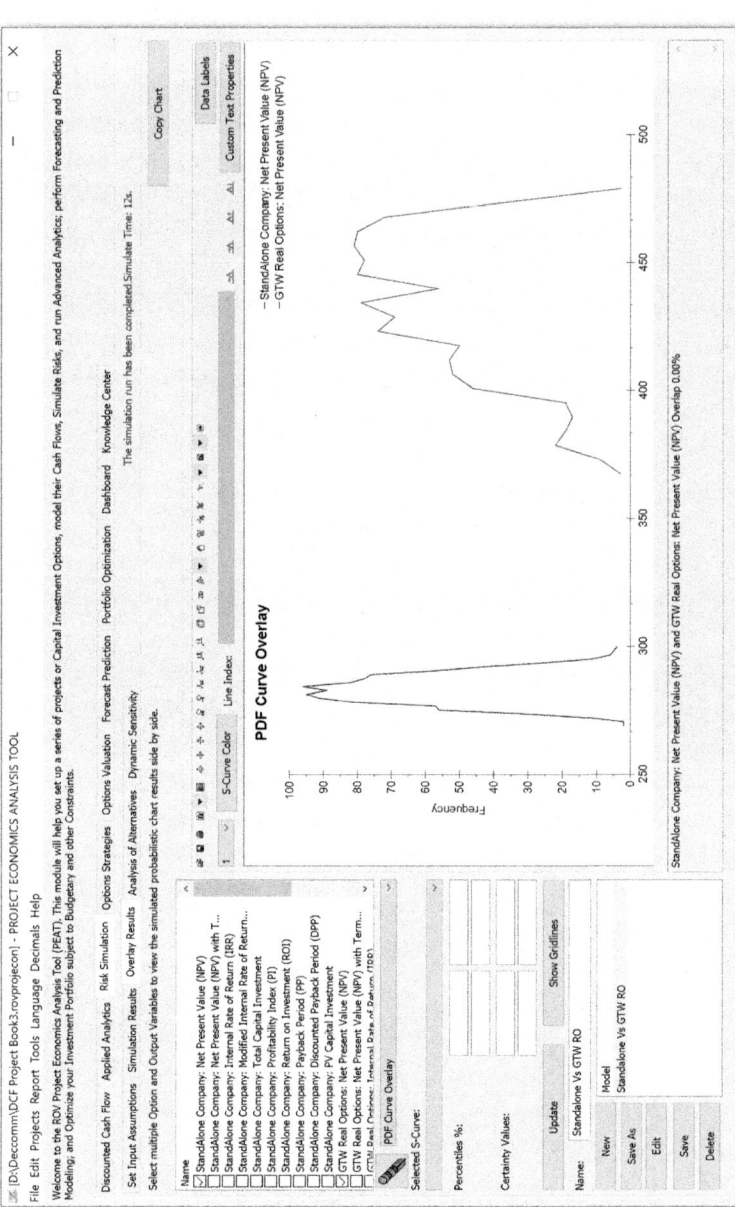

Figure 5.14: Overlay Results – Projects Comparison

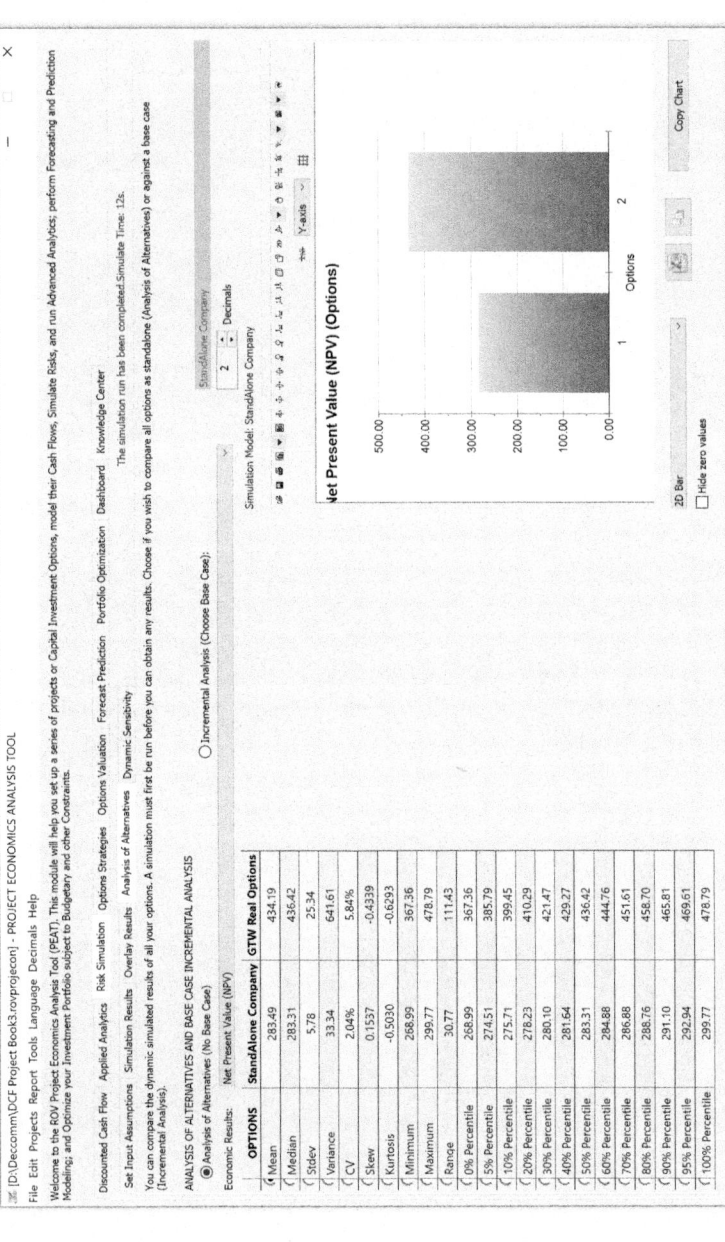

Figure 5.15: Strategic Management – Risk Metrics on Project Portfolio

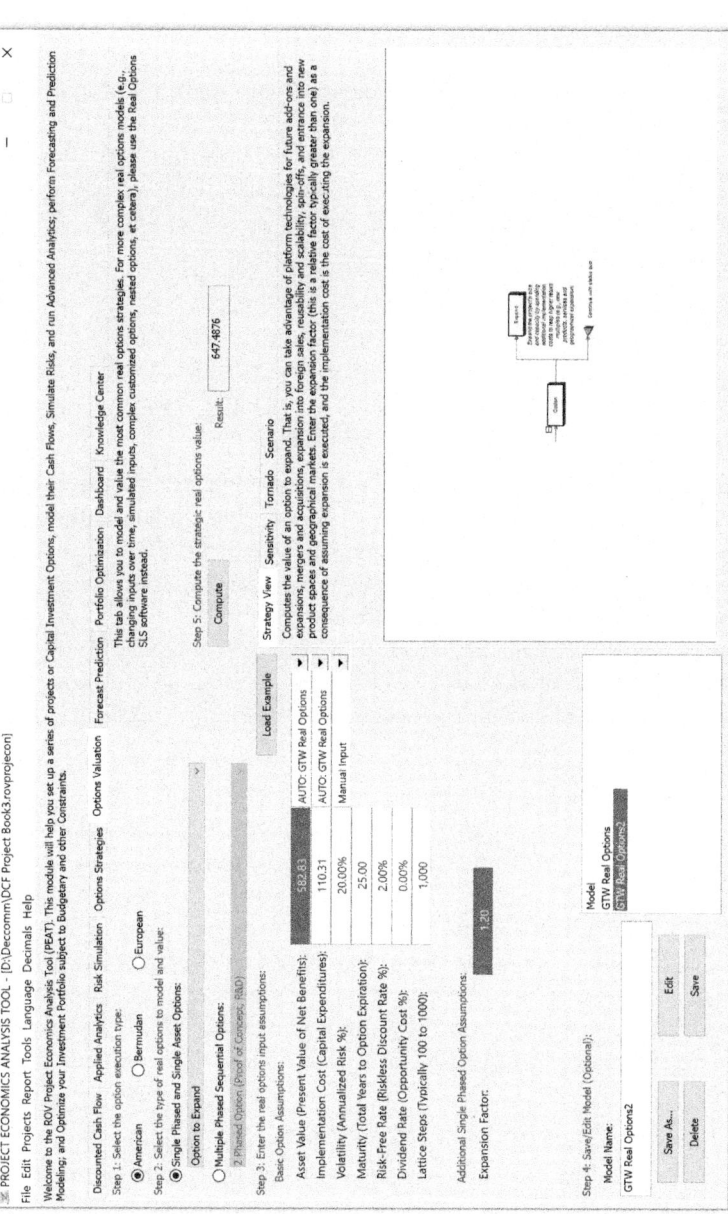

Figure 5.16: Strategic Real Options in Oil and Gas

DECOMMISSIONING STRATEGIES — RISK AND LEARNING

Active managers need to regularly evaluate their decommissioning strategies regardless of the life of the asset, operational conditions, and asset integrity. Emerging strategies and real options not only help managers with decommissioning timing but also enhance company value when real options (uncertainty and flexibility) are visualised and modeled before project implementations.

To model decommissioning risks, decision makers should understand basic aspects of accounting and auditing (e.g., provisions, depreciations, residual value, taxes, and so on) for either analysing conventional decommissioning strategies or valuing emerging options with traditional financial or real options methods.

Analysing risk-based projects and businesses and turning the results into decommissioning strategies requires a full understanding of the associated uncertainties (e.g., environmental conditions, project management, asset integrity, inspections, surveys, compliance, waste materials, land remediation, health, safety, and security, among others). Consequently, decisions need to rely on risk analysis, Monte Carlo simulations, applied analytics, predictive modeling, and portfolio management across multiple financial and economic indicators.

Other considerations during the project valuation and analysis around decommissioning include the type of securities and their interest rates to back up strategies (e.g., letter of credit, bank notes, and means of payments); previous or current decommissioning funds and contributions (e.g., withdrawals, fees, applications, currency, and tax implications); government participation (e.g., funding, provisions, taxes, budget, regulatory framework, and so forth); roles of incumbent companies (e.g., contractors., asset operators, parent companies, assets' owners); contracts management including adjudications and litigations provisions; and type of insurance including premiums.

Note that a consistent and cost-efficient decommissioning strategy requires a holistic uncertainty analysis and risk management practices. PEAT-DECOMM has been developed to help managers improve decisions focused on both business performance and decommissioning improvement (costs, schedule, health, environment, and safety). Therefore, the recommendations, strategies, and methodologies outlined here are not meant to replace managerial expertise or traditional discounted cash flow analysis but to complement them when the situation and the need arise. The entire analysis could be done, or parts of it could be adapted to a more traditional approach. In essence, the process methodology outlined starts with conventional analyses and continues with value- and insight-adding analytics, including Monte Carlo simulation, forecasting, real options analysis, and portfolio optimisation. The real options approach outlined is not the only viable alternative nor will it provide a set of infallible results. However, if utilised correctly with the traditional approaches, it may lead to a set of more robust, accurate, insightful, and plausible results. The insights generated through real options analytics provide significant value in understanding a decommissioning project's true strategic value.

REFERENCES

Berk, J., DeMarzo, P., Harford, J., Ford, G., Mollica, V., & Finch, N. (2013). *Fundamentals of Corporate Finance*. Pearson Higher Education AU.

Choudhury, H., Fjellsa, O., Sanger, C., and Twomey, B.G. (2016). *Guidance Note on the Tax Treatment of Decommissioning for the Extractive Industries*. Retrieved October 26, 2019, from https://www.un.org/esa/ffd/wp-content/uploads/2016/10/12STM_CRP3_AttachmentA_Decommissioning.pdf

IAS. (2019). *IAS 37 — Provisions, Contingent Liabilities and Contingent Assets*. Retrieved October 10, 2019, from https://www.iasplus.com/en/standards/ias/ias37

IFRIC. (2019). *IFRIC 1 — Changes in Existing Decommissioning, Restoration and Similar Liabilities*. Retrieved October 26, 2019, from https://www.iasplus.com/en/standards/ifric/ifric1

ISA. (2009). *ISA 330 The Auditor's Response to Assessed Risks*. Retrieved October 30, 2019, from https://www.ifac.org/system/files/downloads/a019-2010-iaasb-handbook-isa-330.pdf

Mun, J. (2015). *Modeling Risk: Applying Monte Carlo Risk Simulation, Strategic Real Options, Stochastic Forecasting, Portfolio Optimisation,*

Data Analytics, Business Intelligence, and Decision Modeling, Third Edition. Thomson-Shore.

Mun, J. (2016). *Real Options Analysis: Tools and Techniques for Valuing Strategic Investments and Decisions with Integrated Risk Management and Advanced Quantitative Decision Analytics,* Third Edition. ROV Press.

Mun. J. (2018). *Applied Analytical Project Economic and Financial Evaluation* (Applied CQRM Book Series). IIPER Press.

National Audit Office. (2019). Oil and Gas in the UK – Offshore Decommissioning. Retrieved November 28, 2019, from https://www.nao.org.uk/wp-content/uploads/2019/01/Oil-and-gas-in-the-UK-offshore-decommissioning-Summary.pdf

Oil and Gas Authority. (2018). Gas-to-Wire: UK SNS & EIS. Retrieved December 12, 2019, from https://www.ogauthority.co.uk/media/5049/oil-gas-gas-to-wire.pdf

Oil and Gas Authority. (2019). OGA Overview 2019. Retrieved November 10,2019, from https://www.ogauthority.co.uk/media/5407/oga-overview-2019-low-res.pdf

Rogers, D. S. (1992). After-tax equity returns for non-qualified nuclear decommissioning trusts. *Financial Analysts Journal, 48*(4), 70–73.

Sui, D., Wiktorski, E., Røksland, M., & Basmoen, T. A. (2019). Review and investigations on geothermal energy extraction from abandoned petroleum wells. *Journal of Petroleum Exploration and Production Technology, 9*(2), 1135–1147.

Vrålstad, T., Saasen, A., Fjær, E., Øia, T., Ytrehus, J. D., & Khalifeh, M. (2019). Plug & abandonment of offshore wells: Ensuring long-term well integrity and cost-efficiency. *Journal of Petroleum Science and Engineering, 173*, 478–491.

CHAPTER 6: PROJECT RISK MANAGEMENT IN DECOMMISSIONING

Project management does not mean simply listing a number of tasks with single-point best schedule estimations into a project planner tool such as Microsoft Project®, Primavera P6®, or Open Project®, for example, even though those tools have a high level of usability and flexibility for project control and milestones tracking. Managing decommissioning projects in particular requires visualising how the assets were built (backward-looking) and how the assets can be dismantled (forward-looking), with the main focus on a safe reverse engineering, plugging, and abandonment, including land remediation.

Project risk management in decommissioning not only deals with planning, design, engineering, permitting, plugging and abandonment (P&A), mobilisation, demobilisation, reuse of facilities, legal requirements, among other activities, but also involves identifying uncertainty factors and managing the risk associated with these activities. Decision makers and project managers must prepare budgets, estimate project schedules, comply with the health, safety, and environment (HSE) requirements, create the mothballing strategies, and support the financial decisions (Taboas et al., 2004; Kaiser, 2019).

Safety, schedule, and costs are critical for managing decommissioning operations. A decommissioning schedule does not escape the fact that completion time is uncertain; it depends on project management strategies, marine (offshore) and assets conditions (offshore or onshore), logistics, personnel, contractors' management, and other aspects that decision makers need to deal with. Not having a clear decommissioning strategy and project planning leads to inaccurate schedule estimations and a high likelihood of cost overruns.

Decommissioning initiatives, including well P&A, requires two complementary decision-making procedures to increase the odds of completing a project on time, on budget, and safely. First, decision makers, managers, and work teams need to understand project networks, interrelations among activities, project flexibility, alternative strategies, contingencies plans, team integration and leadership, and the value of communication. Second, they require identifying and modeling the impact of uncertainty sources and risk factors on project schedule, cost, and safety.

It is important to emphasise that dealing with the second part of the approach, which is the aim of this chapter, relies on Monte Carlo simulations, tornado analysis, sensitivity charts, and other advanced analytics to quantify and manage project risks.

TRADITIONAL PROJECT MANAGEMENT IN DECOMMISSIONING

A decommissioning process is usually initiated either because of the company's strategic plans, normally around three years before the end of the life cycle of an asset, or because of a *force majeure* (e.g., natural disaster, disruption, environmental issue, regulatory fulfillment). Therefore, estimations and deterministic assessments on costs, schedule, and potential risks and opportunities are part of the routine management activities until a decision to decommission is made.

Traditional Schedule Management

Traditional P&A project management starts with a list of decommissioning activities in a project planner tool, following a specific order and linked from predecessor and successor for each task, to introduce some estimated duration and completion times as illustrated in Figure 6.1, where a GANTT chart is produced by a common planning tool.

Although GANTT charts are important for project control and monitoring, this approach can be problematic for decisions makers and managers considering decommissioning mainly because of the visualisation of hundreds of project tasks, overlapping of critical paths with multiple milestones, and management of a large number of pages and extensive reports to support the decommissioning plan. Even if GANTT charts are used to model level-two and level-three of the project plan, non-interconnected and overlapping macro-activities will increase the lack of understanding of the P&A plan.

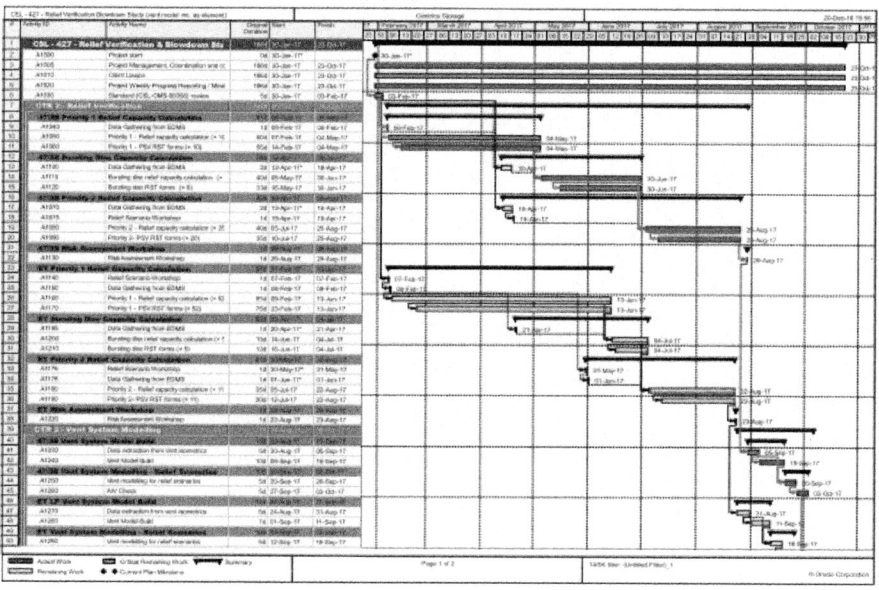

Figure 6.1: Illustration of a GANTT Chart

Another method is to start working with a project network in order to guide the decision-making process. It is particularly recommended that project networks are prepared before the detailed project plan to address the P&A strategy and interrelationships among activities and, consequently, to build the detailed decommissioning plans, and not the other way around. Figure 6.2 shows a generic P&A network diagram that helps not only decision makers and project managers to visualise and understand the macro-plan and potential critical path (the longest estimated path to complete the project—critical path method, or CPM), but also helps project planners to build the detailed plans and specific milestones (Mun, 2018).

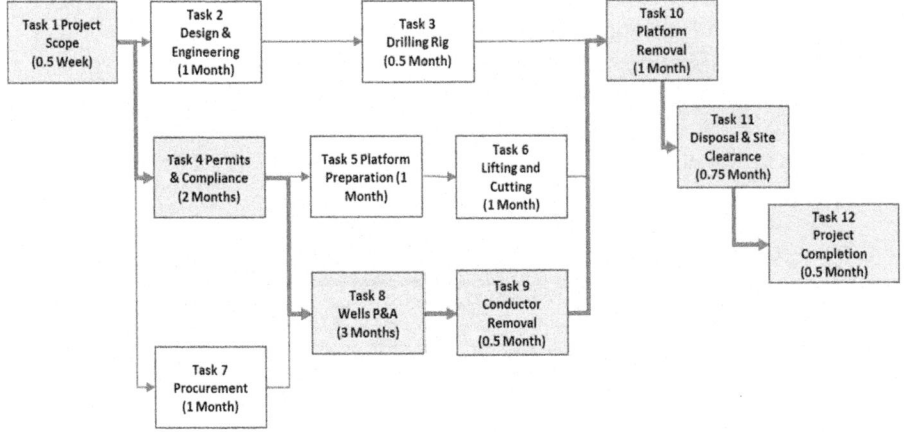

Figure 6.2: General P&A Project Network and Critical Path

Decision makers can mismanage a decommissioning project not only because of their lack of understanding of the complex P&A tasks, but also because of the uncertainty of project schedules. Projects often take longer than expected; and controlling a deterministic critical path is not enough to manage the decommissioning dynamics (e.g., parallel and sequential activities, redundancy in resource management, time acceleration in the critical path, and project inefficiencies and flexibility).

These dynamics need to first be considered and included in the project network, and then they should be incorporated into the detailed plan. Note that changing task orders or links among interrelated activities can distort the full P&A plan and project awareness, which increases the project risk levels in terms of time to completion.

In traditional schedule management, schedule risks are uncovered when a project's incumbents start providing single-point base case estimations, even though they believe these estimations have variability or ranges. The more tasks a decommissioning project has, the lower the chance a P&A project will complete within the base-case estimations. Therefore, some project managers consider that shortening the critical path is not enough to protect the base-case schedule, because a critical path changes due to the passage of time, actions, flexibility, and task completion, and when new events are contemplated.

A relevant step in mitigating the usage of single-point estimates is using Monte Carlo simulations and decision-making analytics to enhance risk management in P&A projects, where each activity's schedule has variability, the critical path is stochastic (not deterministic), and an analytical expression to determine the effect of the uncertainty sources and risk factors can be explored using tornado analysis, risk profiles, and sensitivity charts that show a probabilistic approach to the P&A completion and project management.

Traditional Cost Management

Cost analysis is another area of uncertainty in decommissioning projects (Ahiaga-Dagbui et al., 2017). In parallel, a company receives quotes from multiple contractors, service suppliers, the project manager, independent specialists, and others in charge of multiple activities (e.g., lighting, cutting, removals, work packs, bulk materials, equipment, site clearance, and so forth). With all the information in hand, project incumbents start estimating total costs, sometimes without performing further classifications of said costs, for example, fixed costs (e.g., equipment or construction material) and variable costs (time-driven costs such as project management or control activities). Decision makers, project managers, and cost engineers deal with contingency analysis, inflation variations, multiple tenders for the same task but in differentiated bundle prices, discounts, different time constraints and activity completions, platform weights, personnel on board, mobilisation and demobilisation assumptions, and other aspects that impact P&A cost estimations.

Table 6.1 shows some common forms of services quotes à la carte provided by the contractors or service suppliers. Procurement and project managers centralise that information to start estimating the total P&A cost or capital expenditure. Some of the common project management mistakes made at this point include considering that prices and costs are constant (single-point estimates adjusted by a percentage of contingencies) and assuming these quotes apply globally and do not follow an activity-based approach.

A relevant step in enhancing risk management in P&A costs, overcoming the usage of single-point estimates, is using Monte Carlo simulations and decision-making analytics. Note that uncertainty affects both fixed and variable costs; fixed costs through inflation and price variation because of changes in scope (e.g., multiple bids estimations), and variable costs because of schedule estimations, delays, environmental conditions, and other sources of uncertainty. As a result, each activity's total cost has variability, and decommissioning risk can be analysed using tornado analysis, risk profiles, and sensitivity charts, among other risk management approaches.

Table 6.1: Forms of Contractors' Quotes

Quote PA001 - Company XYZ
Conductor removals

No.	Water Depth (ft.)	Piles	Type of Barge	Method	# of Conductors	Cost w/ Conductors
1	50	3P	DB300	Complete Removal	1	£1,835,703
2	118	4P	DB600	Complete Removal	1	£3,171,086
3	156	4P	DB800	Complete Removal	6	£4,039,831
4	400	4L-1P-4SP	DB4K	Complete Removal	6	£8,893,674
5	410	8P-12SP	DB4K	Complete Removal	5	£10,239,277
6	484	4P	DB2K	Tow to Shallow	2	£6,836,169
7	523	4P-4SP	DB2K	Tow to Shallow	7	£9,375,800
8	619	4P-4SP	DB4K	Tow to Shallow	8	£15,790,690
9	693	4L-8SP	DB4K	Jacket Sectioning	3	£15,093,830
10	774	8P-12SP	SSCV	Jacket Sectioning	24	£41,194,940

Apply contigencies of 10%

Quote PA002 - Company AAB
Wells Preparation

No.	Description	Days	Cost
1	Flush, Purge and Clean Facilities, Tanks and Vessels	4	£130,000
2	Prepare Modules for Removal	3	£79,000
3	Replace Tension Units for Tendons	21	£870,000
	Total		£1,079,000

Apply contigencies of 15%

Quote PA003 - Company ZXB
Site Clearance and Verification

	Activity	Hours	Days	Costs
1	Mob Vessels to Site	30	2	£100,000
2	Side Scan at Platform Location	32	2	£98,000
3	Inspect and Clean up	48	2	£230,000
4	Demob Vessels from Site	24	2.5	£81,500
5	Weather Downtime		0	
	Total			£509,500

Prices valid for 3 months

As can be seen, uncertainty analysis and decision analytics are required to manage the decommissioning cost and schedule risks. Therefore, both activity-based costs and activity-based schedules are recommended perspectives for modeling risk and contingencies, not only to guide risk workshops, discussions, and engagements during decommissioning planning, but also to determine the most influential factors in the decision-making process.

MODERN PROJECT RISK MANAGEMENT IN DECOMMISSIONING

As noted in the preceding discussion of the traditional approach to managing projects, including decommissioning projects, there are two major sources of project risk: schedule risk and cost risk (in asset dismantling and well P&A, safety, of course, is another major risk factor). However, how to deliver a project on time and under budget is an important question always considered by managers and decision makers. The following sections present a general approach for dealing with cost and schedule risk and demonstrate how to use the PEAT PM solution to model these sources of risk.

Schedule and Cost Risk Modeling

Cost and time can vary across well P&A projects depending on the decommissioning strategies, price changes, delays, and other uncertainties and risk events, all of which should be considered in project management. Quantifying the impact of these uncertainties on cost and time requires creating probability distributions for each project task. Consequently, Monte Carlo simulation techniques can be applied to forecast the likely range of project schedule and cost and to determine the main risk drivers of these performance indicators (Mun, 2010; Hollmann, 2016).

Although many probability distributions (normal, lognormal, PERT, uniform, triangular, BETA, Weibull, etc.) can be used in project management, for P&A projects, a simple triangular distribution is a practical probability distribution to quickly describe uncertainties around costs and time.

For instance, regarding schedule, the natural fit of a triangular distribution relies on the fact that decision makers and decommissioning specialists can provide a range of task durations (minimum, maximum, and most likely) that are easy to understand. Therefore, they control finite and limited values in project durations using regular project engagement and controls, or, as a last resort, they move the most likely and maximum durations as the project progresses and uncertainty is resolved.

In costs risk modeling, a triangular distribution is also a reasonable alternative to analyse activity costs, especially because it allows managing uncertainties and scenarios as follow: % of contingencies around the best-case estimates, multiple vendors' quotes, assumptions on cost ranges and most likely values associated with both inflation and contractors' rates, and other decommissioning aspects. Moreover, in well P&A, this information can be obtained from multiple surveys related to vessel weights, piping specifications, and asset integrity conditions, which, alongside the engineering, construction, and design norms, provide data to determine the minimum, most likely, and maximum activity-based costs.

Figure 6.3 serves as a guide to interpret the inputs of a triangular distribution. The minimum means optimal utilisation of resources, no problem in project cost or schedule. The most likely contains the base-case scenarios and project plan assumptions (single-point plan estimations). Finally, time and cost are more likely to overrun than underrun due to uncertainties, inefficiencies, and adverse events.

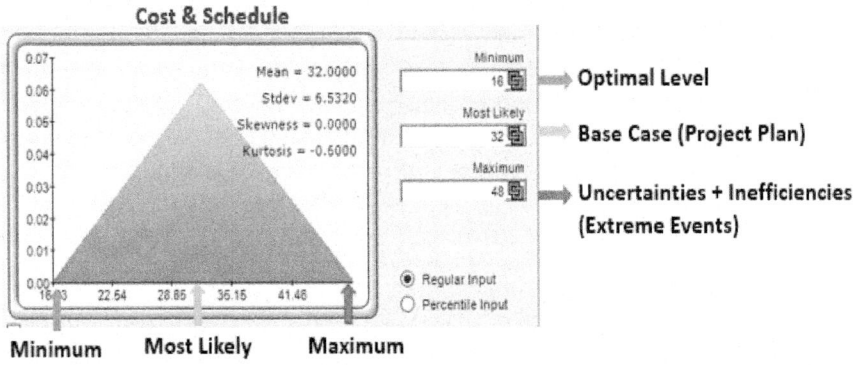

Figure 6.3: Triangular Distribution in Well P&A

To estimate these inputs, we should use multiple sources. For example, we can talk with contractors, project managers, and people doing hands-on work, as well as different vendors and suppliers. We can use construction norms and scenario analysis. Historical data can also be used, but with caution because past results do not imply the same future performance (different time, actions, events, people, and sources of uncertainty). Please note that the PERT distribution requires as inputs, minimum, most likely, and maximum, is also widely used to emphasise the most likely values (planners' or experts' information) over the extreme values or minimum and maximum estimates (Mun, 2010).

Monte Carlo Simulations and Risk Profiles

With probabilistic schedule and nondeterministic cost management, thousands of trials are run using Monte Carlo risk simulation. It allows exploring the range of likely outcomes (risk profiles) for schedule and cost in decommissioning projects, and determines risk drivers through probabilistic path analysis, tornado and sensitivity charts, and other techniques.

Figure 6.4 shows some of the risk profiles that can be obtained from simulations, illustrating in a chart the expected or most likely values, percentiles, and confidence interval. These charts allow decision makers to visualise whether a P&A project overruns or potential contingencies are expected around schedule and cost. Note that deviations above expected values (or central tendency measures) are considered unexpected or risky.

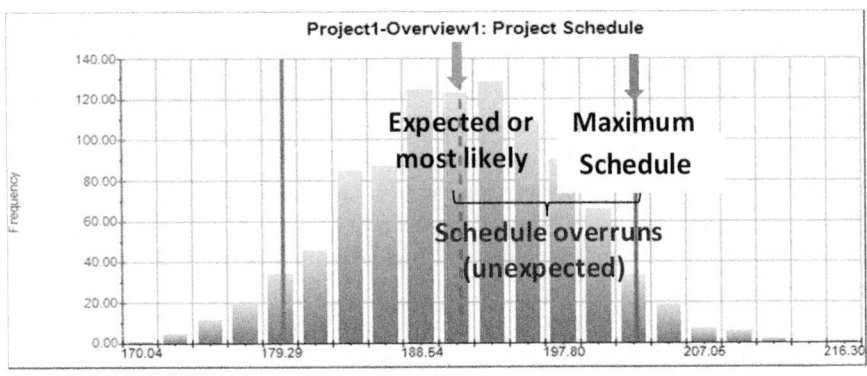
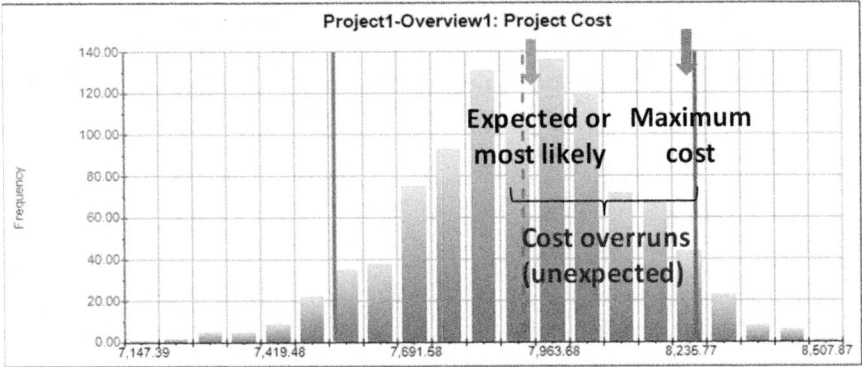

Figure 6.4: Risk Profiles on Cost and Schedule

HANDS-ON PEAT PROJECT MANAGEMENT

To illustrate how quantitative risk management can be applied in well P&A projects, PEAT-DECOMM (PM module as shown in Figure 6.5) is also used to model decommissioning. A dynamics on cost and schedule risk (e.g., estimating confidence intervals, exploring critical paths and contingencies, analysing tornado, sensitivity charts, and risk profiles). This IT risk management solution has been used by the authors to implement various quantitative decommissioning risk analyses.

Figure 6.5: PEAT – Project Management Platform

Projects with Complex Tasks and Critical Path

Projects can be implemented using either a linear path (sequential activities, one task after the other) or a complex task (combination of parallel sequential activities) approach. Decommissioning projects make use of the complex task approach, where activities can be executed linearly and simultaneously, and can be recombined at any point in the project network.

PEAT-DECOMM not only allows considering linear and complex tasks, but also, in an integrated form, running both activity-based schedule and activity-based cost analyses in the same project risk model. Moreover, activity-based cost can be split into fixed and variable. The model incorporates estimations on minimum, most likely, and maximum values into a project complex task.

After several decommissioning consultations and plan revisions with contractors and service providers, 15 tasks were developed into a general decommissioning plan to run safely, on time, and under budget. Table 6.2 lists the activities, and Figure 6.6 shows the probability distributions of cost (fixed cost and variable cost) and schedule of a general well P&A project. Figure 6.7 shows the complex tasks network diagram resulting from adding activities and combining them in a visual map. Note that after running the model using Monte Carlo simulation, the complex path shows the highlighted critical path.

Table 6.2: List of Generic Well P&A Tasks

Task 1	Project Start
Task 2	Scope of Work (FEED Study)
Task 3	P&A Design
Task 4	Engineering Planning
Task 5	Procurement
Task 6	Decommissioning Permits & Compliance
Task 7	Drilling Rig Arrival
Task 8	Platform Preparation
Task 9	Well P&A
Task 10	Conductor Removal
Task 11	Heavy-Lift Vessel Arrival
Task 12	Platform Removal
Task 13	Disposal & Site Clearance
Task 14	Handover
Task 15	Project Completion

From Figure 6.7, it can be observed that Tasks 1, 2, 4, 6, 8, and 12–15 represent the critical path, which matches with the project plan in Microsoft Project®. However, PEAT-DECOMM indicates that there is only a 52% probability the critical path will be along these tasks. The model also uncovers that Tasks 1, 2, 4, 6, 7, and 9–15 have the second-longest duration in terms of project completion (48% probability). Resolving uncertainties around the tasks' performance can increase or decrease the critical paths' probabilities or uncover new ones as the project progresses and updates.

In fact, most of the oil and gas decommissioning projects centralise the highest source of uncertainties on schedule around Task 8 (Platform Preparation) and Task 9 (Well P&A). A probabilistic critical path, then, provides valuable information to managers associated with potential bottlenecks and delays in project completion.

Finally, PEAT-DECOMM can help decision makers to create additional strategies, insert new intermediate tasks, change activities' connections, and implement project variations around the initial model or create new ones. Hence, probabilistic critical path analysis shows preliminary warnings for risk-based decisions in terms of how strong the bottlenecks are, and how accurate and understandable or logical is the detailed P&A plan. *Overrun Assumptions* (budget buffer in each task) and *Probability of Success* (task failures and cancellation impact on subsequent tasks) can be modeled to improve the decision analysis under risk and uncertainty.

Applied Analytics: Tornado Analysis

Tornado analysis is a static approach to identify the critical tasks in projects. In other words, tornado analysis can detect the most influential activities, in size or weight, impacting schedule and cost.

For example, Figure 6.8 exhibits a tornado analysis of the defined well P&A project, using 10% variation around the base-case estimations and an activity-based schedule approach. For the case study, Task 4 (Engineering Planning), Task 6 (Decommissioning Permits), Task 8 (Platform Preparation), and Task 2 (Scope Work) are the risk factors or activities most influential on project schedule. They deserve important attention during the risk discussions, engagements, and quantification in terms of project duration, and create important guidance and decision support around the critical path.

In the same way, Figures 6.9, 6.10, and 6.11 provide information about those critical tasks impacting total cost, fixed cost, and variable cost, respectively. Particularly, Task 12 (Platform Removal) has the highest impact on total costs, fixed costs, duration, and weekly variable cost (Figure 6.9). In addition to Task 12, Task 8 (Platform Preparation) and Task 9 (Well P&A) are the main drivers of project fixed costs (Figure 6.10). Therefore, from the variable cost's perspective, Task 9 and Task 12 are the time-driving activities with the most critical impact (Figure 6.11).

Combining the critical path report with the tornado analysis on activity-based cost and schedule, you can see that Task 8 and Task 12 are important tasks driving the decommissioning project and require planning, monitoring, control, and scenario and sensitivity analysis.

Applied Analytics: Scenario Analysis

Scenario analysis, also called *what-if* analysis, helps decision makers to explore how changes in certain project management tasks (Mun, 2010) impact schedule and cost (total, variable, and fixed).

PEAT-DECOMM can be used to run scenario analysis based on variations around task estimations. Figure 6.12 shows the cost and duration scenario setting for Task 12 (Platform Removal). Inserting changes around the base-case estimation, Figure 6.13 presents the scenario results in the form of heat maps for the total cost estimations of the well P&A project. For instance, if the preliminary budget estimation of the total decommission cost is £41.5M, generating some scenarios on cost and time for Task 12 indicates that duration above 1.8 weeks and fixed costs larger than £17.2M, with the others remaining constant, ceteris paribus, the total cost exceeds the budgeted values (dark area in the numerical heat map).

Risk Identification and Risk Quantification

During data gathering, contractor and project meetings, and well P&A risk analysis, risk and project managers need to interpret information and assumptions in terms of optimal project conditions, most likely durations and costs, project inefficiencies, and worst-case scenarios. In other words, they analyse triangular or PERT distributions' inputs. As a best practice, project incumbents need to justify and provide, by activity or task if possible, reasons about deviations against from the most likely estimations.

For instance, any difference between the maximum and most likely values (cost and schedule) might be associated with uncertainties, inefficiencies, and risk events. One way to also chase these deviations and validate extreme values is reviewing previous projects or the current risk register (see Chapter 7), if available. Doing so enhances the decision making by taking full advantage of the information available and pushing forward towards an integrated risk management approach, starting from the risks identified through to their quantification in terms of costs and schedule effects.

Finally, observe that activity-based analysis also allows identifying, mapping, and quantifying the impacts of extreme events on project management (cost and time). For example, pandemic risks (e.g., Coronavirus – COVID19, Influenza – H1N1), adverse weather conditions (e.g., winter, flooding), among other infrequent events. Particularly, in pandemic risks and decommissioning, it is recommended one first determines what activities (e.g., construction, engineering, site works, testing, procurement) are exposed the most in terms of cost and schedule due to human and operational factors; namely, people with symptoms, homeworking, sick-pay policy, ICT limitations, time management, government lockdown mandatory time, procurement and suppliers' management, travel arrangements, layoff or furlough scenarios, and so forth.

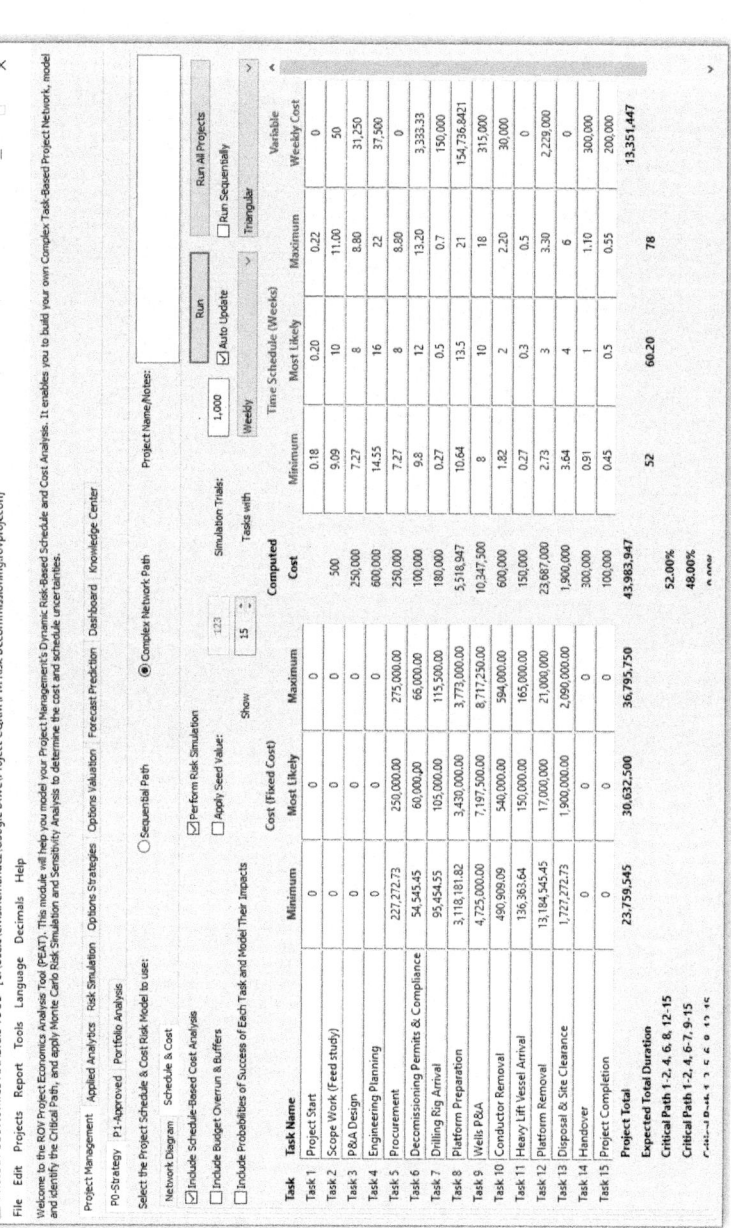

Figure 6.6: Complex Project Simulated Cost and Schedule with Critical Path (Assumptions)

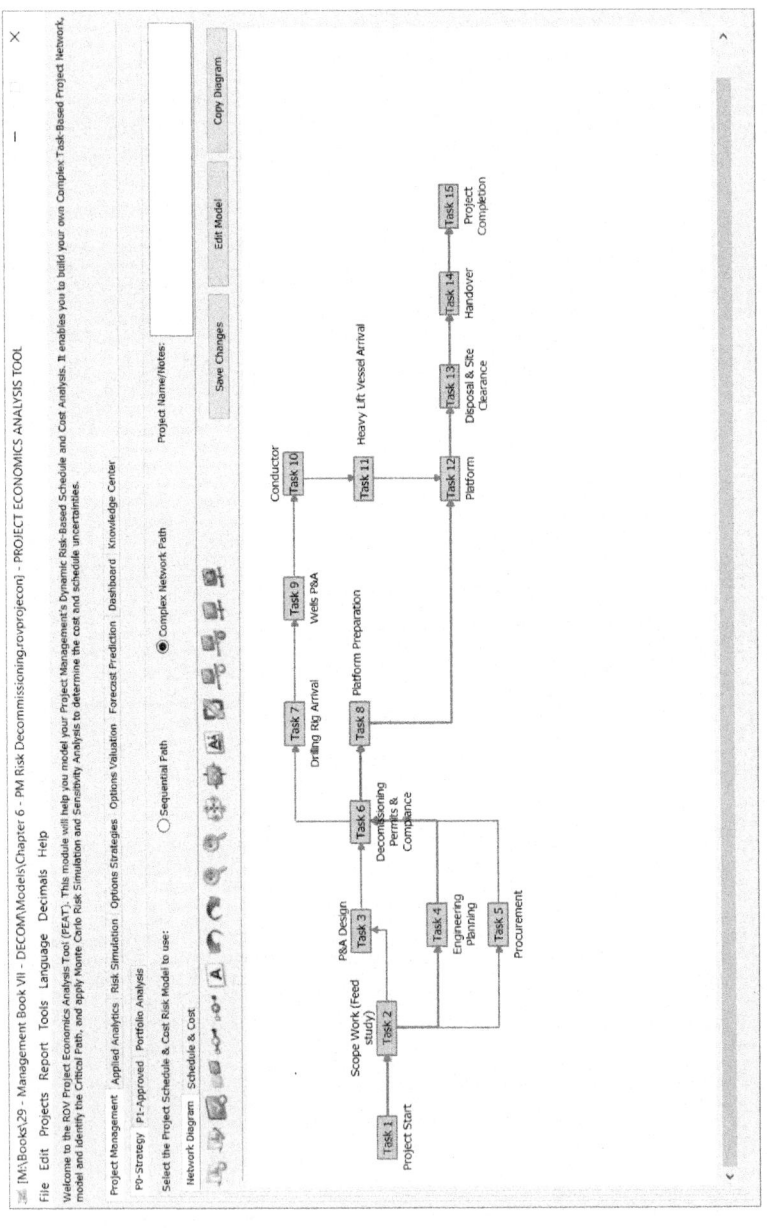

Figure 6.7: Complex Project Critical Path

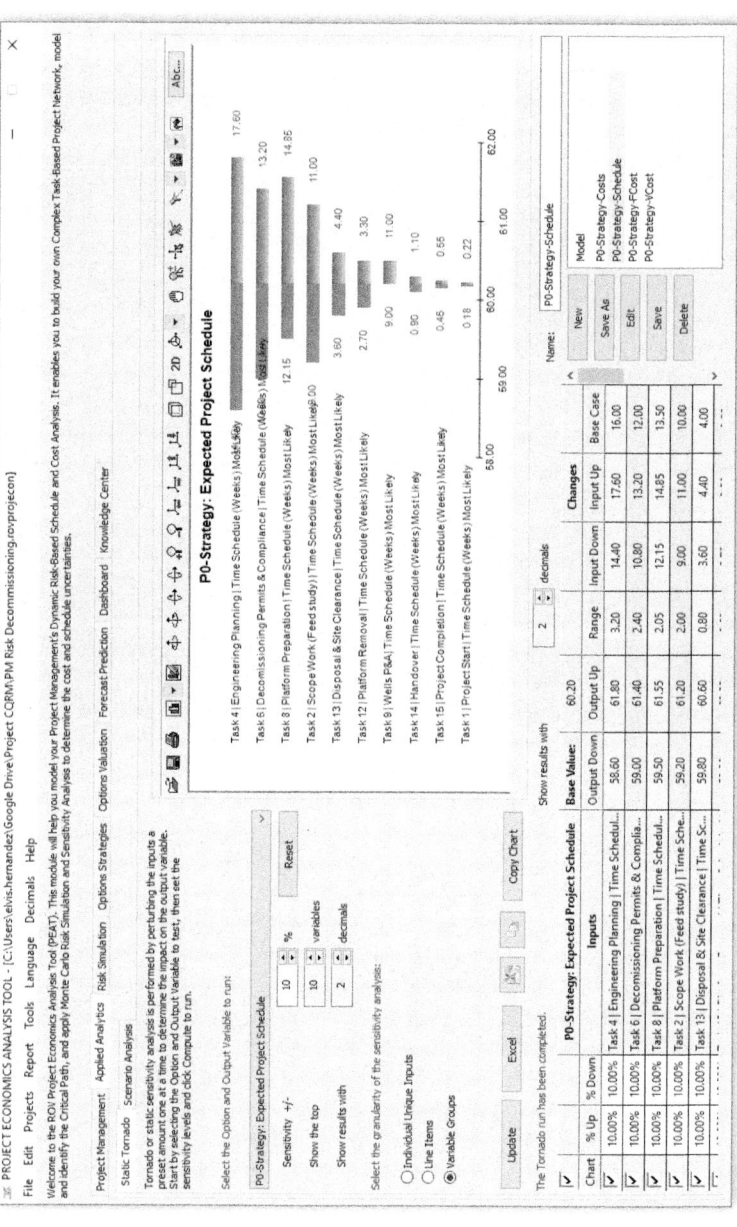

Figure 6.8: Tornado Analysis (Schedule)

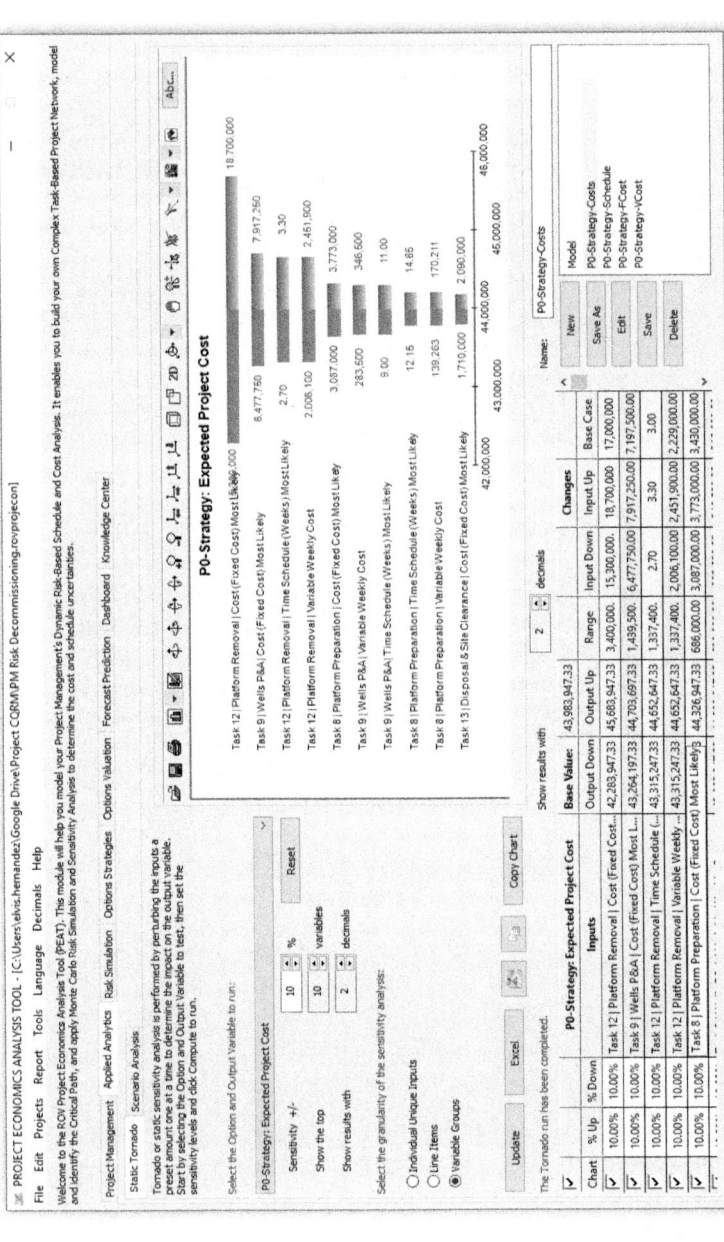

Figure 6.9: Tornado Analysis (Total Cost)

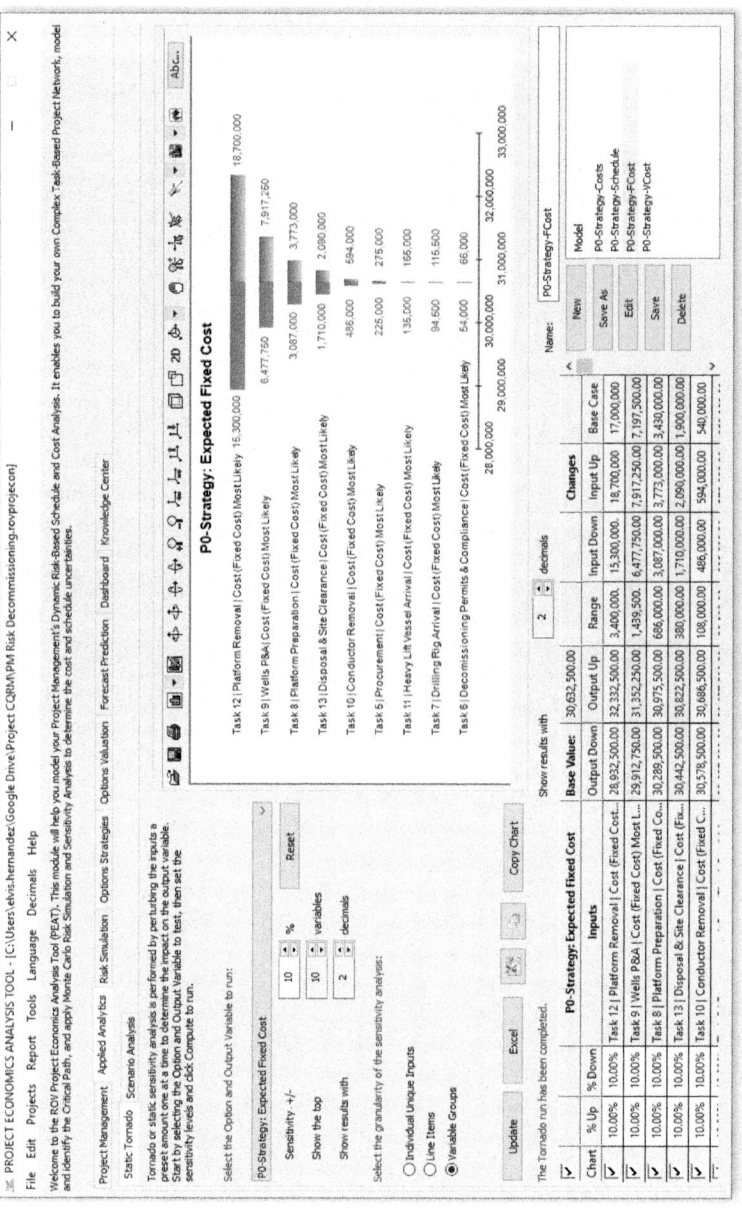

Figure 6.10: Tornado Analysis (Fixed Cost)

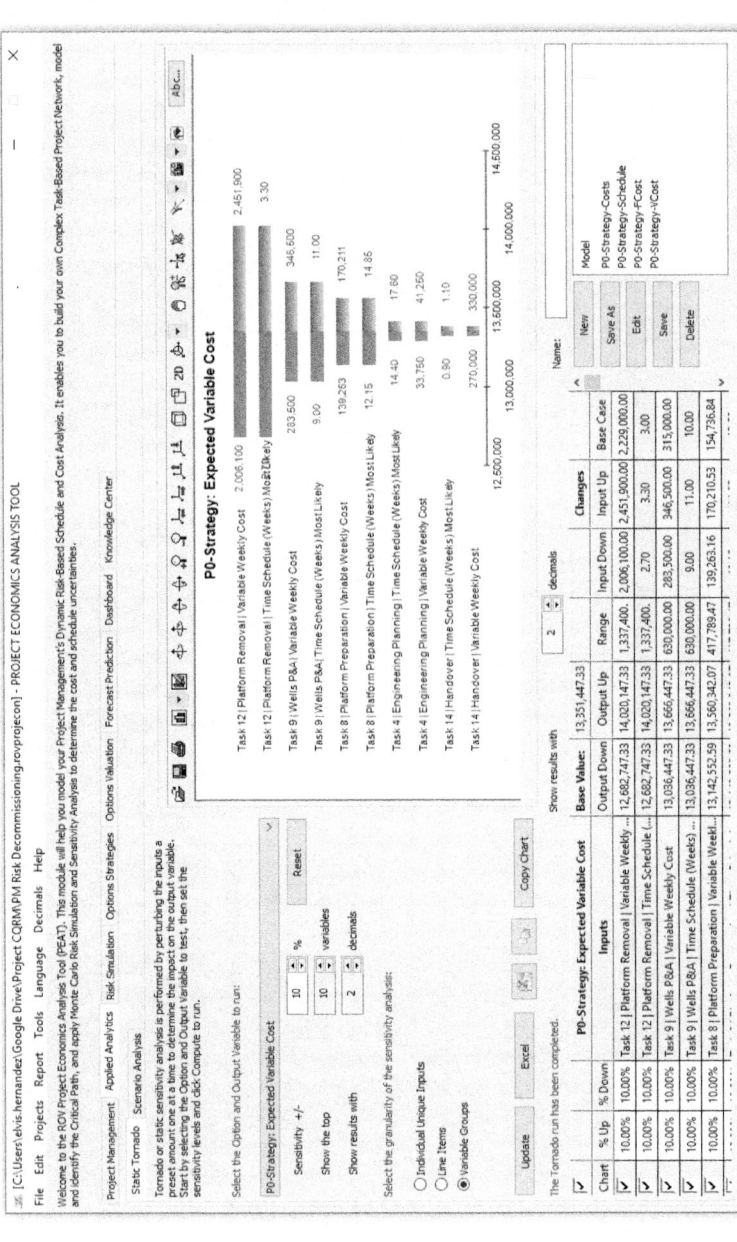

Figure 6.11: Tornado Analysis (Variable Cost)

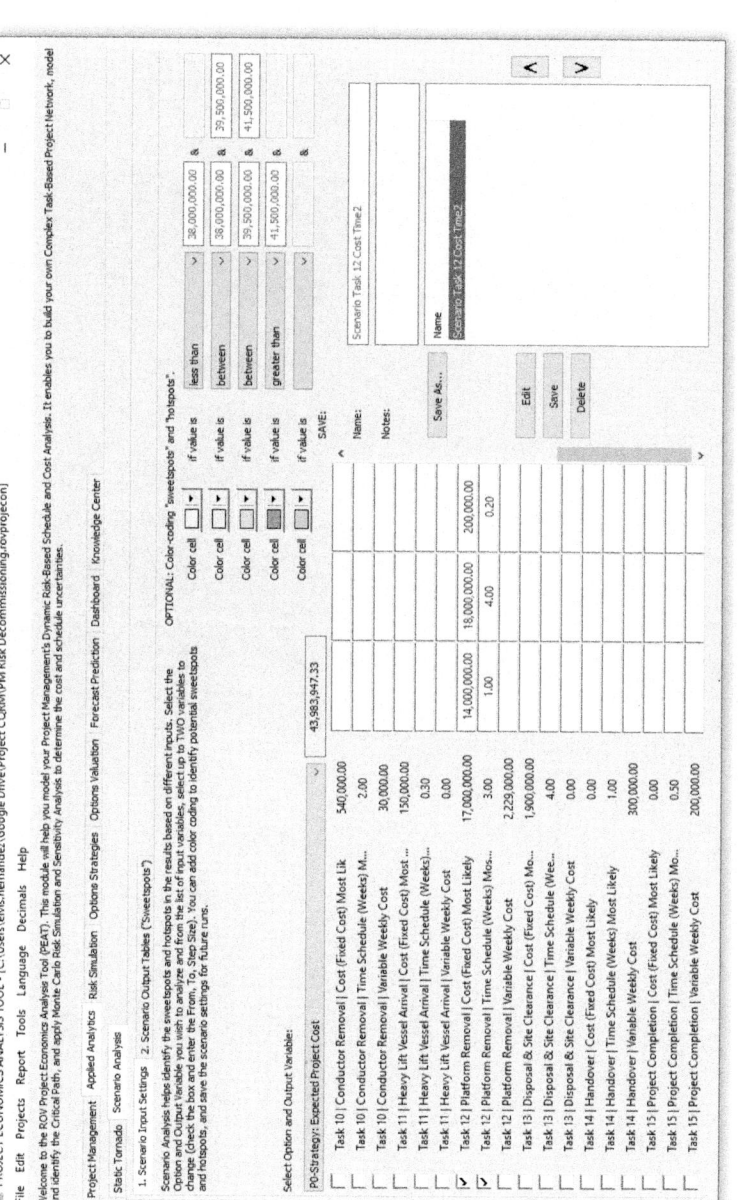

Figure 6.12: Scenario Analysis (Changes on Task 12, Schedule and Total Cost)

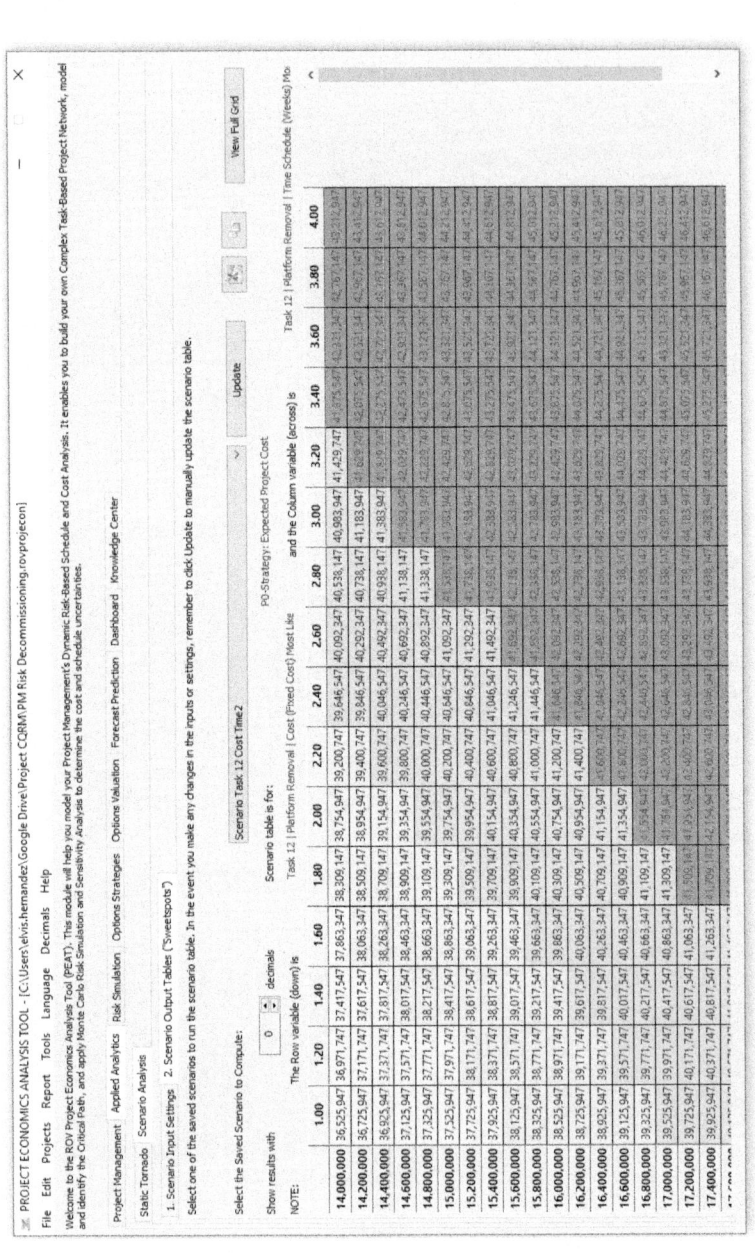

Figure 6.13: Scenario Analysis (Heat Map on Schedule and Total Cost)

Note that decommissioning risk should not rely solely on experience, data vendors, contractor estimations, previous projects, and decommissioning norms. Risk registers can be integrated into the risk analysis to provide quick guidance for mapping causes and consequences in terms of cost and duration, selecting some preliminary events that impact on the tasks' performance such as: potential fires and hazards, lifting and cutting strategies, safety process, people on board, likelihood of accidents, environmental disruptions, and so forth.

A comprehensive and integrated risk management view allows for getting more information, validating the probability estimations, cost and time forecasts, contingencies, and reducing biases while enhancing risk modeling and quantification based on Monte Carlo simulations.

Risk Simulation: Risk Profile

PEAT-DECOMM implements Monte Carlo risk simulations and decision analytics to propagate the uncertainty from the individual well P&A activities to schedule and cost. In fact, the PEAT-DECOMM can also implement this quantitative approach by automatically using the assumptions and estimations shown in Figure 6.6.

Decommissioning managers need to continuously determine, report, and monitor cost and schedule estimations based on their assumptions in the activity-based plan, milestones, and progress. Confidence intervals (e.g., 99%, 95%, 90%) and descriptive statistics (mean, median, standard deviations, skew, kurtosis, etc.) guide them during the project analysis and decision making.

For example, for a well P&A project involving 6 wells, 25-year facilities, a North Sea location, and 7,000 tons of weight, Figure 6.14 shows that there is 90% confidence the project will last between 60 and 69 weeks with a most likely value of 64 weeks. Still using the preliminary task-based duration, there is a 5% chance the project will surpass the 69 weeks. Similarly, Figure 6.15 highlights that there is 90% confidence the project cost can vary between £41.7M and £47.7M. The distance between those cost figures (95th percentile or any other percentile above the 50th percentile), including the expected value, provides information for contingencies. In our example, the company needs around £3M budgeted in case costs overrun or unexpected changes in the capital expenditures become tangible.

While risk profiles on schedule and cost outcomes are important for assessing the confidence intervals and contingency analysis, it is also necessary to know the most influential factors affecting the variability of these forecasts. Consequently, dynamic sensitivity analysis provides a guide for decision makers to control and manage cost and duration. This sensitivity analysis uses both "correlation analysis" and the "percentage of variation explained," among the decommissioning outcomes and the changes on well P&A tasks.

Risk Simulation: Sensitivity Analysis

Dynamic sensitivity analysis is performed after running simulations. It considers variations in all individual tasks in terms of how those variations affect and impact the main project indicators, cost (total, fixed, variable), and schedule. These fluctuations can be assessed using nonlinear rank correlations and percentage of variations explained. The first captures nonlinear effects between the risk events and the project indicators, and the second indicates how relevant each of the uncertainties may be to individual tasks after considering decommissioning schedule and cost.

Figure 6.16 shows the sensitivity charts for a well P&A schedule. We see that more than 90% of the variability in the schedule is influenced by Task 4 (Engineering Planning), Task 8 (Platform Preparation), and Task 9 (Well P&A), and, so, reducing their schedule duration would pay the most dividends as far as reducing the overall schedule length. In fact, controlling and managing the uncertainty on Task 4 not only reduces the variability in the project's schedule but also lessens the potential delay spread on future activities located on the critical path (e.g., Tasks 6, 8, and 12).

Additionally, Figure 6.17 shows the sensitivity charts pertaining to an analysis of the tasks' variability on the project's total cost. Task 12's (Platform Removal) fixed costs and Task 9's (Well P&A) fixed and variable costs amount to nearly 90% of the cost risk. Hence, further reviews of contractor cost, project management expenditures, and cost control, as well as potential days on the plug and abandonment process are required.

The platform removal's most-likely fixed costs are generally difficult to minimise. However, the project management position should be that of avoiding increases in these costs or of enhancing their predictability around the most likely estimations.

Dynamic sensitivity analysis can be applied to both fixed and variable costs. It helps significantly to narrow the number of the potential tasks affecting cost and time simultaneously, reduce the effort needed to manage activity-based risks, and increase the early warnings and monitoring aspects to keep decommissioning projects on schedule and under budget.

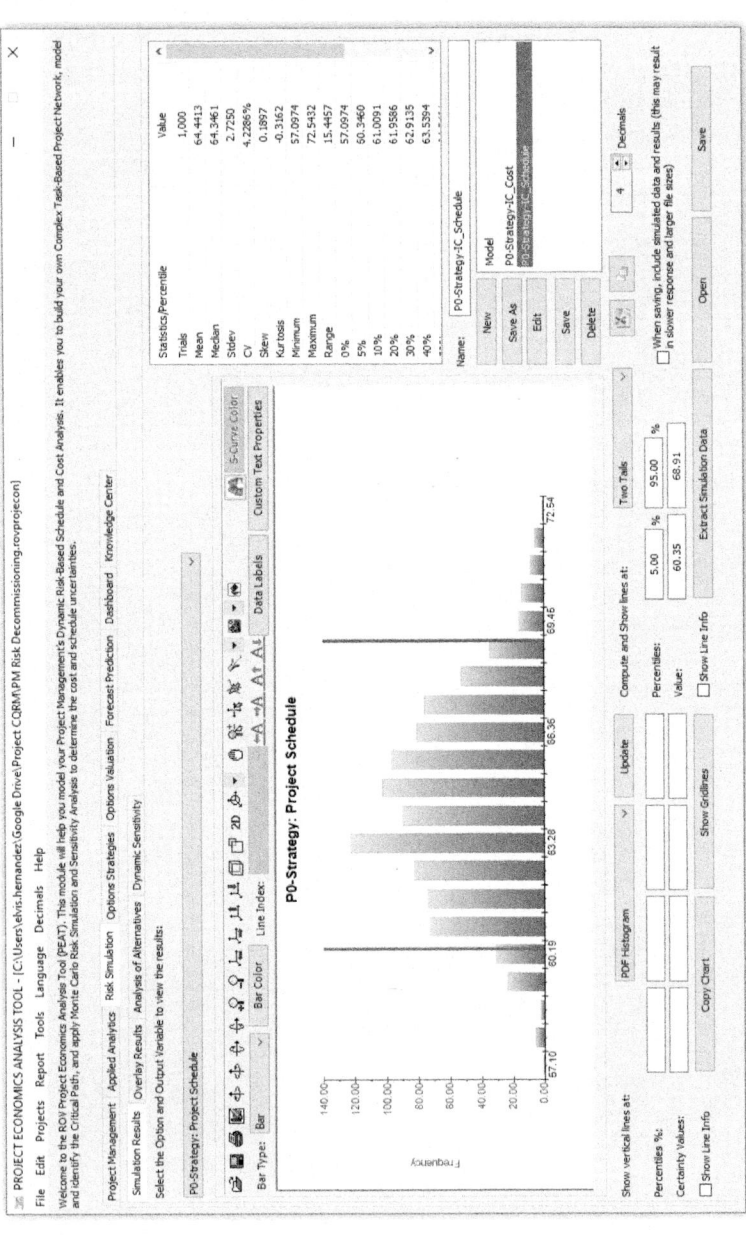

Figure 6.14: Risk Profile – Well P&A Schedule

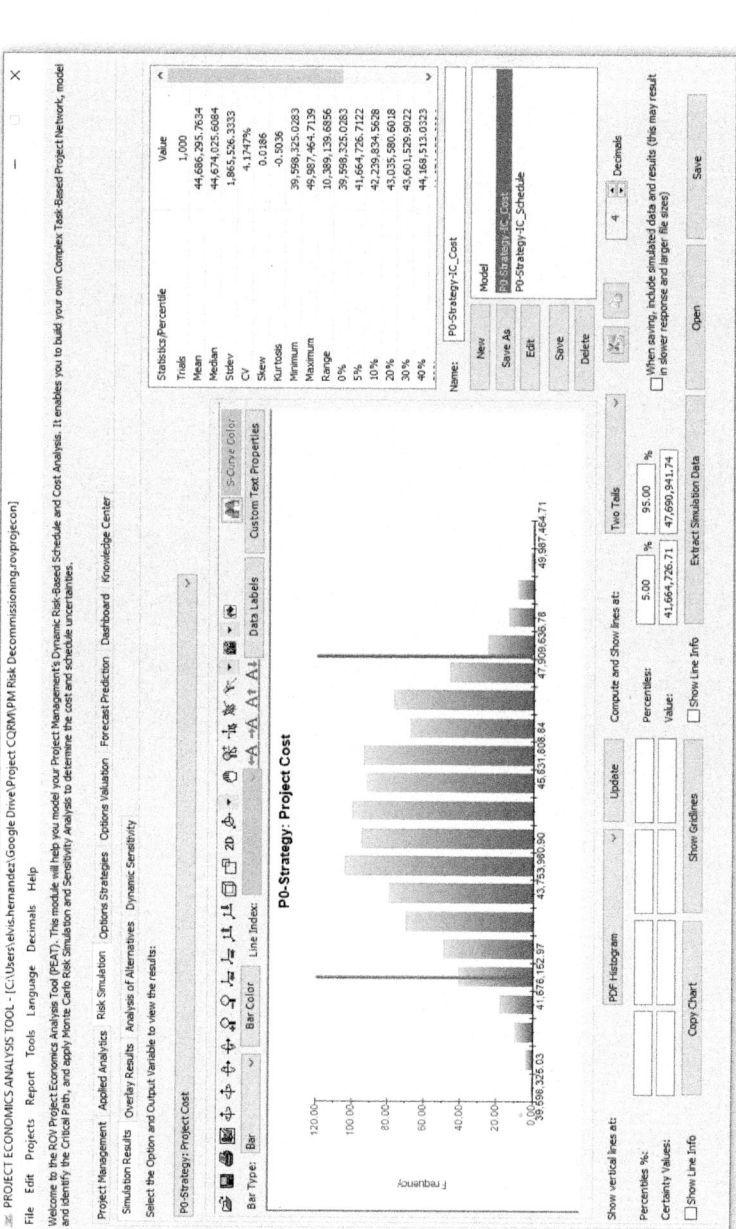

Figure 6.15: Risk Profile – Well P&A Total Cost

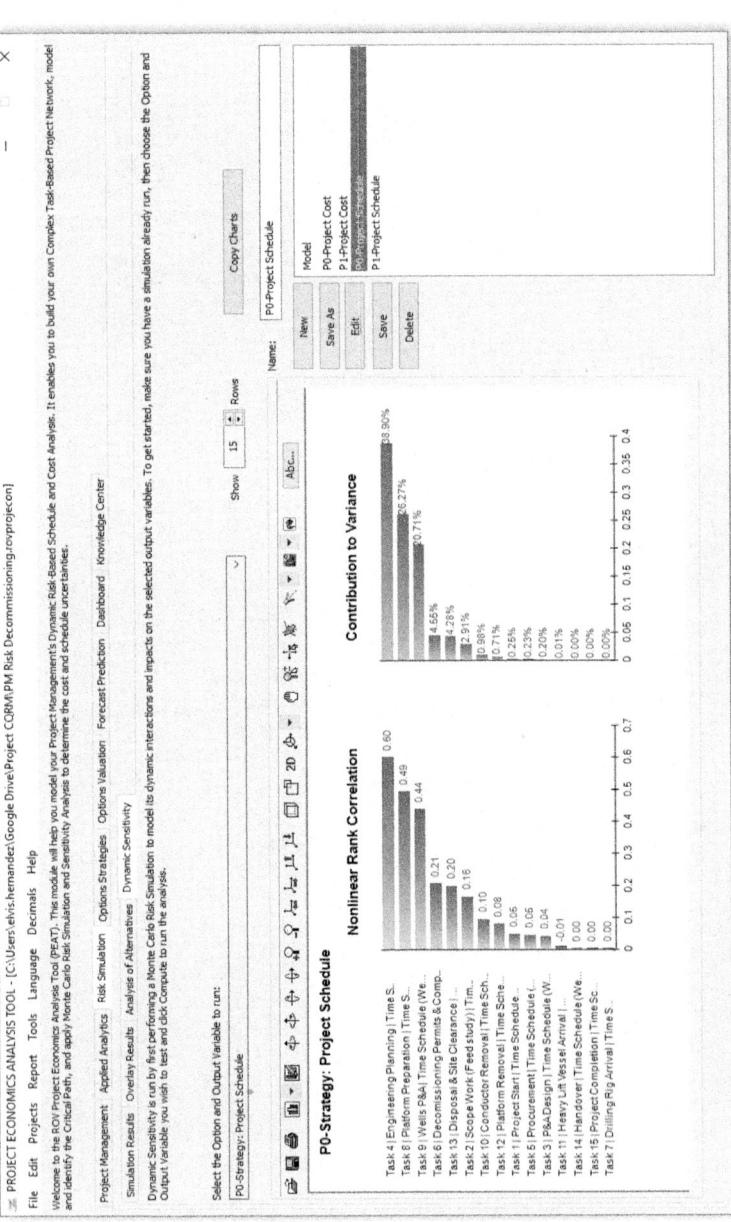

Figure 6.16: Dynamic Sensitivity Analysis – Well P&A Duration

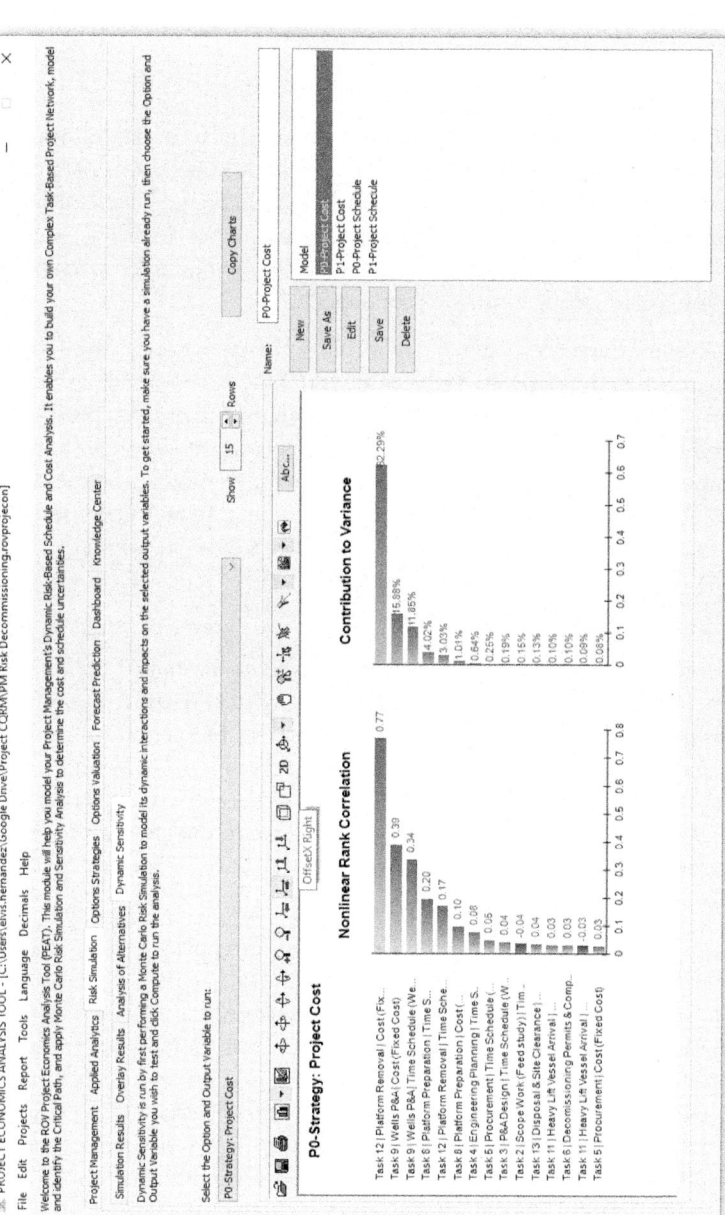

Figure 6.17: Dynamic Sensitivity Analysis – Well P&A Total Cost

DECOMMISSIONING PROJECT STRATEGIES, CONTROL, AND MONITORING

Any decommissioning project requires managers to understand both how uncertainty sources impact cost and schedule (and safety) and how to manage these uncertainties using flexibility (e.g., accelerating some task completions, considering parallel activities with resource redundancy, changing interconnections among tasks, and working on the long-lead items, among other aspects).

Flexibility enhances savings by looking for new means for cost minimisation and schedule reduction and by creating managerial strategies that reduce the impact of risk events on project performance. Therefore, flexibility implies that decision makers can start decommissioning risk management early in the process, enhancing control and monitoring to ensure the start dates, protect the most likely schedule, and reduce the likelihood of extreme durations.

Strategies and Critical Path

In general, one common task for decision makers is that of creating strategies to reduce randomness around the critical path. A decommissioning project that does not have a clear implementation path can suffer severe consequences in time and cost. Figures 6.6 and 6.7 show that there is low likelihood of occurrence of the main critical path (52% probability). Thus, a quick strategy is re-evaluating the initial model and its underlying assumptions around the critical path and tornado analysis.

Strategies around the longest duration require up-to-date project information from contractors, managers, and risk events. Figure 6.19 and Figure 6.20 show how having more consistent and accurate information on engineering planning, decommissioning permits, project compliance (surveys implementation), and lifting and cutting strategies reduce randomness in the critical path (Tasks 1, 2, 4, 6, 7, and 9–15), with a 100% probability of occurrence. Of course, this probability will change as the project evolves and activities complete.

In PEAT PM, decision makers can follow the same approach to compare multiple strategies, implementation options, project assumptions and evolution, project subsections, or interrelationships among activities. In other words, PEAT-DECOMM follows the same structure as that of the Project Management Institute's (PMI) project, programs, and portfolio to keep projects on time and under budget. For example, Figure 6.21 compares the initial well P&A engagement (Figure 6.6) against the updated project (Figure 6.19) and combined them into a portfolio to analyse the strategic objectives (cost and time). Note that the same project scope but different assumptions and implementation options result in a reduction of expected project costs from £44.6M to £41.4M and project schedule from 64 weeks to 61 weeks.

Control and Monitoring

A final aspect that deserves attention is how to control and monitor decommissioning projects. The first control and monitoring activity is to measure project progress by comparing and contrasting actual progress with the planned cost and schedule. The second step is not only to check for progress but also to ensure that we keep a well P&A project within scope and with lower level of risk exposure (schedule, cost, safety, and deliverables).

PEAT PM enhances the basis for project monitoring and control at any decommissioning stage. For instance, decision makers can pair different project options and implementations (flexibility) with project assumptions and evolutions in terms of the same project versions, programs, and portfolio. In addition to the portfolio outlook in Figure 6.21 (project control), Figure 6.22 shows the *Overlay Results* (illustration of relative spread, location, and skew of the results), and Figure 6.23 displays the *Analysis of Alternatives* (comparisons of risk simulations among projects or implementation options).

These figures exhibit how the project progresses after improving the task estimations around the critical path and main risk factors. Observe that there is a risk enhancement because the cost risk profile moves to the left (Figure 6.22), lowering the relative risks or coefficient of variability (CV) from 4.17% to 3.76% (Figure 6.23).

Likewise, Figure 6.24 illustrates the overlay results for the project's schedule. It can be observed that the schedule variability has not changed significantly (width between the tails). However, the expected schedule length has reduced from 2.6 weeks using *Analysis of Alternatives |Incremental Analysis* (Figure 6.25), where one project is selected as a base case and another as a comparison across different statistics (mean, median, skew, kurtosis, percentiles, etc.). *Incremental Analysis* can be also applied for cost monitoring.

Finally, Figure 6.26 and Figure 6.27 show that sensitivity charts can enhance project control and monitoring on cost and schedule, respectively. Note that in Figure 6.17, Task 12 (Platform Removal) is 62% of the cost variability, and after improving the assumptions, it constitutes only 24% (see Figure 6.26). In the same manner, Task 4 (Engineering Planning) in Figure 6.16 incorporates 40% of the schedule risk, and after the project evolves, it accounts for around 16% (see Figure 6.27).

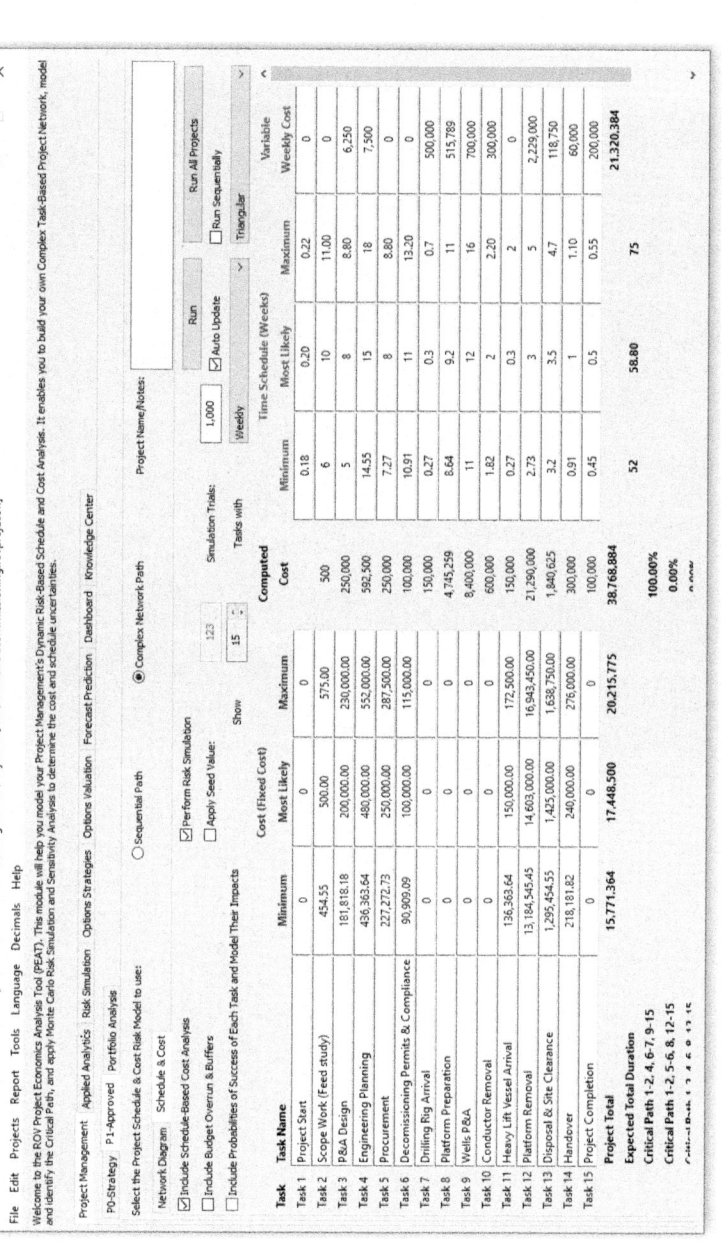

Figure 6.19: Project Assumptions – New Strategy Implementation

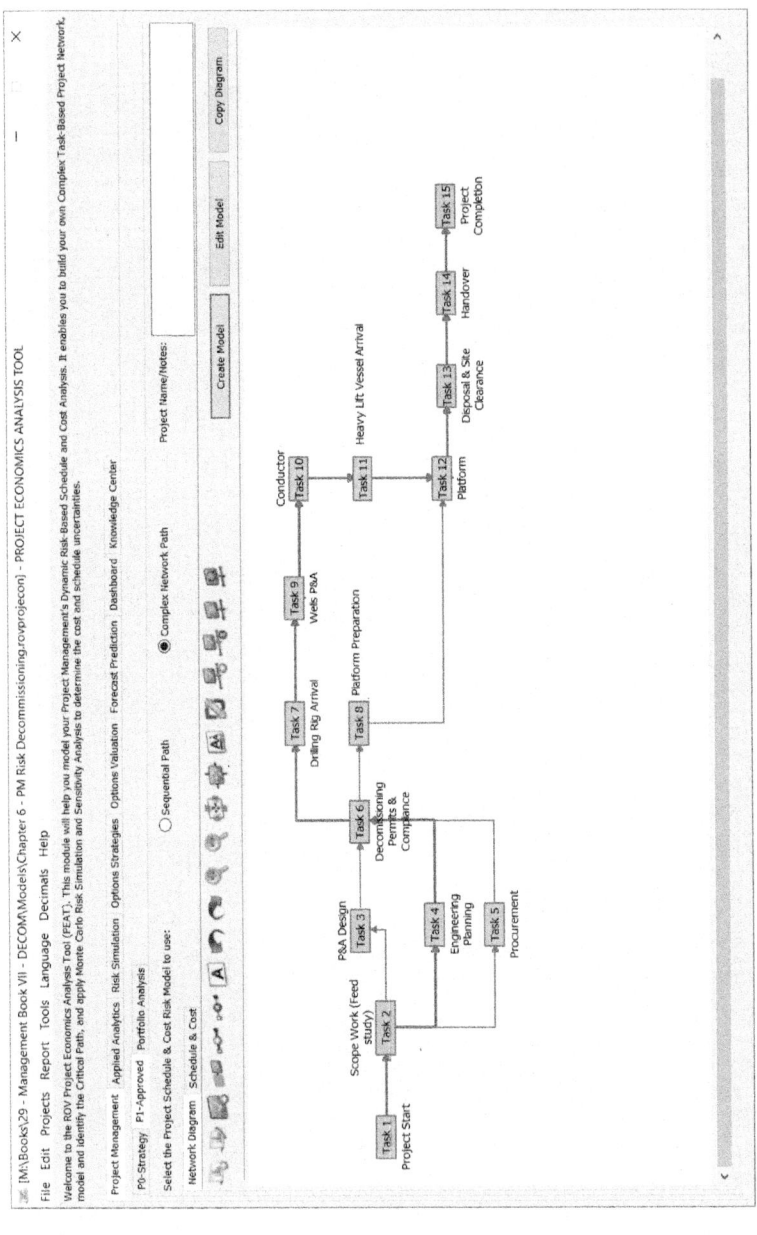

Figure 6.20: New Strategy Implementation – Critical Path

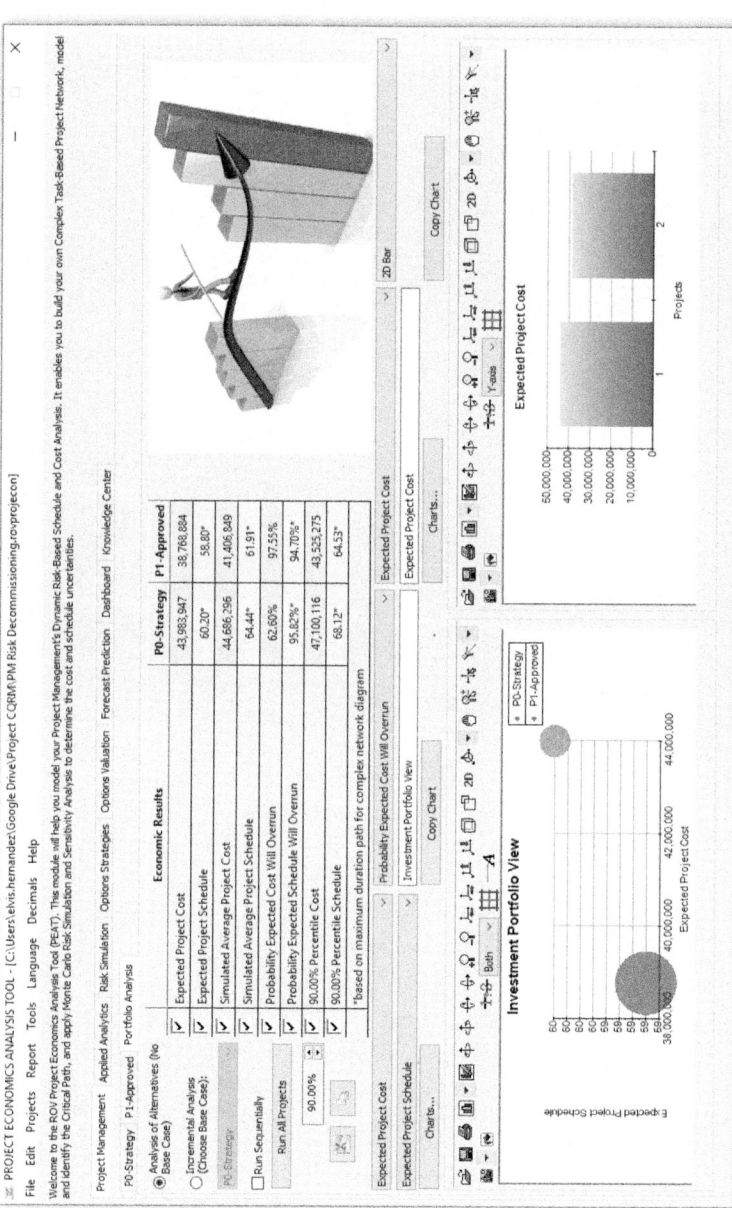

Figure 6.21: Strategic Management – Project Portfolio

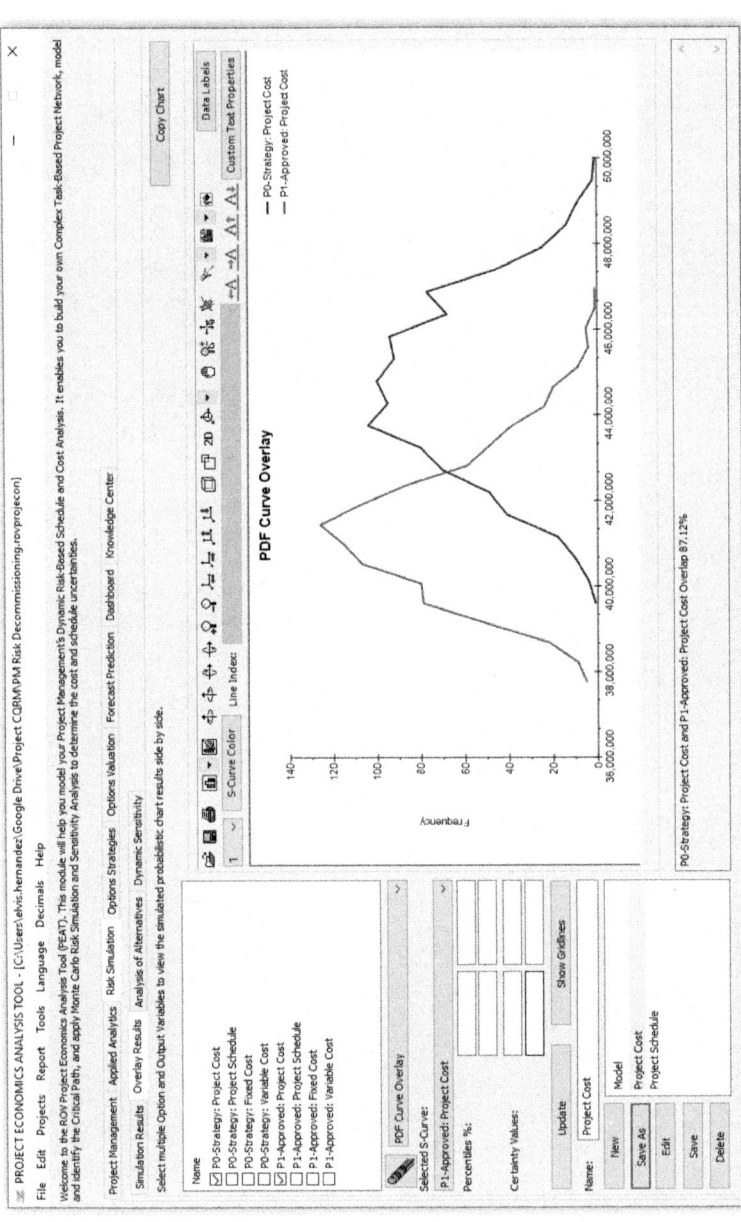

Figure 6.22: Overlay Results – Total Project Cost

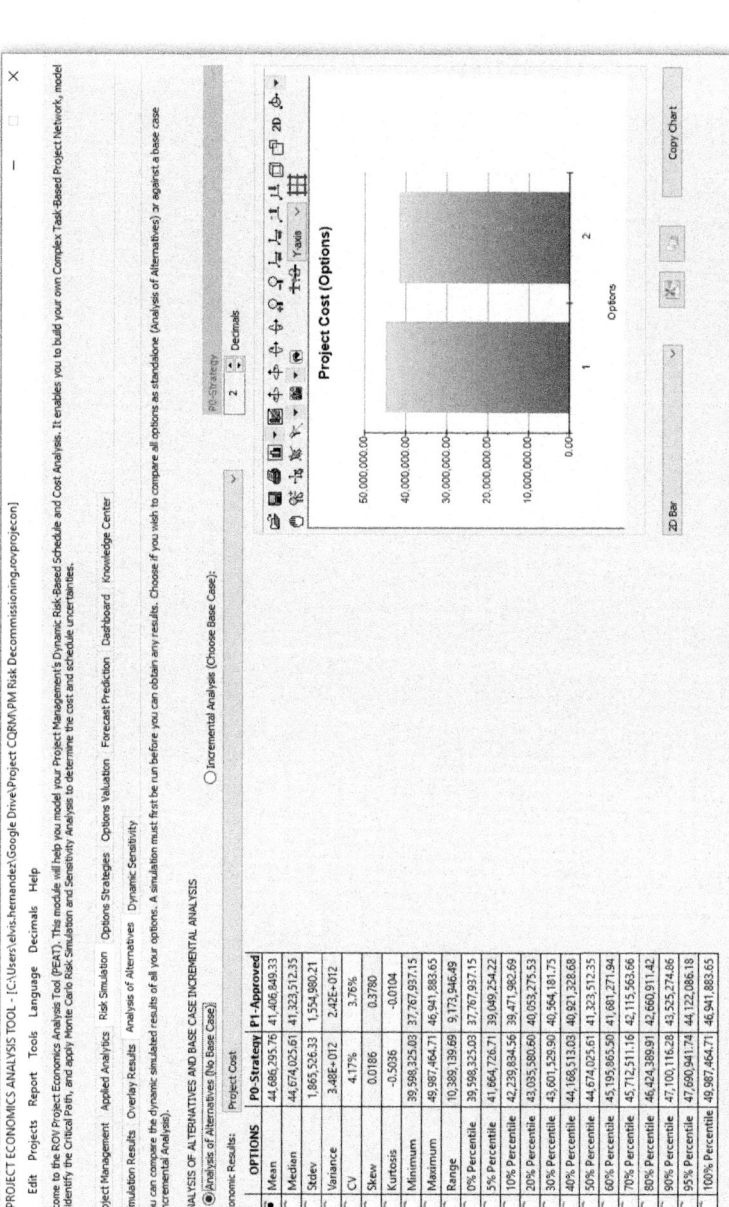

Figure 6.23: Analysis of Alternatives – Total Project Cost

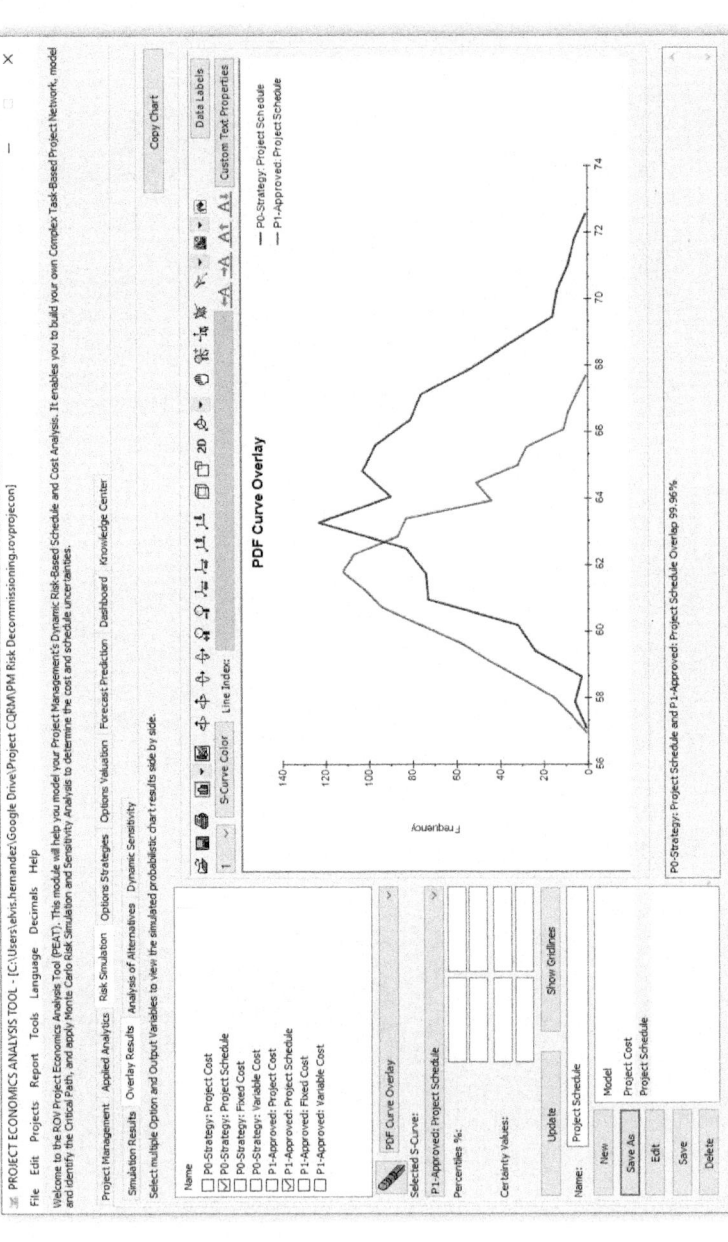

Figure 6.24: Risk Profile – Total Project Risk Exposure (Schedule)

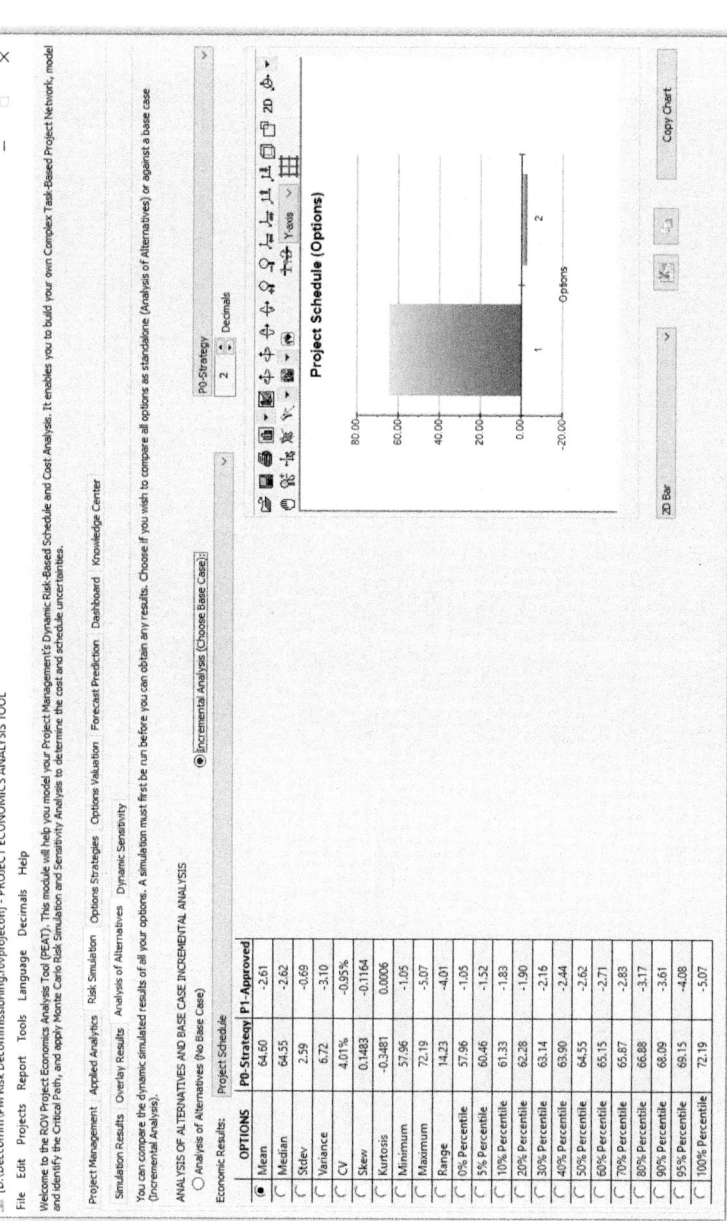

Figure 6.25: Risk Profile – Analysis of Alternatives

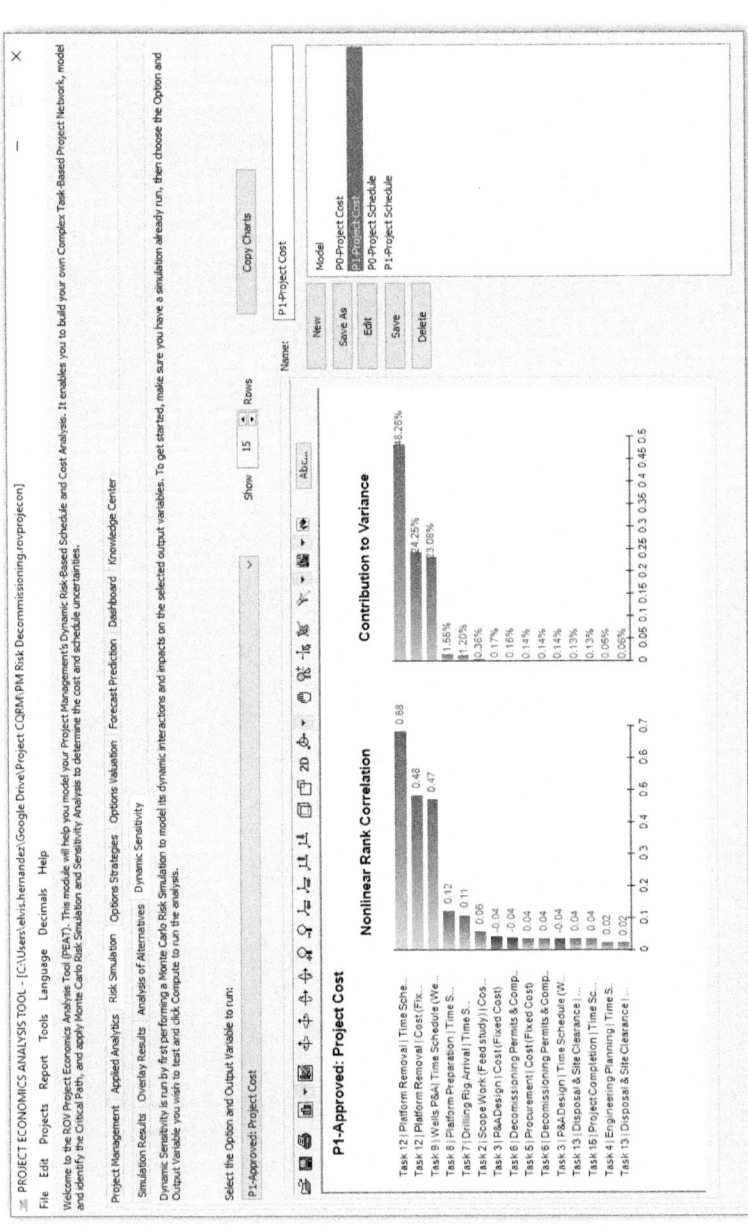

Figure 6.26: Dynamic Sensitivity Charts on Project Costs

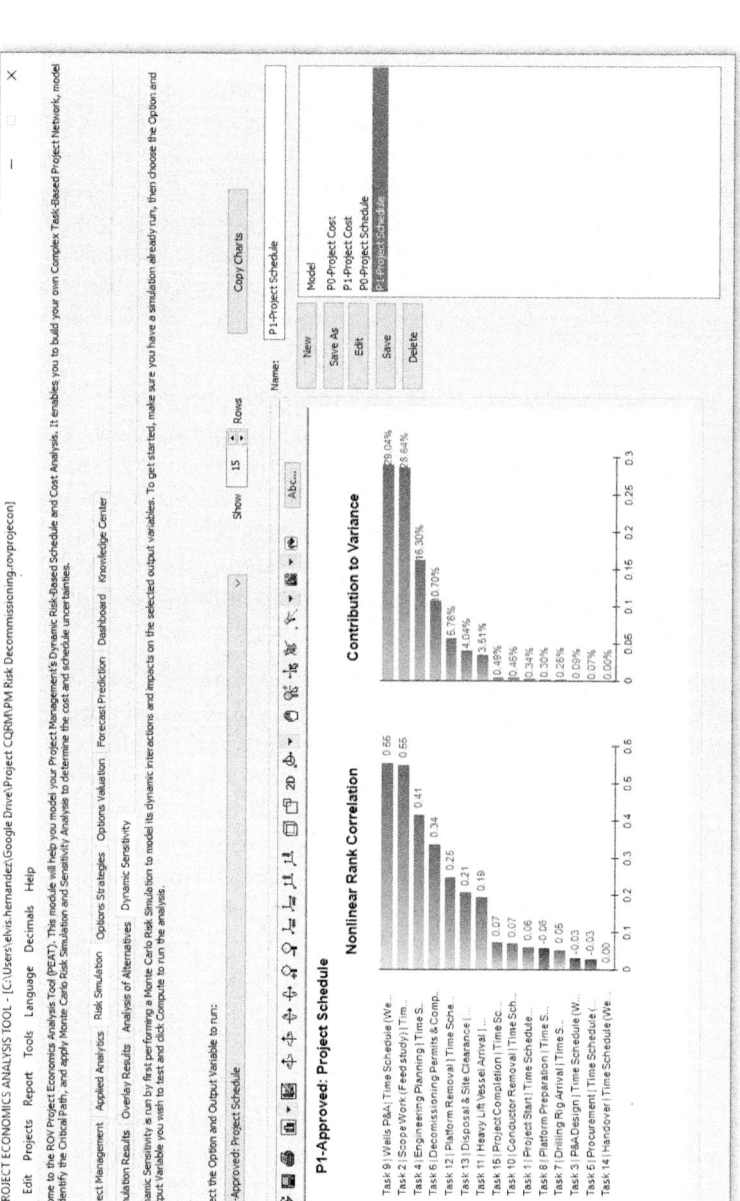

Figure 6.27: Dynamic Sensitivity Charts on Project Schedule

DECOMMISSIONING RISK AND LEARNING

Not only are there many risks associated with a decommissioning project, but using a solely traditional single-point estimates approach to project management—believing that there is just one final cost and one completion date—can lead to risky decisions. The modern advanced analytics approach provides more flexibility and accurate information because decision makers can try different scenarios of project implementations, chase the decommission assumptions, and create new strategies. In fact, thousands of trials and scenarios can be run to explore the range of possible outcomes for schedule and costs.

Under the supposition that each task in a decommissioning network might receive a time and cost estimate assumption, which is a reflection of the uncertainty sources, decision makers can implement risk quantification, control, and monitoring. The faster they can integrate tornado analysis, Monte Carlo simulations, sensitivity charts, and other decision analytics into well P&A decisions, the better the chances of having the decommission process be on time and under budget.

Working with incorrect cost and schedule estimates can result in accelerated cost escalations (fixed and variables costs), adjudications and litigations costs, wrong insurance premiums, and ambiguous project requirements, thus increasing control and monitoring costs and undermining the budgeted cash flows and future investments in the business. The PEAT-DECOMM comprehensive project management framework has been developed to manage potential risks and their quantification related to cost and schedule for decommissioning projects. So, while decision makers work collaboratively across teams, managing multiple resources (whether assets or people), they take actions, safely and effectively, to reduce the overall cost and duration at high certainty levels.

Decommissioning failure is costly and disruptive, not to mention that the dismantling of end-of-life assets must comply with environmental, health, and safety regulations. Hence, performing risk quantification early in the asset planning phase, which also captures the knowledge of the staff and engineering specialists who managed the assets during their life cycle, is almost a mandatory approach.

REFERENCES

Ahiaga-Dagbui, D. D., Love, P. E., Whyte, A., & Boateng, P. (2017). Costing and technological challenges of offshore oil and gas decommissioning in the UK North Sea. *Journal of Construction Engineering and Management, 143*(7), 05017008.

Hollmann, J. (2016). *Project Risk Quantification: A Practitioner's Guide to Realistic Cost and Schedule Risk Management*. Probabilistic Publishing.

Kaiser, M. J. (2019). *Decommissioning Forecasting and Operating Cost Estimation: Gulf of Mexico Well Trends, Structure Inventory and Forecast Models*. Gulf Professional Publishing.

Mun, J. (2010). *Modeling Risk: Applying Risk Simulation, Strategic Real Options, Stochastic Forecasting, Business Analytics, and Portfolio Optimisation*, Second Edition. John Wiley & Sons.

Mun. J. (2018). *Applied Analytical and Project Management* (Applied CQRM Book Series). IIPER Press.

Taboas, A. L., Moghissi, A. A., & LaGuardia, T. S. (2004). *The Decommissioning Handbook*. The American Society of Mechanical Engineers (ASME).

CHAPTER 7: ENTERPRISE RISK MANAGEMENT IN DECOMMISSIONING

Decommissioning involves managing multiple operational processes, systems, and information sources, such as drawings, piping and instrumentation diagrams (P&ID), maintenance plants, asset conditions, and other documentation, people, financial conditions, and health, safety, environment, and quality (HSEQ) criteria, among other aspects. However, the key criteria or objective is minimising the costs and schedule of the decommissioning, without compromising safety. Taking the necessary steps to manage decommissioning risks is a modern-day approach that provides a safety vs. cost compromise option since both variables need to be controlled during the project.

During a decommission, which requires a large cash outflow, companies rely on business processes and methodologies to identify and quantify risks and, consequently, to manage them. The proposed risk-based methodology is supported by a general Enterprise Risk Management (ERM) framework (Mun, 2019). ERM primarily allows organisations interested in decommissioning to perform quick evaluations of risk registers, hazard and operability studies (HAZOP) (Crawley & Tyler, 2015), layers of protection analysis (LOPA) (Clarin, 2013), and "as low as reasonably practicable (ALARP)" guidelines (see www.hse.gov.uk/risk/theory/alarpglance.htm), or simply classify decommissioning risks in terms of *Likelihood* or *Consequence* through a *qualitative* risk assessment and documentation. Integrated with risk quantification techniques, ERM allows decision makers to analyse the project dynamics of cost and time risk, capital expenditures (CAPEX), and compliance with the stringent requirements of HSEQ where the failure to do so can expose a company to severe penalties.

Project dynamics can be analysed using mathematical, analytical, and statistical methods to quantify the risks identified during decommissioning in terms of savings, schedule, costs, contingencies, cash flows, budgeting, and so forth. For risk identification, decision makers have to rely on different ERM approaches, for example, COSO ERM (Moeller, 2011); ISO 31000:2009/2018 (ISO, 2018); Risk-Based Inspections, RBI 580-581 (API, 2000a, 2000b); ISO 9001 (Avanesov, 2009); and ISO 55000 (Woodhouse, 2014); among others.

The most common concerns associated with decommissioning projects are:

1. Managing uncertainties related to project strategies (e.g., asset sectioning, cutting, lifting, mobilisation, demobilisation).
2. Balancing risk appetite when the job must be done with minimal costs and maximum safety levels (i.e., expected costs vs. contingencies constrained to safety).
3. Revising contingency plans and risk responses (e.g., emergencies, contract management, surveys in place).
4. Understanding operational flexibility (i.e., capabilities to identify, quantify, and manage surprises and losses).
5. Controlling correlated risks (e.g., contractors, vendors, inflation, and fixed costs, parallel and sequential activities, variable costs, and delays).
6. Framing strategic options to mitigate downside risks (e.g., contracting options using third-party contractors who see residual value in the decommissioning materials, switching option for CCUS, and so forth).
7. Improving the ratio of savings/capital expenditure embedded in other key performance indicators (schedule, costs, budgeting, savings, and other criteria).

APPLYING ERM IN DECOMMISSIONING

Although the ERM process mostly involves a qualitative assessment and risk register analysis, it is recommended as a preliminary step in risk management to save time during the risk quantification and risk allocation activities in the main areas of decommissioning, for example, CAPEX, schedule, and financial performance. According to the authors' experience, the qualitative-quantitative integration needs to be deployed using an Integrated Risk Management (IRM)® approach as follows:

- Establish the senior management risk-management culture for the main areas of decommissioning (costs, time, and HSEQ).

- Evaluate and share the board members' and project owners' expectations to discuss the value of risk management in decommissioning.

- Review risk registers and current ERM practices, including areas for improvement.

- Facilitate risk workshops for a quick quantification of the risk registers and integrate them into the decision-making process as they pertain to, for example, cost, time, and budgeting.

- Enhance group discussions with key stakeholders and project managers to identify other uncertainty sources (safety, reliability, lifting, cutting, financial decisions, regulations, environment, asset integrity, etc.).

- Validate project strategies and financial assumptions.

- Coordinate project development, control, monitoring, and key performance indicators (KPIs) for the defined decommissioning objectives.

- Implement risk quantification and analyse unallocated risk from the ERM process or risk registers quantitatively.

- Determine risk profiles on cost, time, and HSEQ by risk categories and project activities by using, for example, coherent and adequate dashboards and reports expeditiously.

- Establish a management working team consisting of board members, project owners, and contractors to manage, report on, control, and mitigate the decommissioning risks.

Note that a simple list of risk registers with risk categories, a general risk classification by *Likelihood* or *Impact*, a report of risk scores, or a generic risk matrix (*Heat Map*) by themselves can mislead decision makers (Thomas et al., 2014). They rely on purely qualitative information, giving decision makers the illusion of control and robustness in the risk management information presented. For this reason, a more integrated risk management framework combining risk identification and risk quantification needs to be applied. Hereafter, a qualitative approach will be called RM-Level1, and a quantitative approach, RM-Level2.

COMPREHENSIVE QUANTITATIVE ERM

A more comprehensive ERM approach in decommissioning not only is supported by qualitative assessments (RM-Level1) or risk registers but also needs to be included in the main decision areas of decommissioning, for example, budget, cost, savings, and project schedule. These aspects require quantitative methods (RM-Level2) for a better understanding of unexpected project outcomes. Risk quantification relies on Monte Carlo simulations, tornado analysis, scenario analysis, dynamic sensitivity analysis, and other decision analytics. They simplify both data-driven and risk-based decisions, empowering decommissioning professionals with insights from powerful quantitative methods.

This quantitative process (RM-Level2) can be implemented on traditional taxonomies from the risk register (Geographic, Activity, Process, Department, Managers, Division, Categories, etc.), and then linking them to decommissioning KPIs. Moreover, decision makers can analyse and integrate them into the economic and project management aspects of decommissioning. For example, lack of permits, terms and conditions, contracts in place, and asset surveys (risk registers) can increase the completion time of the activity *Procurement* by 50% (from 50 days to 75 days). While the traditional ERM enhances discussions around risk engagement and controls, the RM-Level2 pushes discussions forward by using statistical analysis, risk scenarios, and simulation around KPIs to create strategies around contingencies, mitigation responses, and recovery plans.

HANDS-ON ENTERPRISE RISK MANAGEMENT MODELING

Based on the authors' experience and knowledge dealing with risk management and working with other professionals on decommissioning programs, namely, plugging and abandonment (P&A) of oil and gas wells, a comprehensive IRM framework was developed to analyse their risks. The type of well P&A project used as a benchmark comprises six wells, with a weight of 7,000 tons.

A risk management solution called PEAT-DECOMM (ERM module as shown in Figure 7.1) is used to implement the IRM approach in well P&A. It is a desktop and a Web-based application with multiple patents, developed by one of the authors for quantitative risk management in decommissioning.

Global Settings (Risk Classifications)

Energy companies, including oil and gas firms, have significant information on risk registers as a result of common operational risk implementations (HAZOP, LOPA, Failure Mode, Effects Analysis, etc.) that are part of a regular implementation during the design, engineering, construction, and commissioning of assets and facilities. To accelerate the ERM automation and risk integration in decommissioning projects, PEAT-DECOMM allows for a quick setup of the company's organisation and risk structure for mapping risk registers on well P&A projects, if available. Otherwise, risk workshops, with project stakeholders and other active members, are required to identify those general risks affecting the P&A process. Regardless, risk workshops are needed to obtain starting points for risk quantification, which in the end, is the value-added area for decision makers in terms of risk management. We cannot manage something if we do not quantify it first.

The **Global Settings** section starts with *Date Settings, Risk Matrix (Likelihood vs Impact),* the number of categories, colour codes, and global units for the risk registers and key performance indicators or KPIs (currency, time measures, production units, etc.), as shown in Figure 7.2.

Risk Groups (Segmentation and Taxonomy)

As for other risk analysis in engineering projects, analysing decommissioning risks also requires the ERM methodology to have the ability to create divisions, departments, risk categories, risk managers, and other segmentations within the organisation responsible of the well P&A. This capability allows the risk quantification, business analytics, and risk clustering around the taxonomies be created, called risk grouping or clustering.

As shown in Figure 7.3, the **Risk Groups** classification for a generic P&A project should include, at the very least, *Risk Division* (e.g., Company: MJH Decomm); *Risk G.O.P.A.D* (e.g., Department: Decommissioning); *Risk Category* (e.g., Project Management, Operations, Construction, Marine, HSEQ, HR, and other categories); and *Risk Manager* (e.g., "LJackson," "JMun," and "EHernandez"). These areas represent a common Risk Taxonomy for decommissioning projects.

Note that multiple decommissioning projects can have multiple divisions or branches (e.g., UK, Europe, Offshore, Onshore, and so on). *Risk G.O.P.A.D* in PEAT ERM allows risk segmentation around Geographic, Operations, Products, Activities, and Departments. Other risk categories can be obtained from the *Load Risk Inventory Library*.

Risk Mapping (Risk Structure)

With the *Risk Groups* and their taxonomies, decision makers can obtain a risk map to view the defined risk hierarchies, which are relevant to show how certain decommissioning risks permeate the P&A project, as well as how specific risks touch different departments, categories, or project activities. For instance, Figure 7.4 presents a general **Risk Mapping** for a well P&A project. However, numerous decommissioning initiatives with different Risk Categories can simultaneously touch multiple G.O.P.A.D categories, divisions, or managers. Nevertheless, it is always good practice to keep a one-to-one correspondence to avoid double counting in terms of risk profiles and risk quantification. One common way to overcome this potential problem is by allocating the risk event according to the higher impact it has or under what category this risk primarily needs to be monitored or controlled.

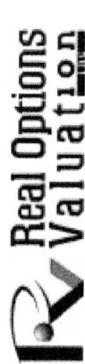

Project Economics Analysis Tool

© Copyright 2012-2018 Real Options Valuation, Inc.

Applying Integrated Risk Management methodologies (Monte Carlo risk simulation, strategic real options, stochastic forecasting, business analytics, and portfolio optimization) to project and portfolio economics and financial analysis.

○ Corporate Investments - Stochastic DCF
● Enterprise Risk Management (ERM) - Risk Register
○ Project Management - Schedule and Cost Risk
○ Goals Analytics - Sales and Pipeline Modeling
○ Banking - Credit, Market, Operational, Liquidity Risk
○ Corporate Investments - Buy vs. Lease
○ Public Sector Analysis - Knowledge Value Added
○ Oil and Gas Economics - Investment Decision Analysis
○ Oil and Gas Economics - Oil Field Reserves
○ Oil and Gas Economics - Remaining Oil Recovery
○ Oil and Gas Economics - Well Type Curves
○ Customized Encrypted Models

Load Example English

Start Selected Module Exit

☐ Healthcare - Health Economics Analysis Tool (HEAT)

Figure 7.1: PEAT ERM Decommissioning – Enterprise Risk Management by ROV

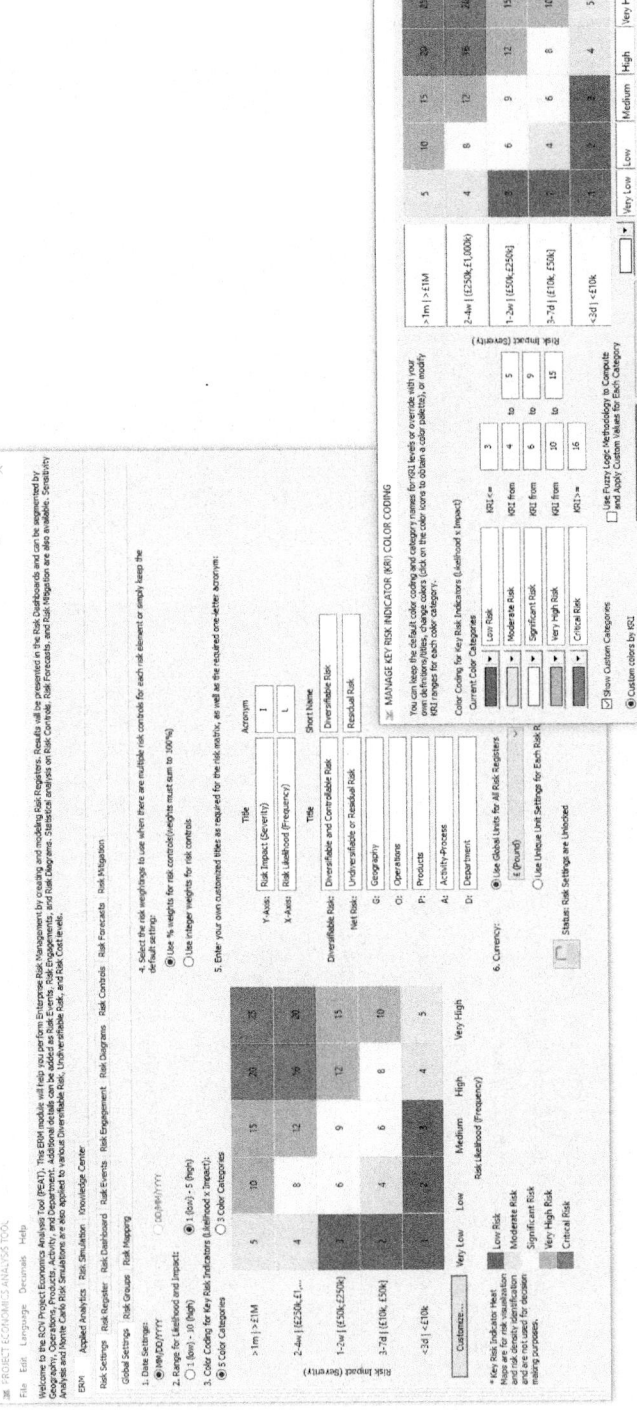

Figure 7.2: Risk Settings

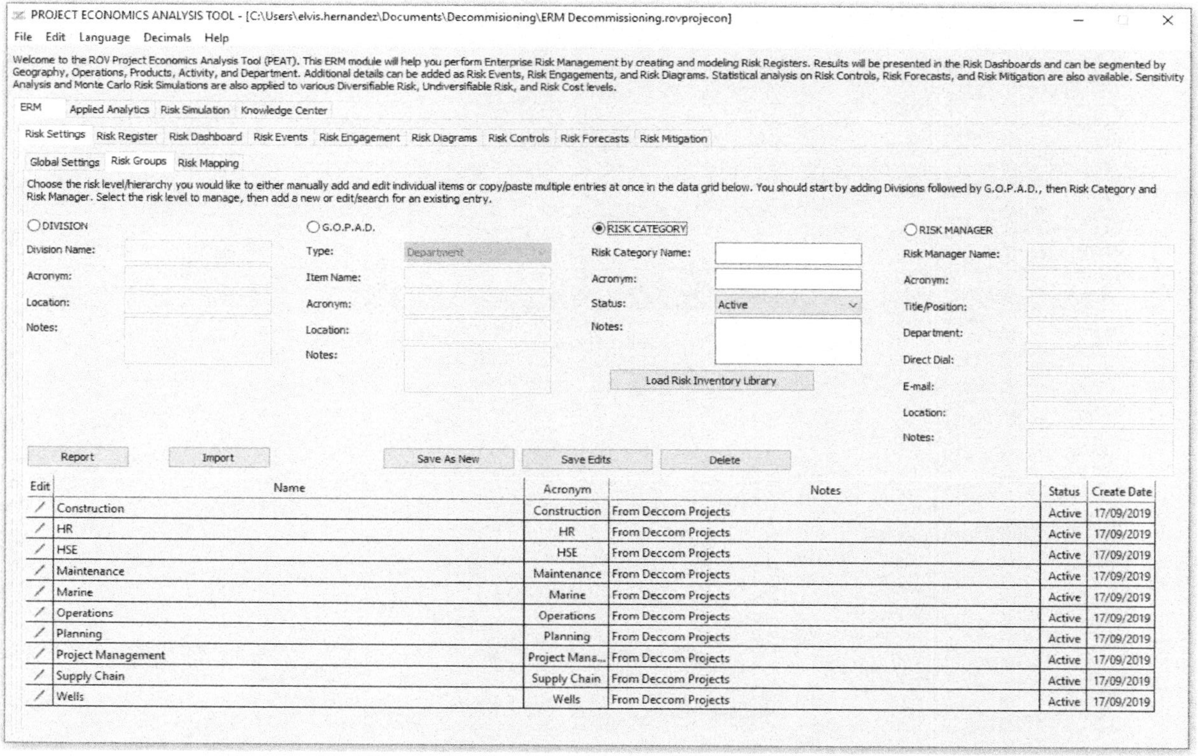

Figure 7.3: Risk Grouping in Decommissioning

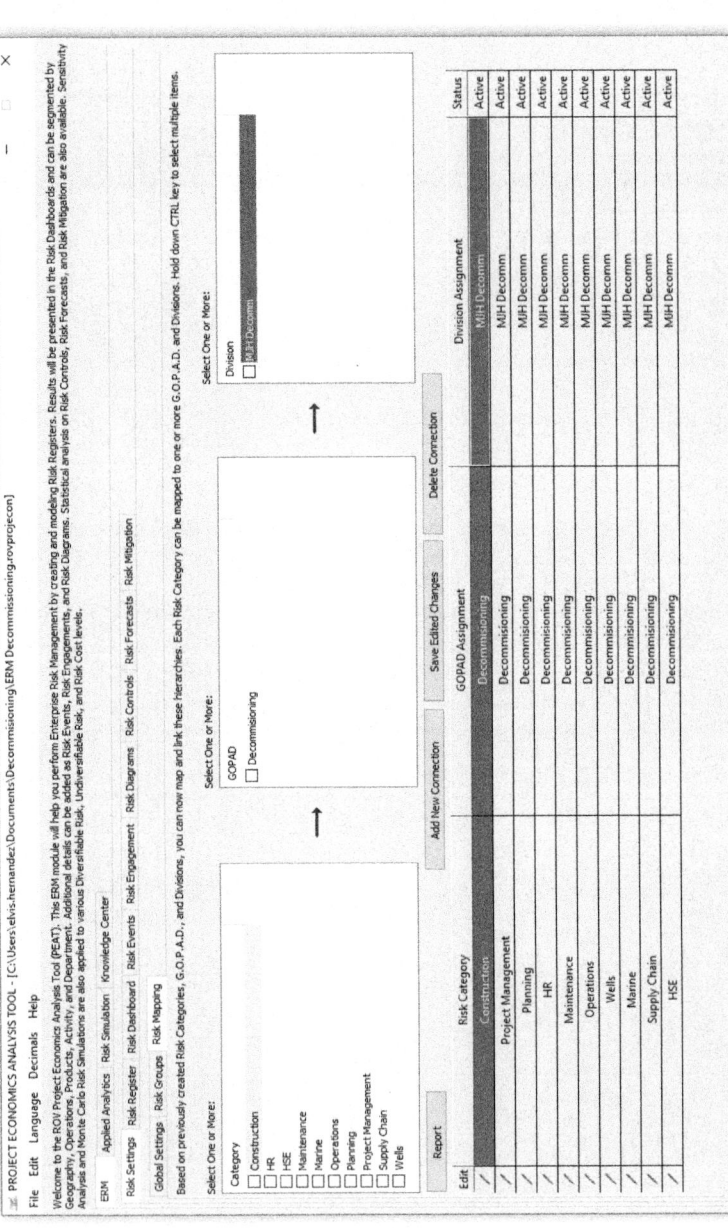

Figure 7.4: Risk Mapping for Decommissioning Projects (Well P&A)

Just as other ERM applications and risk register approaches require the correct inputs to initiate the risk analysis or risk discussions, PEAT ERM requires that *Group Settings, Risk Groups,* and *Risk Mapping* be done with great care to obtain consistent risk classifications, reports, and dashboards. Preliminary project planning and engagements between risk managers, project managers, engineers, and other stakeholders are needed to create a comprehensive ERM model (RM-Level1) that can enhance the quantitative approach (RM-Level2).

Risk Registers

Risk registers are key elements of risk analysis in energy companies, including project and asset integrity analyses, mostly presented in Excel files or spreadsheets. Decision makers, engineers, risk managers, and analysts find and gather multiple risk factors and identify causes, consequences, and mitigation strategies on a qualitative basis (RM-Level1). Nominal scales (e.g., Low, Medium, High) or scores (1, 2, 3, 4, etc.) are simple ways to present risk information to decision makers.

However, risk registers alone cannot properly support decision making because of the subjectivity of their nominal scales and scoring procedures that are based on surveys, interviews, and experience. Despite these constraints, however, risk registers can provide quick guidance for mapping causes and consequences, and also selecting some preliminary events for risk modeling and quantification in terms of P&A costs and schedule, for instance.

A simple analogy for a risk register and its elements would be a to-do list or a check-book with potential risks or opportunities identified. In decommissioning projects, namely, well P&A, risk elements are events and concerns such as fire, lifting, cutting safety, people onboarding, accidents, environmental regulation, mobilisation, demobilisation, logistics, pre-works, gangway, drilling rig, combined operations, and so forth.

For our P&A case study, the risk registers are shown as rows in a data grid and divided into two big decommissioning perspectives: CAPEX (Figure 7.5) and schedule (Figure 7.6) Although listing the risk elements with causes, consequences, and mitigation responses is standard for RM-Level1 implementation, it is important to mention that measurable aspects, such as risk exposure (diversifiable or controllable), uncontrollable or residual risk, mitigations costs, risk controls, expected complexity in terms of risk quantifications, data availability, percentage of mitigation, weights, and so forth, enhance both RM-Level2 implementations and a more comprehensive IRM approach. Otherwise, risk registers become a list of unallocated risks.

One key aspect of the risk registers is their contribution to the discussions and conversations around the risk quantification and their integration into the decision-making process. The risks being integrated refine the estimations on risk quantifications on CAPEX and schedule and, consequently, create priorities for risk control and monitoring, including the financial and nonfinancial implications of lack of compliance with HSEQ aspects.

Regarding monitoring, PEAT ERM helps users to create new profiles (*Change Name / Duplicate* and *Save As*) to either audit the risk revisions and progress during risk engagements or to insert new events during the risk register updates. To illustrate this approach, Figure 7.5 shows two versions of the risk registers on CAPEX. The first contains the preliminary project risk engagements, and the second contains refined estimations after revising in detail the "Project Management" category on the P&A strategy. A similar approach is followed for project schedule in Figure 7.6 to assess the risk category "Operations (Oper)."

Risk Dashboards

Even though risk registers help to organise and centralise risks and opportunities, notably for a large list of events, they can visually mislead the analyses and actions of decision makers interested in well P&A and other decommissioning projects if those events are not presented correctly, especially when they are handled and managed qualitatively in spreadsheets.

With the defined *Risk Groups* and their taxonomies, decision-makers can view risk registers in hierarchies or clusters both qualitatively and quantitatively. This approach is relevant for observing how certain decommissioning risks permeate the project management strategies as well as how specific risk elements touch different taxonomies (e.g., activities, process, managers, and so forth).

Figure 7.7 provides the common risk events in the project management category impacting CAPEX. Uncertainties around logistics, pre-works, leadership, platform conditions, and repair orders can cause P&A budgets to overrun by changes in variable and fixed costs, vendors quotes, and unclear project scopes (e.g., personnel onboarding, milestones, overlapping activities by contractors, and so forth). These events deserve attention and proper risk quantification for both project cost and schedule. Therefore, as shown in Figure 7.8, we can highlight how to address the "scaffold removal" that is critical for cost analysis associated with the category "Construction" in well P&A.

Figure 7.9 and Figure 7.10 show some traditional risk events that require immediate attention during well P&A projects because of their impact on a project's schedule. For instance, in the category "Operations," handover (assets not handed over to the decommissioning team), level of operational knowledge for work scopes, and the platform crane's lifting capability are initial aspects to analyse regarding schedule risk. Besides, in terms of the "Wells" risk category, wells surveys and P&A strategies are identified as important delay factors for this type of decommissioning project.

It is important to realise that the qualitative dashboards for Risk Matrices (Heat Maps), Risk Taxonomies (top-down or bottom-up), and Risk Diagrams (Bowtie, Cause and Effect, Hazard Diagrams, among others) only provide a preliminary approach to guide risk discussions around uncertainty sources, potential risk factors, decision-making concerns, or a potential list of risk events.

Conversely, this qualitative approach adds value or supports the decision-making process not only for well P&A projects, but also for other decommissioning projects when they are integrated in terms of quantitative risk assessments on costs, budget, schedule, and other aspects of performance measurements. However, from an IRM perspective, as has been noted, both RM-Level1 and RM-Level2 enhance risk discussions, pre-engagements, project meetings, lessons learned, and other aspects that maintain the well P&A narrative as well as the risk quantification to estimate the unexpected or potential cost or schedule overruns.

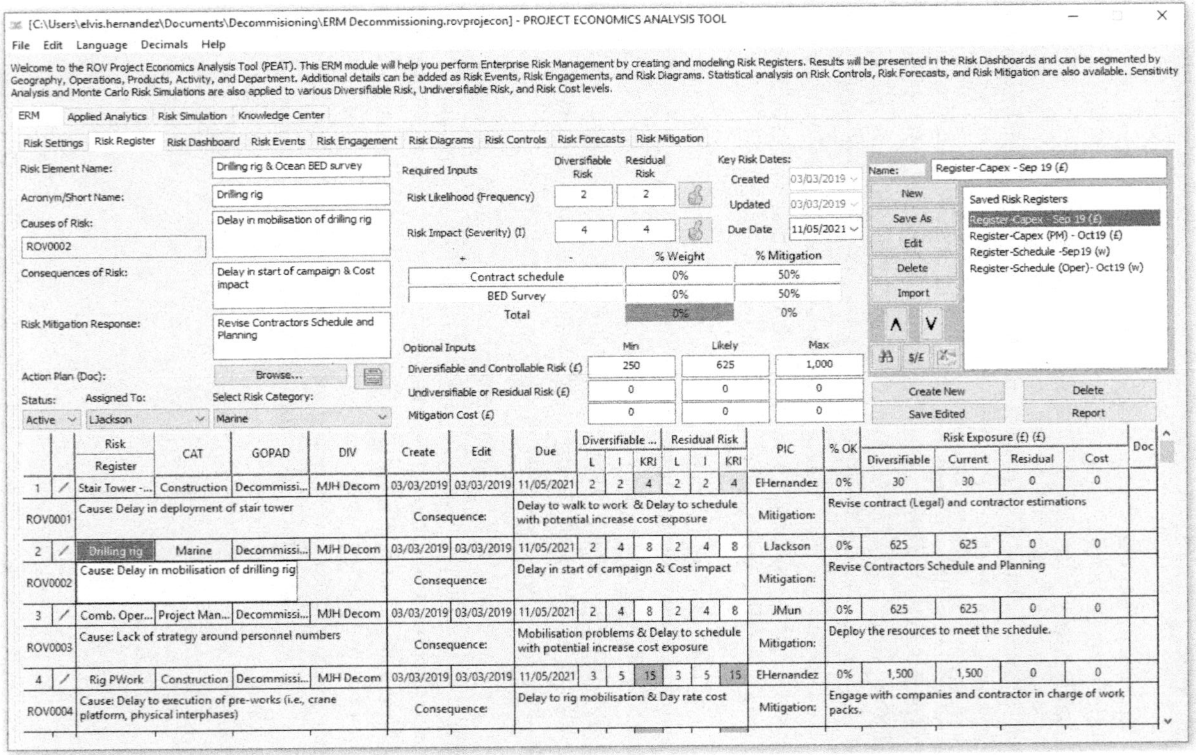

Figure 7.5: Risk Registers for Decommissioning Projects (Well P&A – CAPEX)

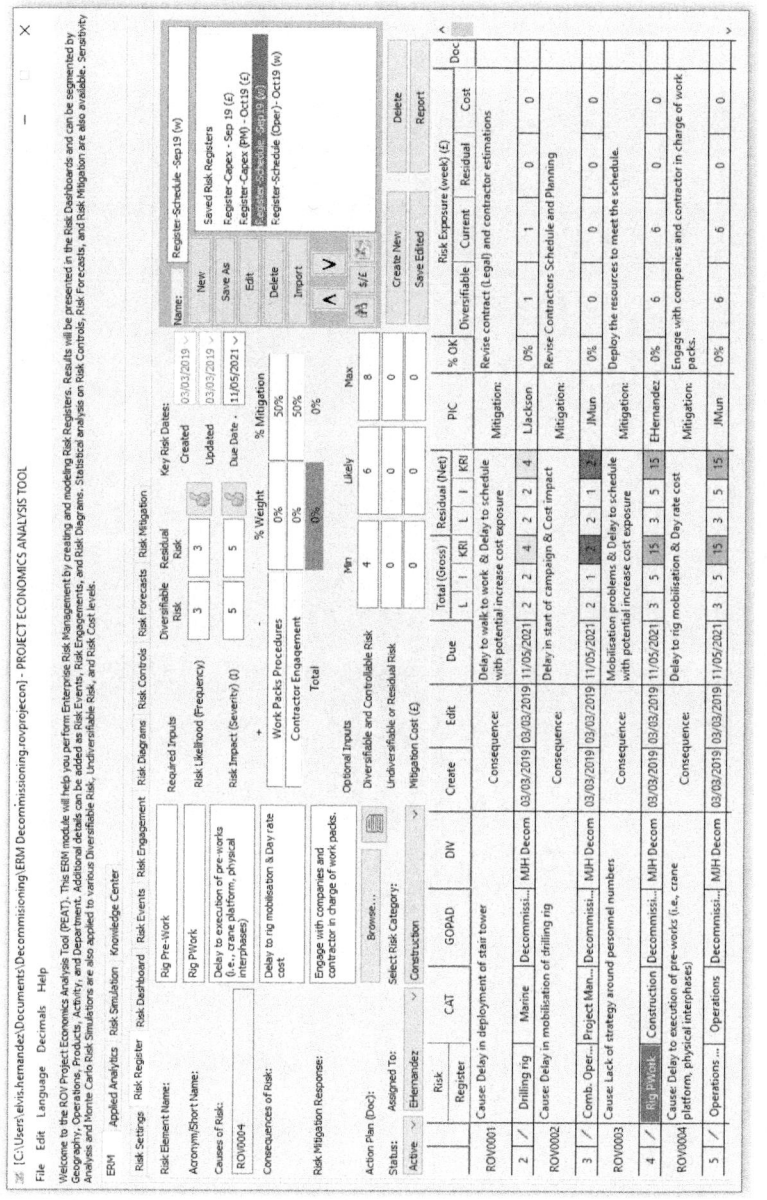

Figure 7.6: Risk Registers for Decommissioning Projects (Well P&A – Schedule)

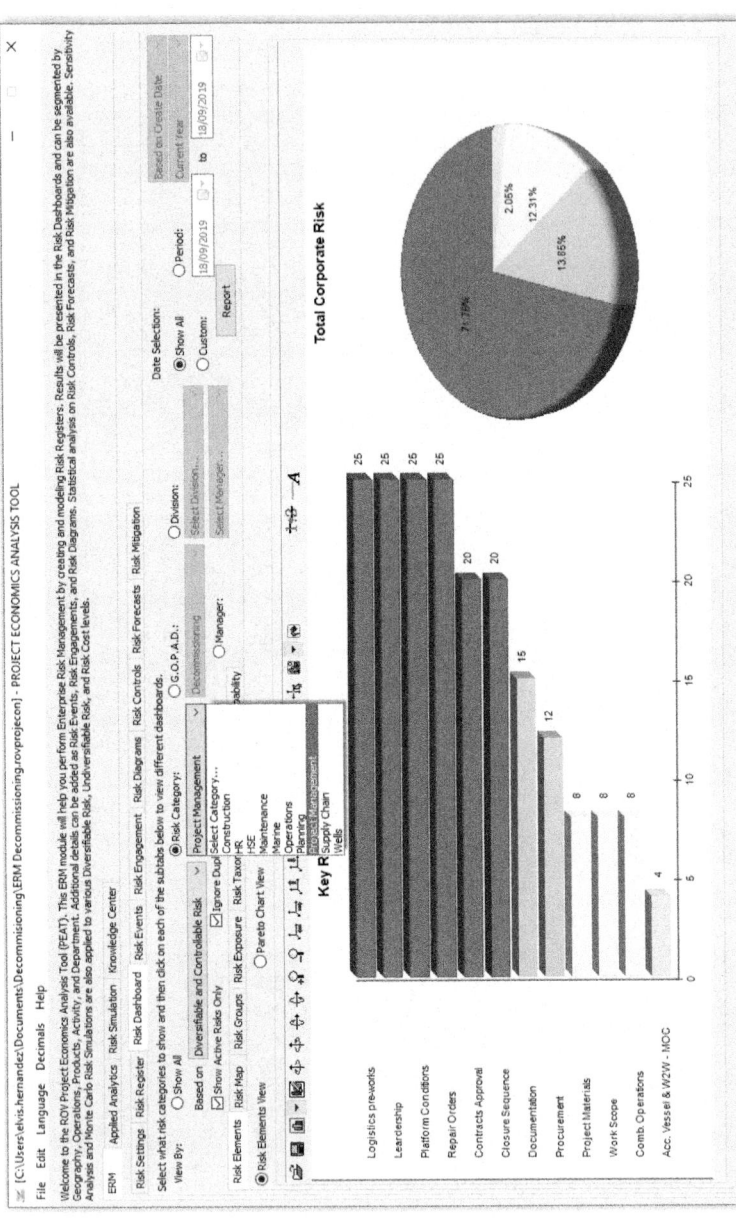

Figure 7.7: Risk Dashboard – Project Management Category (Well P&A – CAPEX)

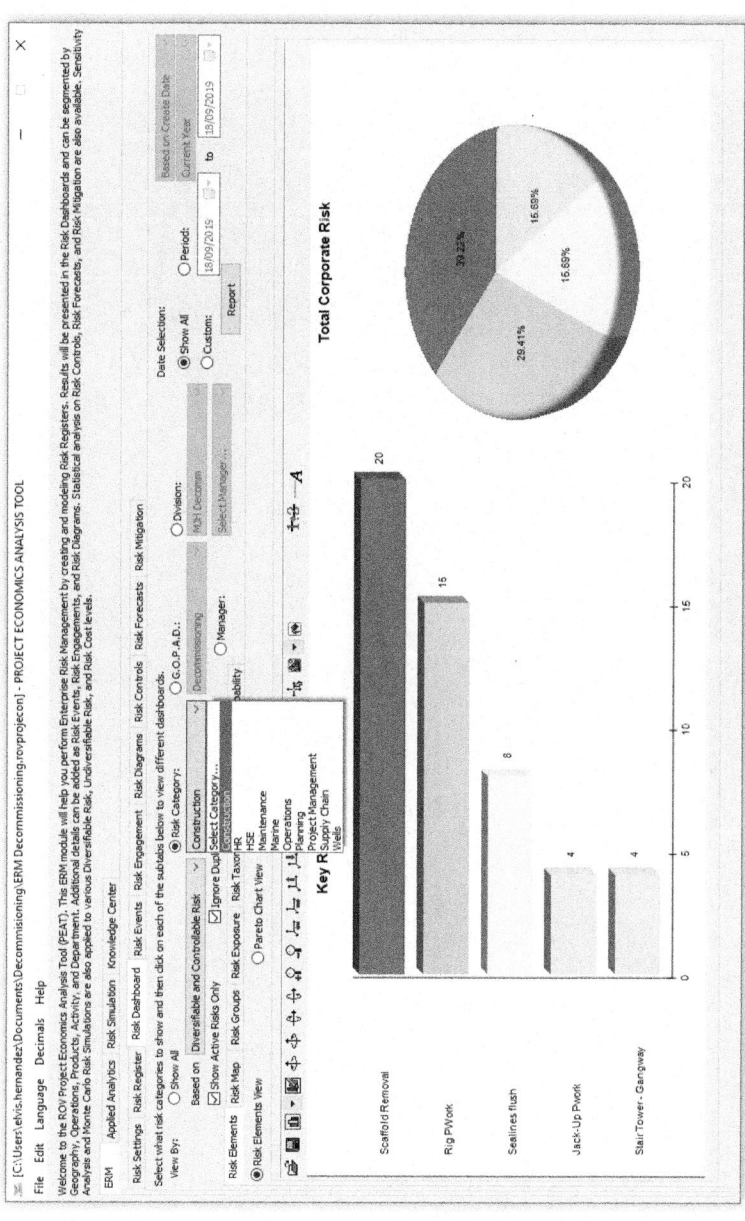

Figure 7.8: Risk Dashboard – Construction Category (Well P&A – CAPEX)

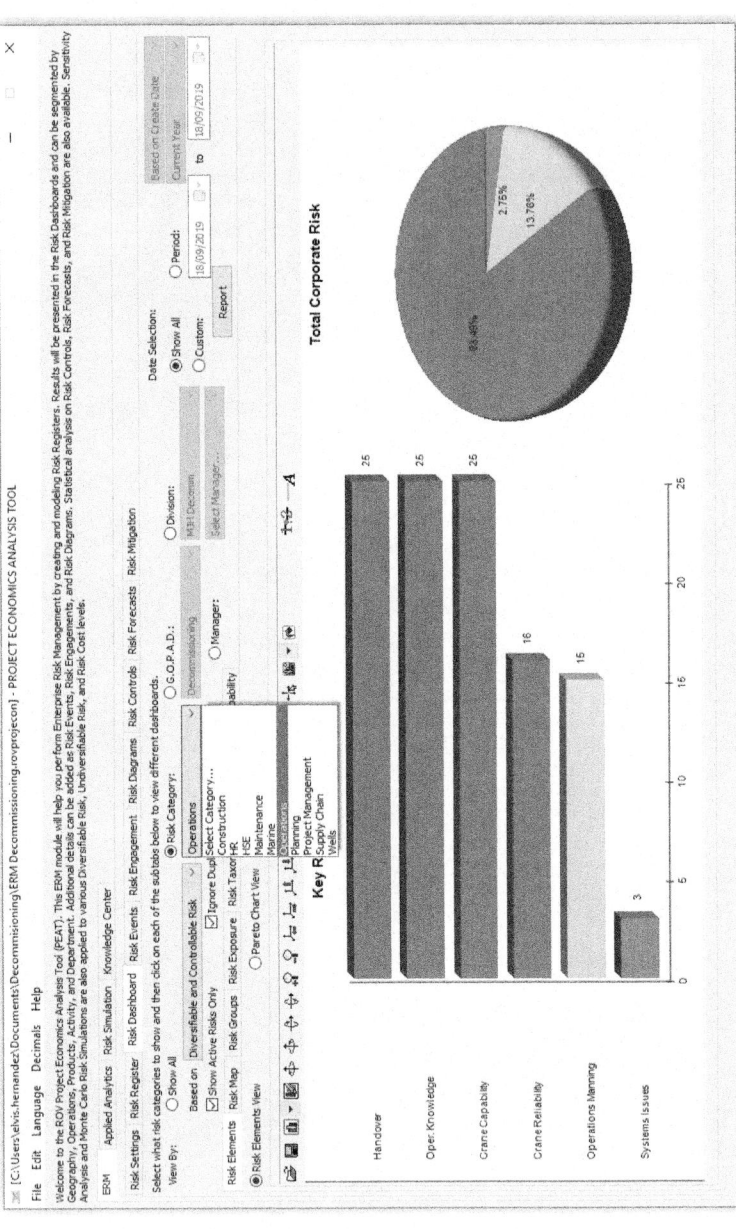

Figure 7.9: Risk Dashboard – Operations Category (Well P&A – Schedule)

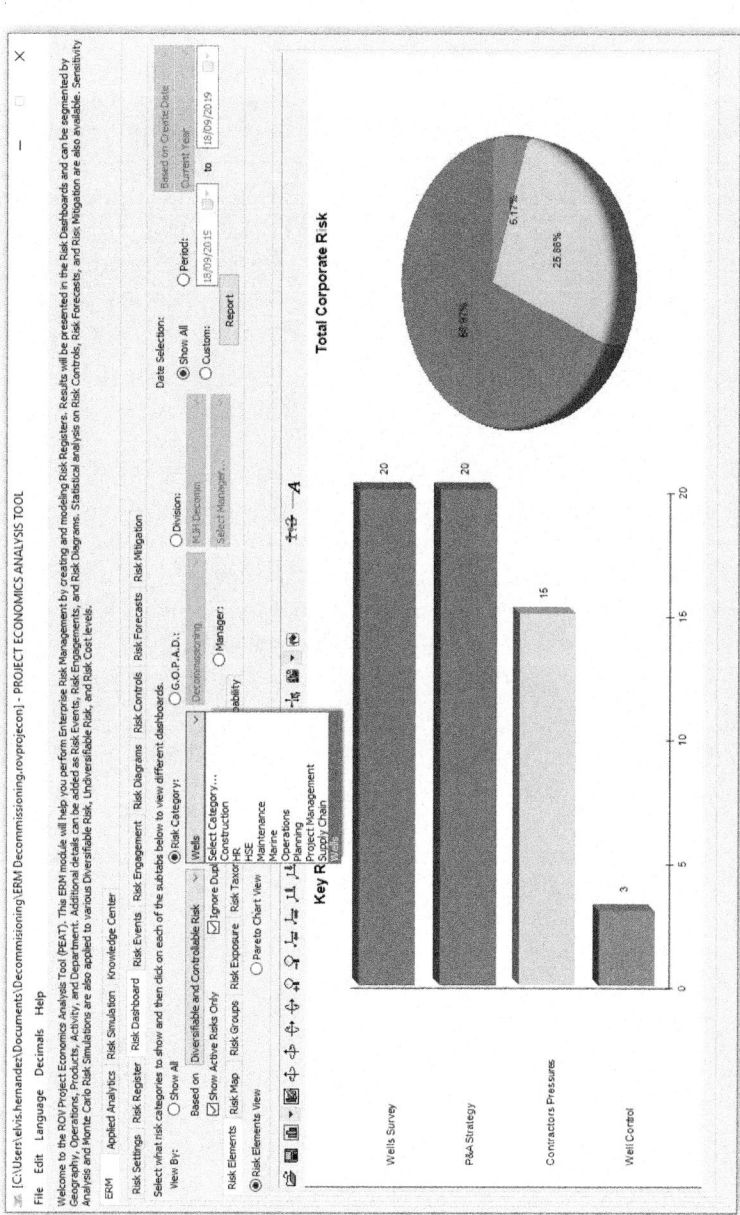

Figure 7.10: Risk Dashboard – Wells Category (Well P&A – Schedule)

HANDS-ON PEAT-DECOMM FOR ENTERPRISE RISK MANAGEMENT

As shown in the previous sections, the use of ERM and risk registers historically have been considered as a qualitative technique. However, in this chapter, Integrated Risk Management (IRM) analytical methods are applied to enhance and reduce uncertainties around decommissioning projects, especially, in well P&A projects. Risk impacts or exposures in terms of CAPEX, operational expenditures (OPEX), fixed and variables costs, schedule, savings, and budgeting impacts are relevant for this quantitative section.

The proposed IRM approach (RM-Level2) to analyse decommissioning risk intersects traditional ERM frameworks and numerical estimations based on data, experience (Delphi-methods) and probabilistic assumptions on risk exposure (diversifiable and uncontrollable), and mitigation costs, among other aspects monitored during the lifespan of the project. These variables are applicable to each *Risk Element* of a risk register, segmented or clustered throughout risk categories, for instance. By doing the above, decision makers, project managers, analysts, and engineers can apply quantitative IRM in well P&A projects.

The IRM framework starts with a quick risk identification of the most influential factors through tornado analysis and consequently implementing some scenario *what-if* analysis. Therefore, a project team can utilise mathematical functions and probability distributions, among other quantitative features, to analyse the risk events and uncertainty sources to quantify and manage P&A risks on cost and schedule, for instance.

Applied Analytics: Tornado Analysis

Tornado analysis is a static approach to identify the critical factors in well P&A and other decommissioning projects. In other words, tornado analysis allows determining which risk elements contribute to a project risk segment or taxonomy (category, manager, activity, product, division, etc.).

In complex decommissioning projects with a large number of risk events in the risk register, more than 10, as a rule of thumb, it is recommended implementing tornado analysis by categories to enhance risk conversations and engagements around the most critical risk factors.

Figure 7.11 exhibits a quick tornado analysis for the "marine" category; 10% variations around the base case are considered. For the P&A case study, platform modifications, collisions, and gangway are critical factors for this risk category, impacting walk to work (W2W), vessel accommodation, and facilities assembly showing cost ranges between £1.35 and £1.65 million. In addition to this, these factors also affect schedule in the same tornado charts (see Figure 7.12). Hence, risk discussions help to verify whether these risk events have significant influence on the wells' marine P&A delays and variable costs.

In the same way, Figure 7.13 presents the usage of static tornado analysis in well P&A to determine schedule risk exposure on HR. We see that "unclear people demobilisation" is the most influential factor in this risk category, which also affects company retention and future resource planning because of redundancy in payment and social burden.

Applied Analytics: Scenario Analysis

Scenario analysis, also called *what-if* analysis, helps decision-makers to explore how changes in the Risk Events–based valuations impact the risk exposure of a decommissioning risk category or segment.

PEAT-DECOMM (ERM module) allows creating heat maps for scenario analysis based on variations around two risk factors. Figure 7.14 shows the scenario settings for two of the most relevant factors in the "marine" risk category. Inserting changes around the CAPEX estimations on "Struct. Facilities & W2W – Gangway" and "Struct. Facilities & W2W – Collision," Figure 7.15 presents the scenario results in the form of heat maps for the cost estimations of the "marine" category.

According to the marine team in charge of the P&A, the dark area results from exploring different combinations of estimated cost values in the gangway and collision where the allocated budget overruns. This mostly requires relevant risk control and mitigations like the implementation of extensive structural surveys and design checks on the walk to work (W2W) access proposals.

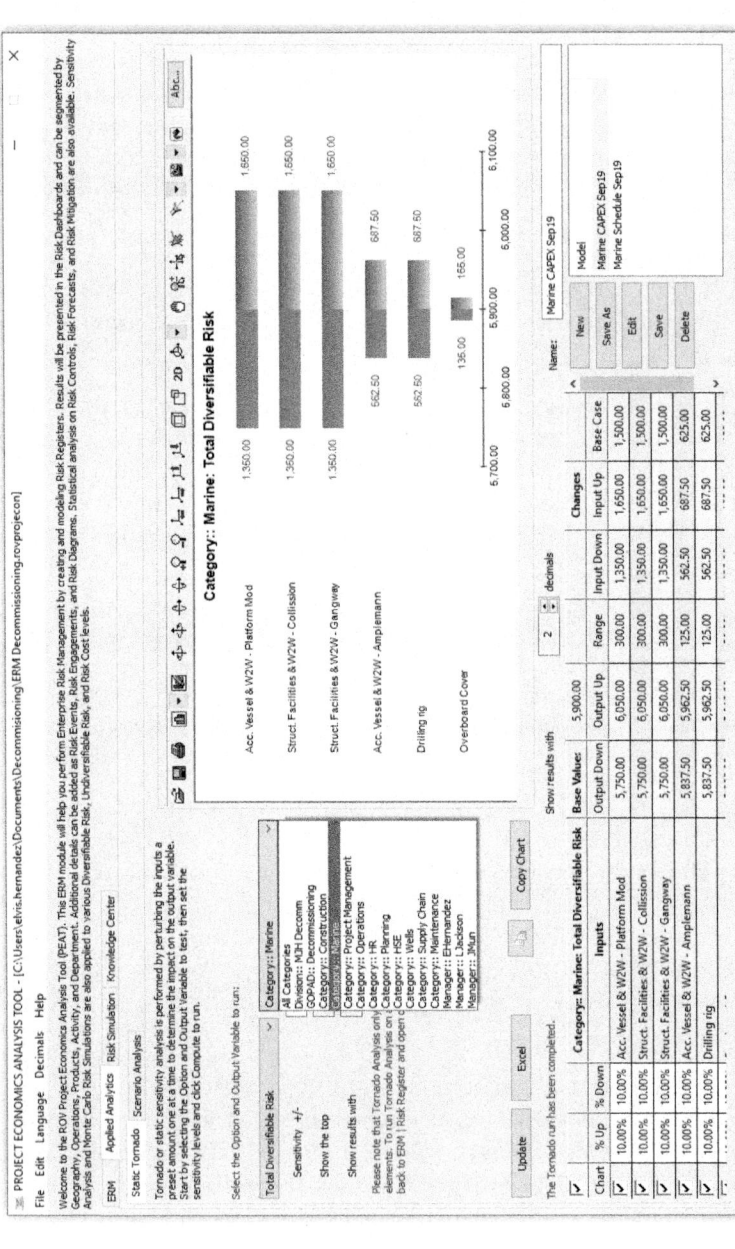

Figure 7.11: Tornado Analysis – Marine Category (Well P&A – CAPEX)

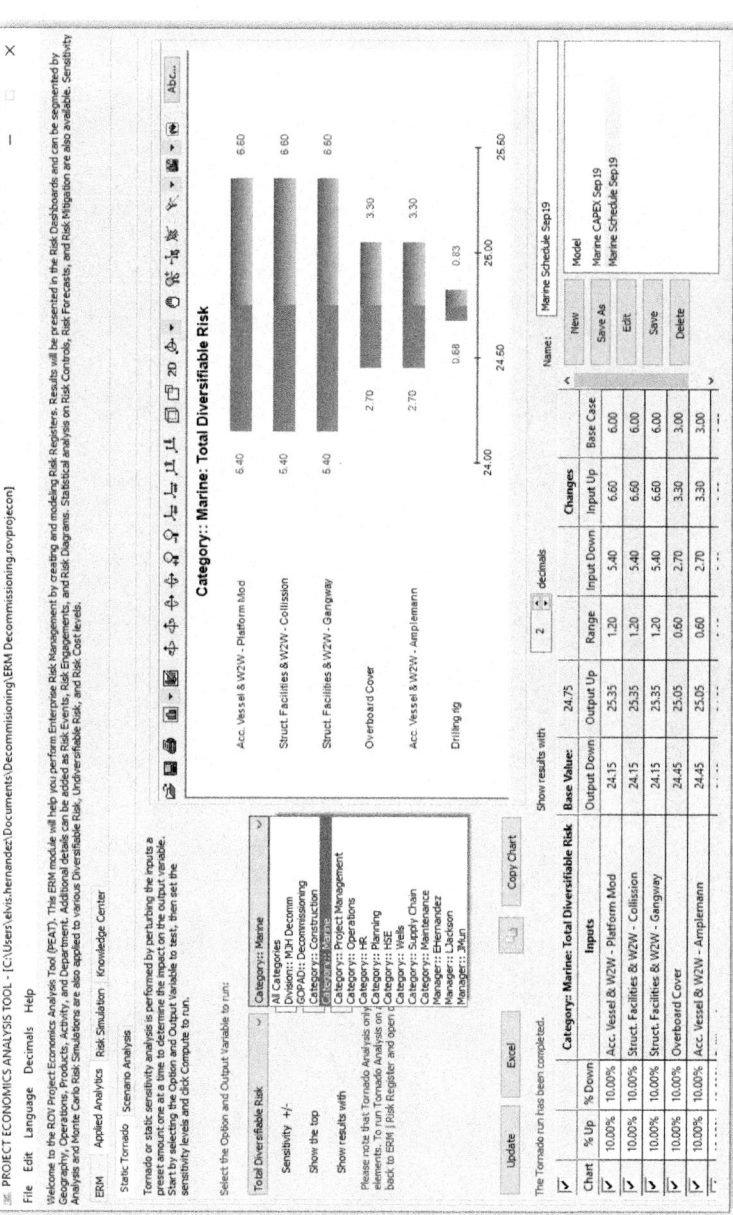

Figure 7.12: Tornado Analysis – Marine Category (Well P&A – Schedule)

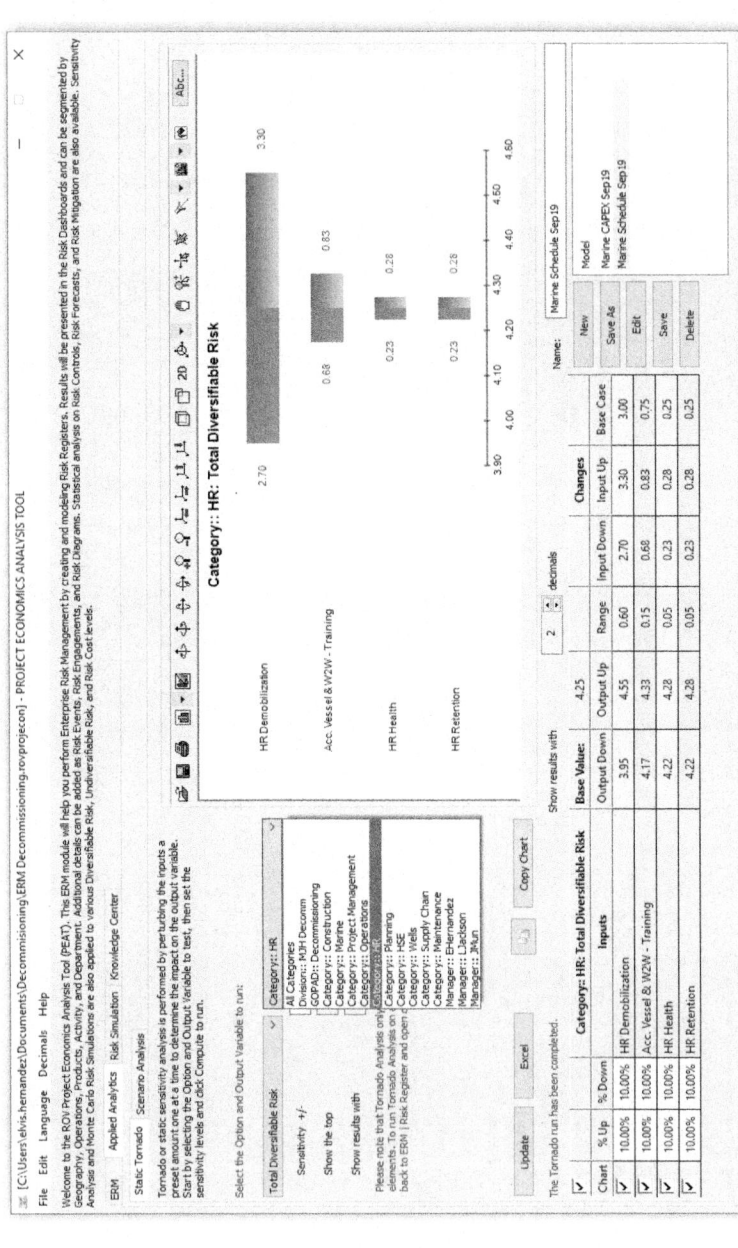

Figure 7.13: Tornado Analysis – HR Category (Well P&A – Schedule)

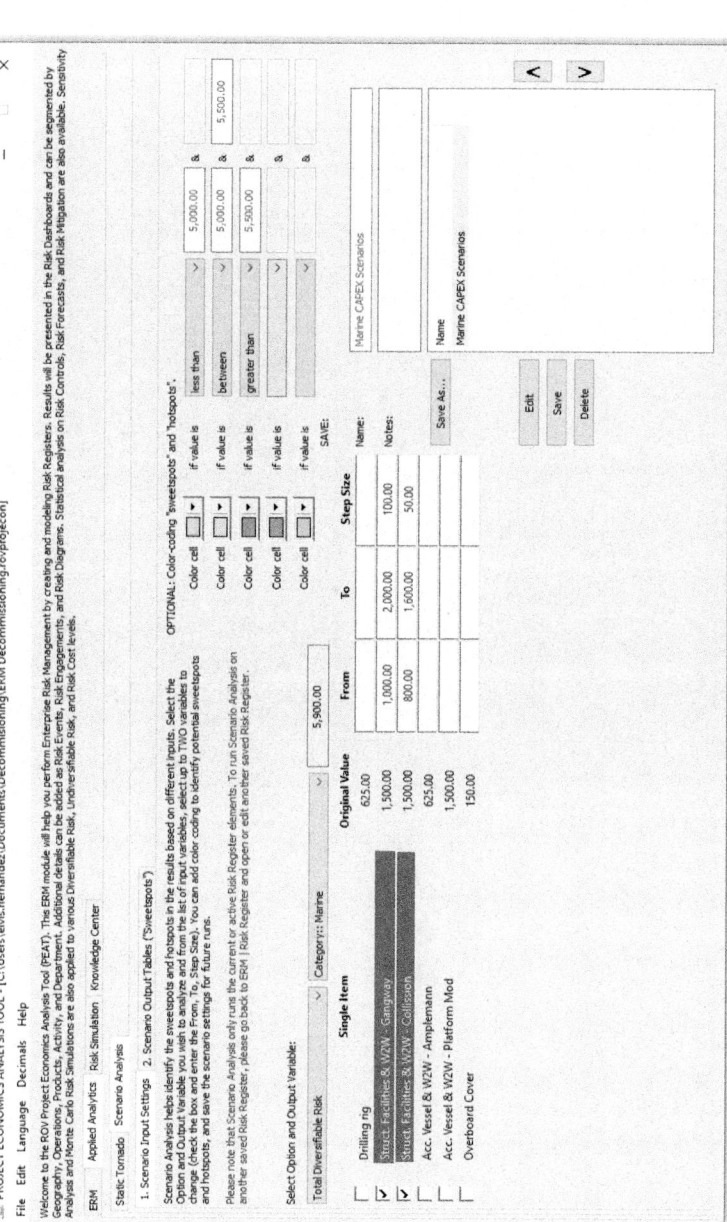

Figure 7.14: Setting Scenario Analysis – Marine Category (Well P&A – CAPEX)

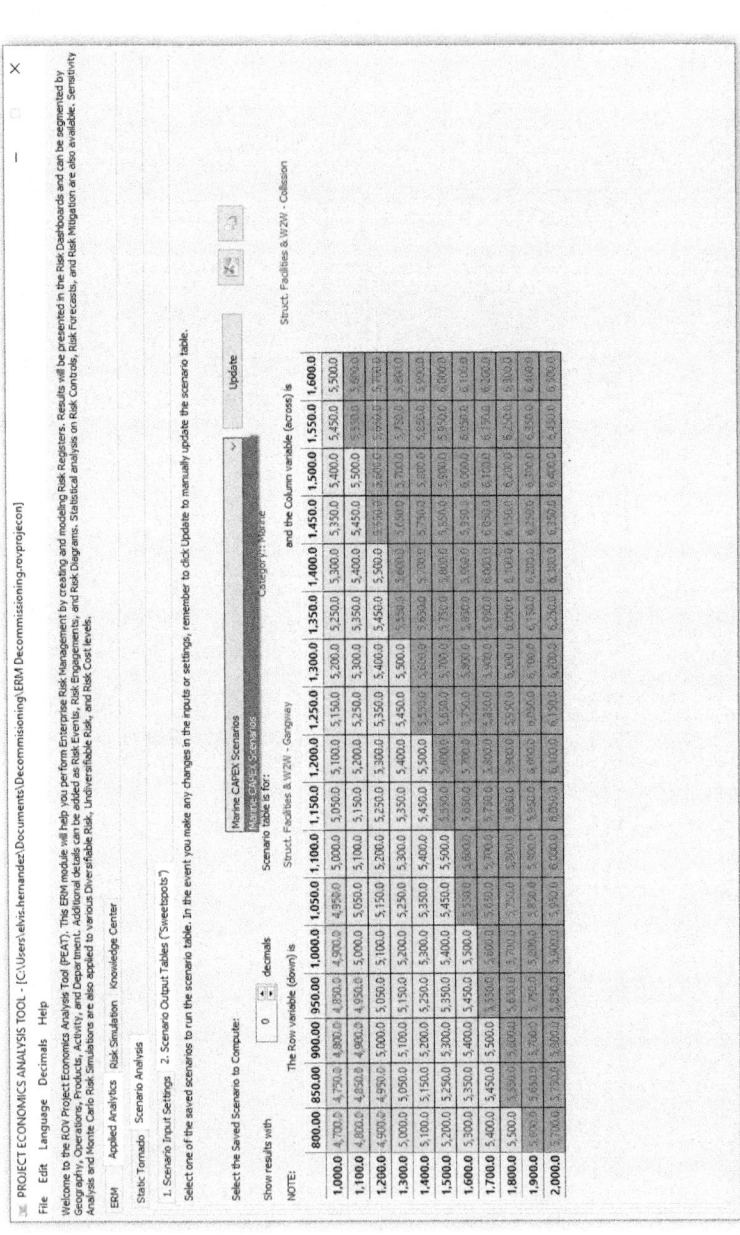

Figure 7.15: Results of Scenario Analysis – Marine Category (Well P&A – CAPEX)

Risk Simulation (Risk Profile)

By implementing Monte Carlo risk simulations and propagating the uncertainties from individual elements of the risk categories to KPI profiles and performance measures, PEAT ERM's users can introduce input assumptions using theoretically or empirically supported probability distribution functions, ranges, and percentiles, among other inputs (e.g., minimum, most likely, maximum, standard deviations, central tendency measures, and so forth). Figure 7.16 shows how assumptions can be set for running Monte Carlo risk simulations.

In fact, PEAT-DECOMM can also implement this quantitative approach by automatically taking the assumptions and estimations considered in total diversifiable and noncontrollable risk and mitigations costs, for instance. Total current and residual risks can be computed based on the controls' weights and percentage of mitigation.

As for other decommissioning projects, decision makers in well P&A projects need to continuously determine, report, and monitor cost and schedule estimations based on their assumptions on project plans, milestones, deliverables, schedule, and risk events. Normally, confidence intervals (e.g., 99%, 95%, 90%), central tendency measurements (mean, median, standard deviations, skew, kurtosis, etc.), ranges (max-min, interquartile, etc.) are elements helping to guide them during the project analysis.

For example, Figure 7.17 shows that there is 90% confidence that the total CAPEX varies between £42M and £45M when only considering a list of *Risk Events* (unallocated risks). Of course, this information needs to be contrasted against project activities, fixed costs, variables costs, vendors, decommissioning norms, procurement estimations, and so forth. Similarly, Figure 7.18 illustrates the confidence interval for a preliminary revision of the P&A schedule. Note that there is 90% confidence that the project schedule remains between 177 weeks and 191 weeks. This information also needs to be reviewed and integrated into the project planning, activity-based schedule, reimbursable and fixed time agreements, contracts management, and other aspects of managing these unallocated risk events.

As good practice, it is always recommended to analyse the risk profiles for cost and time by categories, activities, managerial exposure, or any other bottom-up view, except, of course, not at the risk event-level because of the large number of items P&A involves. With this in mind, Figure 7.19 presents the core risk profile of the "Project Management" category (activity-based or category-based analysis). Decision makers can see that project management costs can vary between £9M and £11M (90% confidence). Similarly, Figure 7.20 reports the confidence interval in terms of schedule for the risk category "Operations."

In the same way that understanding the risk profile is important for assessing the confidence intervals, it also necessary to know the most influential factors affecting the variability of these forecasts. Therefore, dynamic sensitivity analysis provides a guide for decision makers through correlation analysis and relative importance (percentage of variation explained).

Risk Simulation (Sensitivity Analysis)

Sensitivity analysis is also known as dynamic perturbations created after running simulations, considering variations in all the risk events affecting a risk category, profile, or performance measurement. These fluctuations can be analysed using two complementary approaches: nonlinear rank correlations and percentage of variation explained. The first approach captures nonlinear effects between the risk events and outcomes, and the second computes how much of the variation of a risk profile or an outcome can be explained by the simulated assumptions or risk events.

For example, Figure 7.21 and Figure 7.22 show sensitivity charts for project management costs and schedule. Note that more than 90% of the variability of the outcome (see the risk profile in Figure 7.19) is influenced by rig pre-works, sea-lines flush, and scaffold removal, three events that increase the variability of the project's costs (positive nonlinear rank correlation).

These risk events or drivers are not only aligned with the authors' experience and current literature in well P&A, but they also provide strong objective support to decision makers on where to invest time and resources to best manage and control risks. Therefore, dynamic sensitivity analysis can be applied to other risk categories, project representatives, company divisions, etc., is good practice for implementing an IRM approach to decommissioning projects.

A final aspect that deserves attention is how to control and monitor the ERM implementation for P&A projects. Namely, during project engagements, risk discussion, and follow-up meetings, PEAT-DECOMM allows duplicating the current risk register for other risk quantifications, including control and monitoring. For example, Figure 7.23 exhibits the overlay results comparing the project progress in terms of risk management. Specifically, some risk events associated with project management costs are analysed using overlay charts. Note that both variability (width of the distribution profile) and total costs have decreased after getting a better strategy and cost estimations on project management.

Likewise, Figure 7.24 illustrates the overlay results to compare the progress in terms of the risk events associated with schedule. It can be observed that variability has not changed significantly (width between the tails) but the schedule has decreased after getting a better strategy based on operational knowledge in P&A using internal decommissioning training programs and having better estimation of the crane's reliability and capability.

In addition to these overlay results, the PEAT-DECOMM solution also provides other comparative reports for decommissioning projects such as **Analysis of Alternatives** and **Incident Reports** (injuries, accidents, disruptions, equipment failure, etc.). Finally, for P&A applications and accelerated IRM implementations on cost and schedule, Table 7.1 provides a selective list of risk events in well P&A projects that can be used in other decommissioning projects.

Note that other risk factors associated with HSE are also essential in the decommissioning strategies, such as staff injuries from moving materials and machinery, fire and explosions, loud noise, water on staircases, hazards associated with asbestos, fall of large objects, means of escape, evacuation and rescue (EER) progressively unavailable, exposure to toxic substances from transportation to disposal site, and so forth. Not considering and analysing these aspects will cost a company a lot of money if it goes wrong.

Table 7.1: Common Risk Events in Well P&A Projects

Risk ID	Risk Register Item
RR01	Stair Tower or Gangway
RR02	Drilling rig & Ocean BED survey
RR03	Combined Operations
RR04	Rig Pre-Work
RR05	Operations Manning
RR06	HR Demobilisation & Contract Life
RR07	Repair Orders
RR08	Jack-up pre-works
RR09	Logistics pre-works
RR10	Personnel on Board (POB)
RR11	Vessel Safety Case
RR12	Drilling Rig Contract Approval
RR13	Installations Safety Case
RR14	Well Abandonment Execute Strategy
RR15	Wells Survey
RR16	Environmental Impacts from Decommissioning
RR17	Structure of facilities & W2W
RR18	Accommodation vessel & Walk to Work (W2W) - Appleman
RR19	Heavy and Large Equipment removal
RR20	Construction and demolition waste
RR21	Accommodation vessel & Walk to Work (W2W)- Platform Modification
RR22	Accommodation vessel & Walk to Work (W2W) - HSE
RR23	Accommodation vessel & Walk to Work (W2W) - Training
RR24	Personnel Retention
RR25	Personnel Health
RR26	Crane Reliability
RR27	Platform crane's lifting capability
RR28	Operational Knowledge for work scopes
RR29	Handover from Operational Team
RR30	Availability of key project materials
RR31	Decision Makers and Project Leaders
RR32	Lack of integrated plan (People, Information, Cost & Time)
RR33	Communication & Culture
RR34	No schedule for shutting down systems
RR35	Sea-line flush
RR36	Walkway and dropped object hazard risk to decommissioning teams
RR37	Removal points and structural strengthening and scope problems
RR38	Renovation and repair survey to be completed
RR39	Delay of Closure Sequence due to Well P&A delay
RR40	Scaffold removal
RR41	Field stand-by vessel additional crew cover
RR42	Existing platform structure may be unable to support equipment loading
RR43	Interface between vendors and operations
RR44	Fragmentation of documentation
RR45	Contractor and Client roles and responsibilities
RR46	P&A permits, license approvals, notifications and consents register
RR47	Hire of dedicated supply vessel for Well P&A Campaign
RR48	Well Contractor affected by time and cost constraints
RR49	Well control issues cannot be managed by the platform

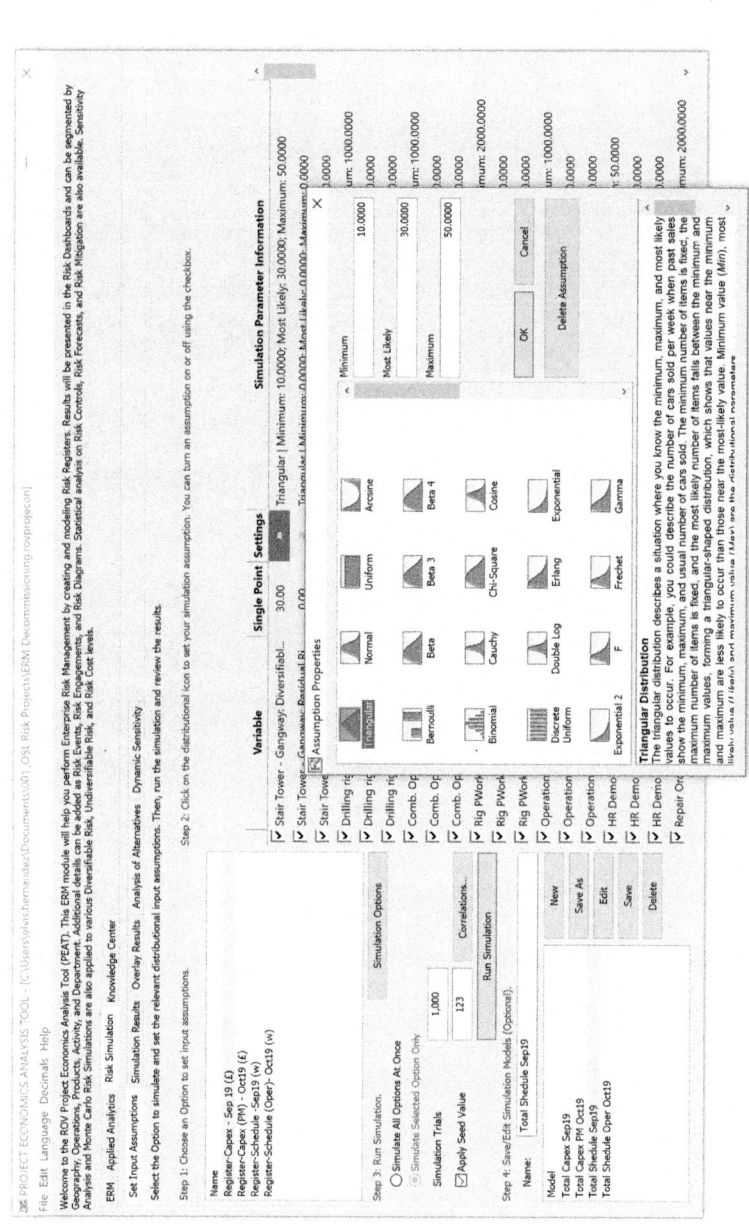

Figure 7.16: Risk Simulation Assumptions

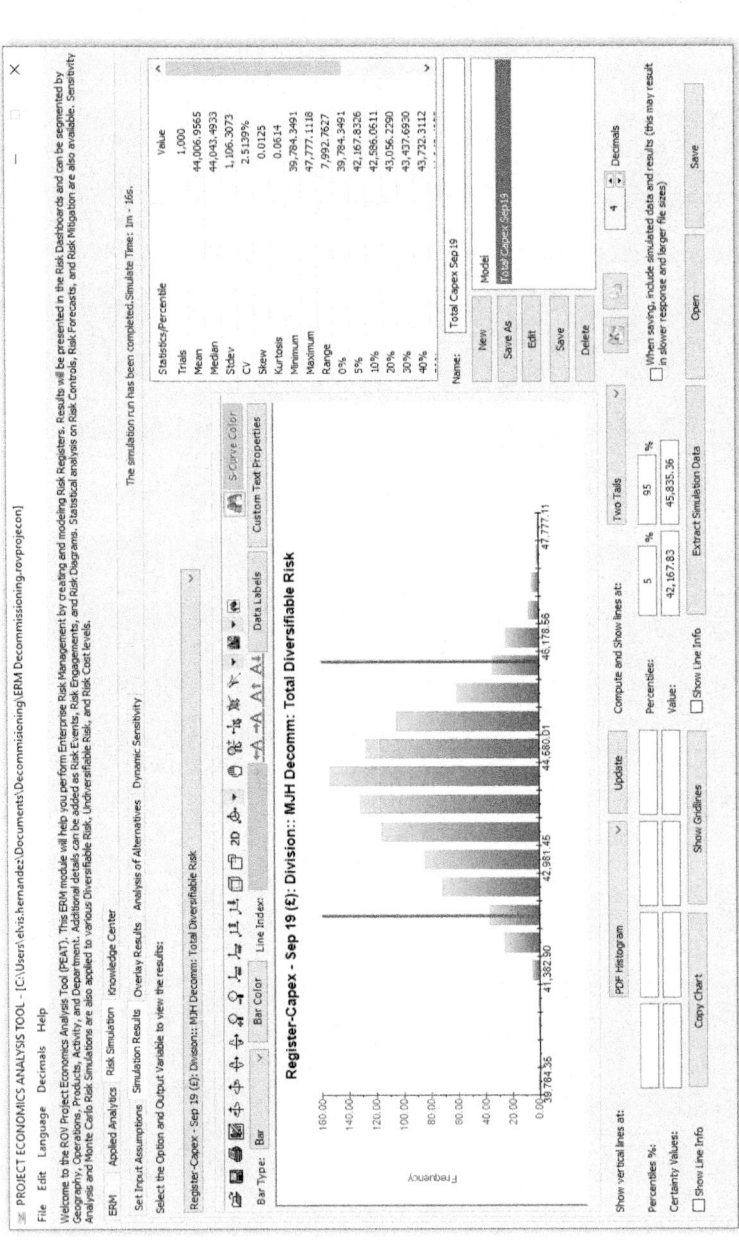

Figure 7.17: Risk Profile – Total Project Risk Exposure (CAPEX)

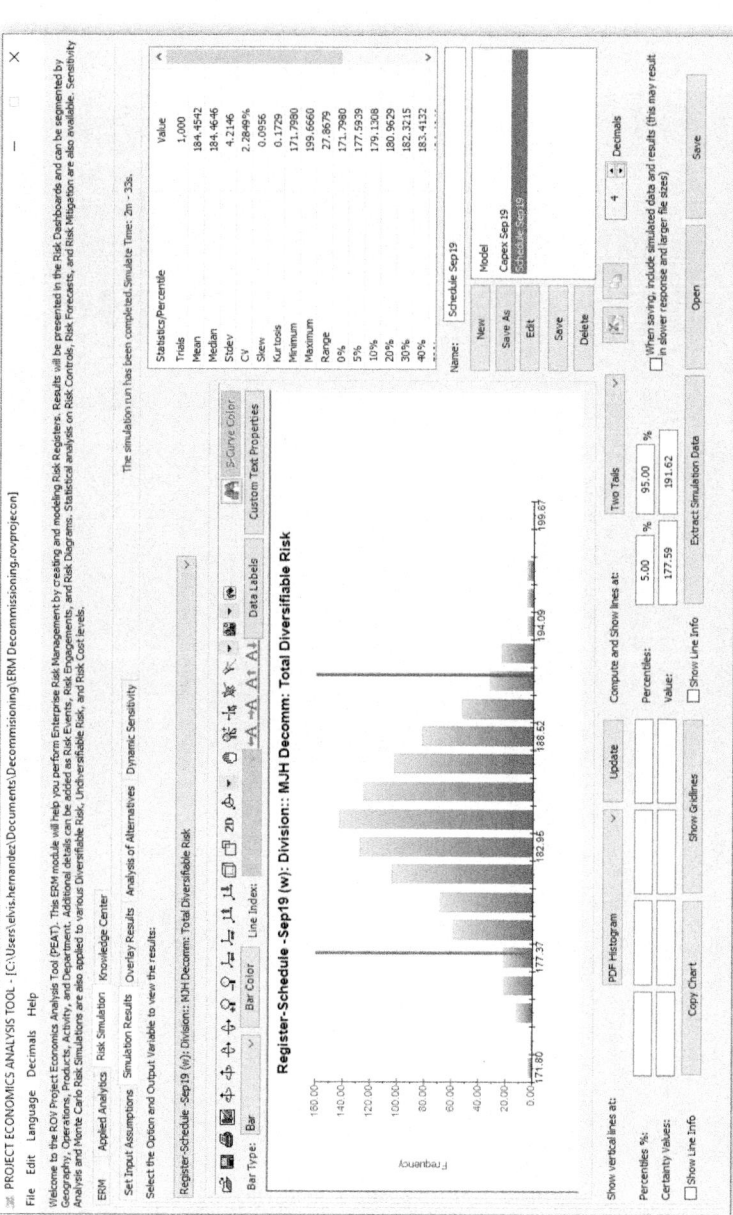

Figure 7.18: Risk Profile – Total Project Risk Exposure (Schedule)

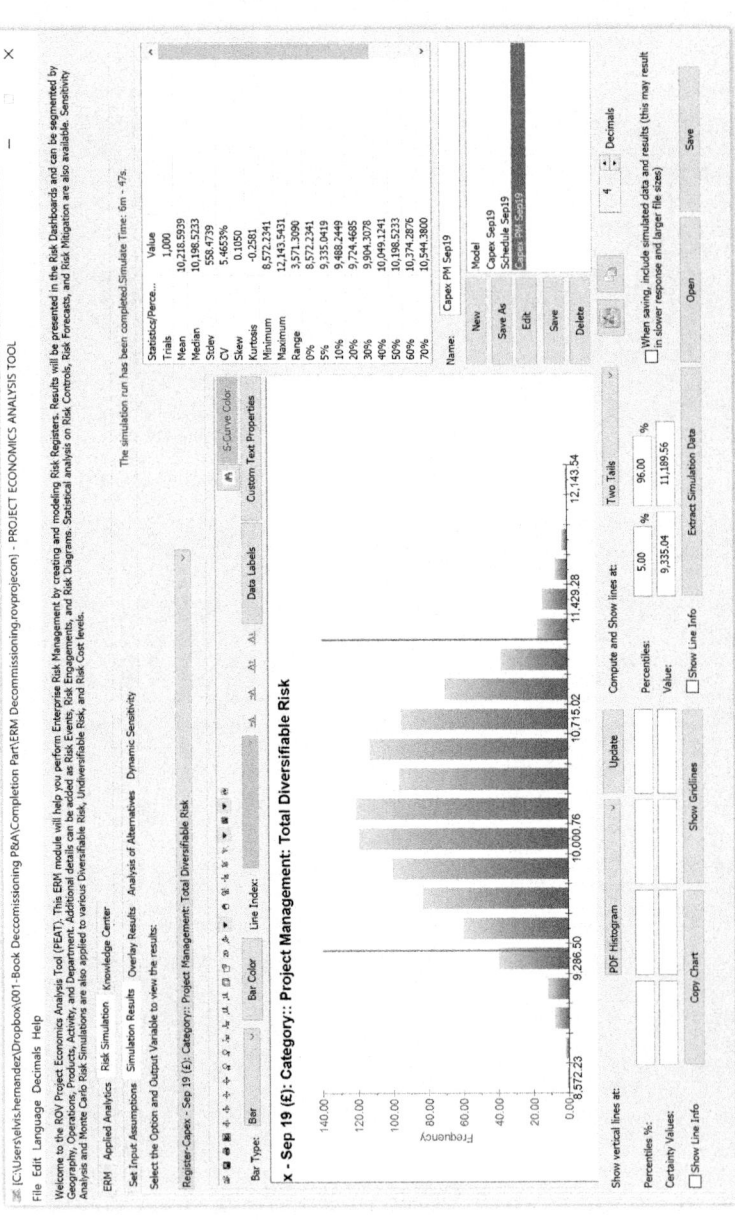

Figure 7.19: Risk Profile – Project Management Risk Exposure (CAPEX)

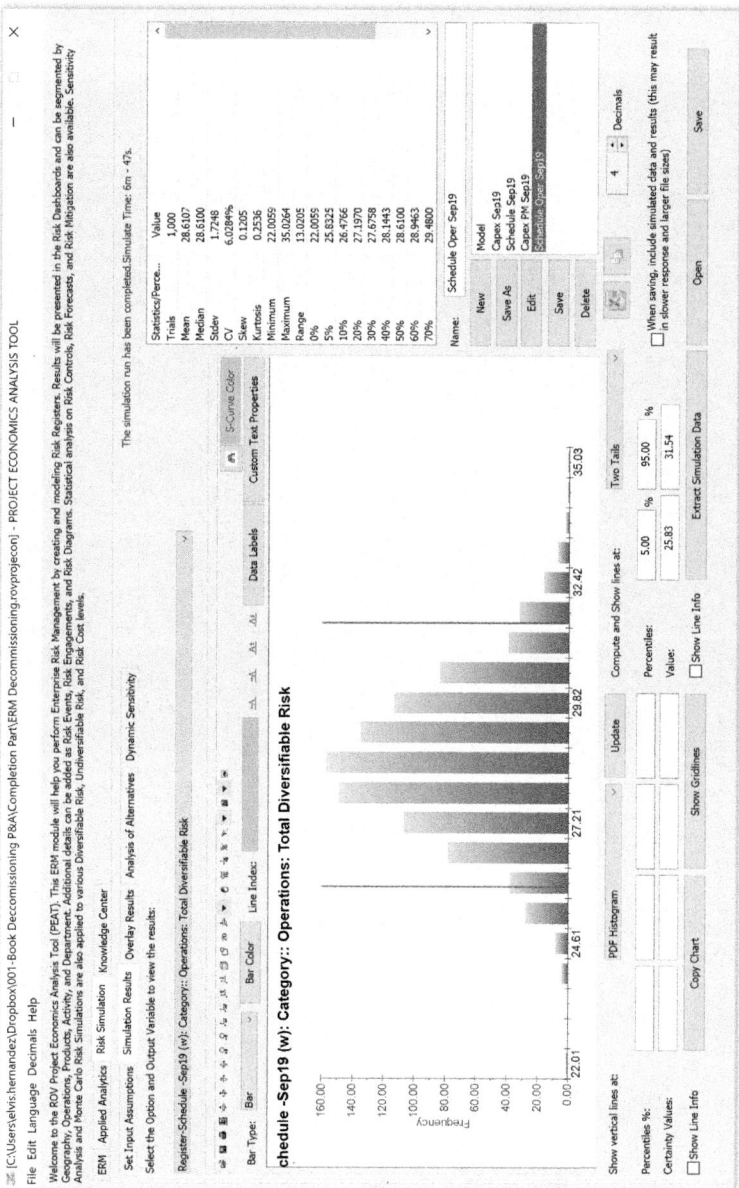

Figure 7.20: Risk Profile – Operations Risk Exposure (Schedule)

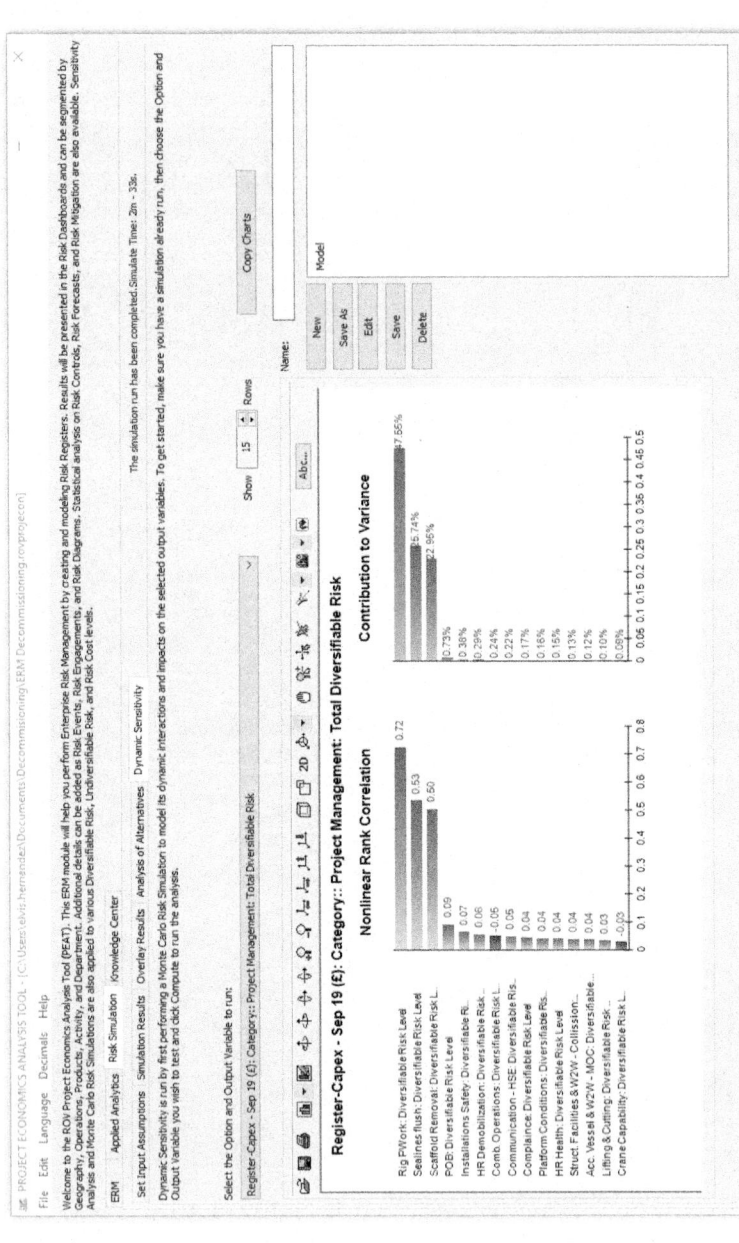

Figure 7.21: Sensitivity Analysis – Project Management Risk Exposure (CAPEX)

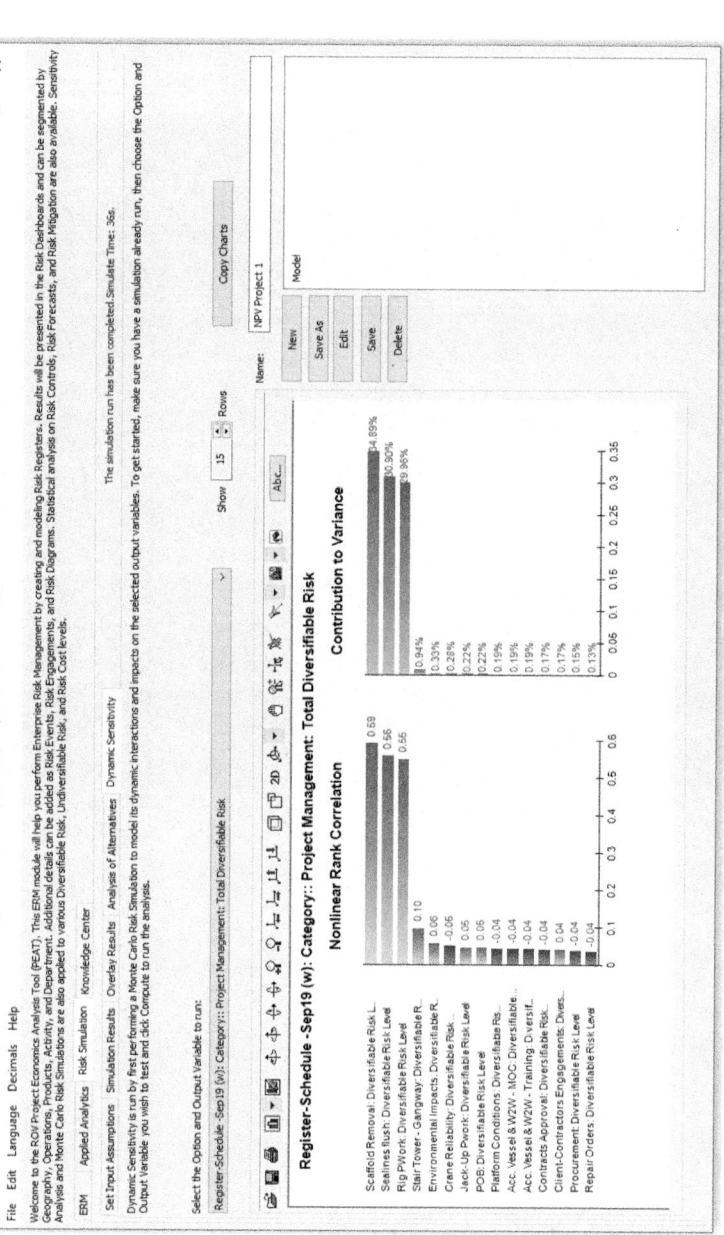

Figure 7.22: Sensitivity Analysis – Project Management Risk Exposure (Schedule)

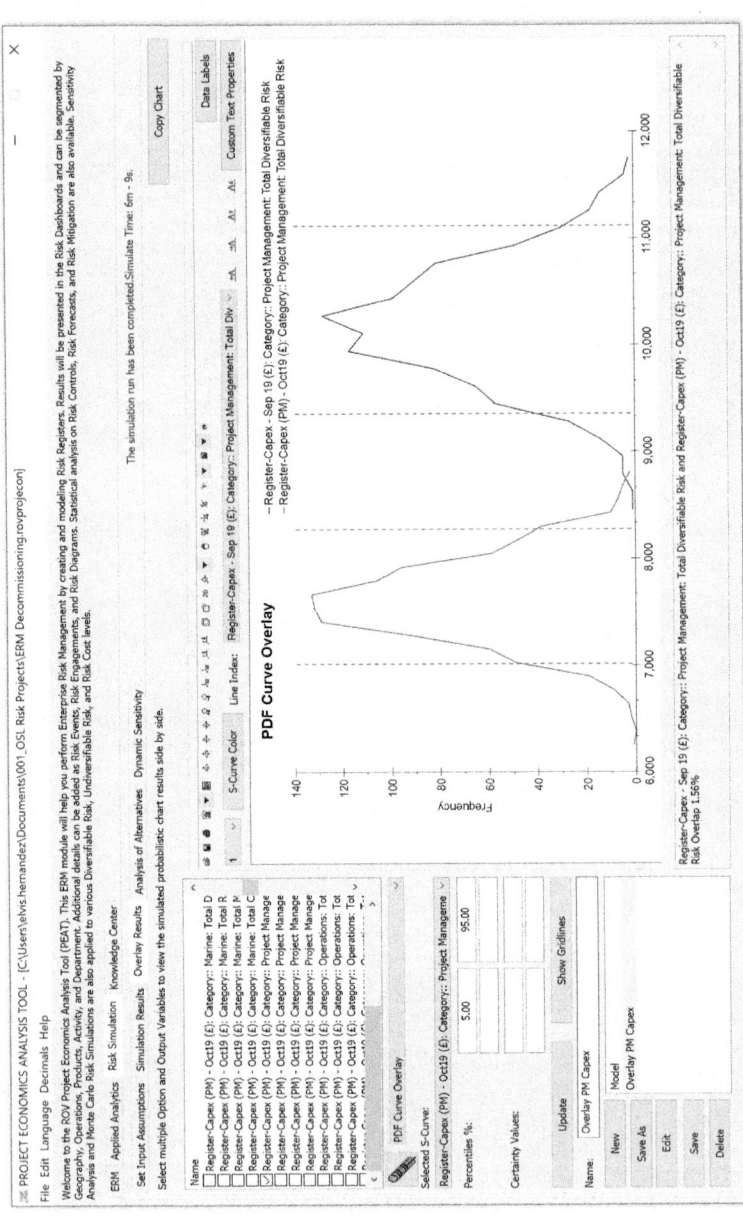

Figure 7.23: Overlay Results – Comparative Analysis on Project Management (CAPEX)

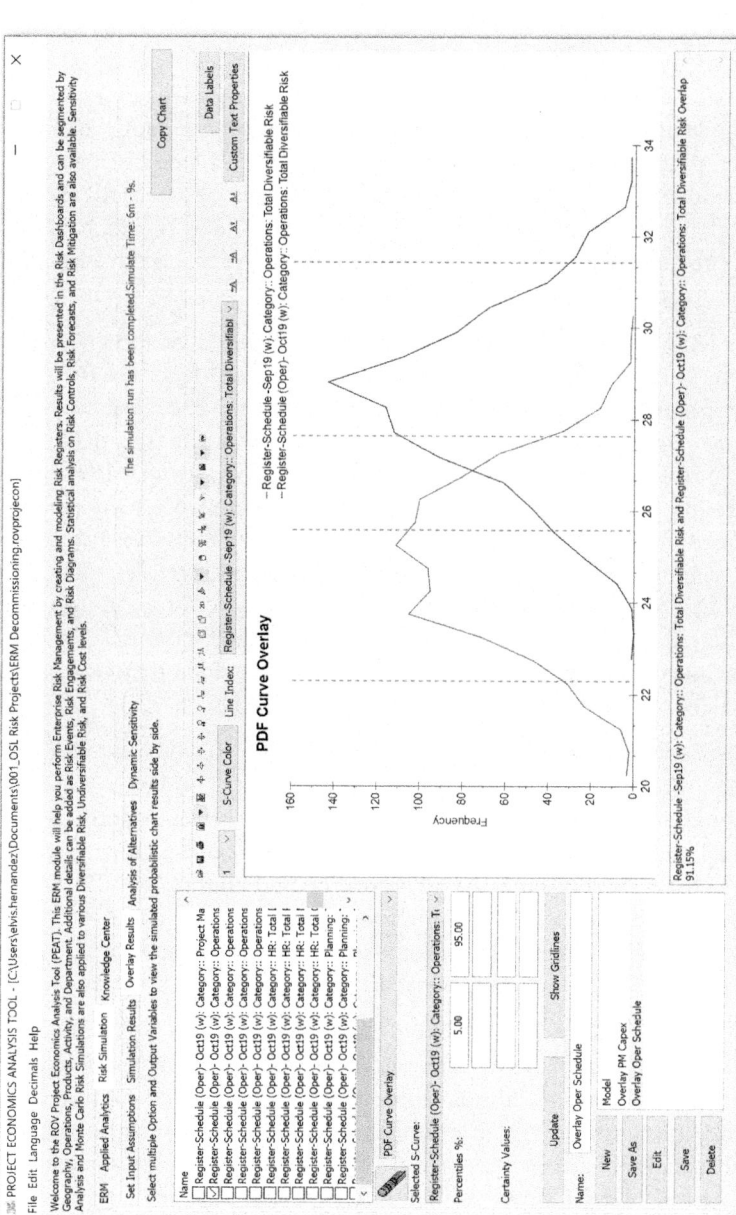

Figure 7.23: Overlay Results – Comparative Analysis on Operations (Schedule)

INTEGRATED RISK MANAGEMENT AND DECISION SUPPORT

The PEAT-DECOMM (ERM module) software solution extends the concept of expected values in risk quantification, enabling risk-mitigating plans for decommissioning and well P&A. Decision makers use statistical evaluations, real options, analysis of alternatives, and static and dynamic sensitivity analysis to manage key risk factors on cost, time, budgeting, and other KPIs, following risk taxonomies and risk categories.

This IRM approach moves the risk register qualitative approach (RM-Level1) out of the realm of the usage of *Heat Maps* and *Risk Matrices* or simple scoring implementations based on *Likelihood* and *Consequence (Impact or Severity)* to a more quantitative approach (RM-Level2). Note that decommissioning risks, especially in well P&A, require managing the uncertainties around the risk events to make them more predictable, but usually not with absolute certainty. Moreover, when such uncertainties become more predictable, using mathematical functions, probability distribution functions, or best estimates that follow statistical properties and reduce cognitive biases, they need to be integrated into the decision-making process to manage decommissioning risks, mainly on time and cost.

Decision makers can view traditional ERM approaches and risk events as a preliminary system of unallocated risks. The faster they are integrated into decisions, the more agile the risk management process is, not only to reduce monitoring and mitigation costs but also to increase the potential savings on time and cost of well P&A projects. The qualitative part is something that can be done in Excel, however it slows the risk engagements and discussions and inhibits the quick identification of relevant risk factors and implementation of tornado and sensitivity analysis.

The comprehensive IRM framework visually displays potential risks in well P&A, and their quantification can be extended to other decommissioning projects, for example, wind turbines, onshore assets, industrial and chemical plants, and other capital-intensive facilities. Either Risk Events or Risk Registers can also be classified in Risk Categories (e.g., Construction, Project Management, Planning, HR, Maintenance, Operations, Wells or Type of Assets, Marine or Onshore, Supply Chain, HSE, and other categories).

When some risks are not fully integrated into costs and schedule analyses, further information about controls, weight or relative importance of the controls, and % of mitigations complement other analyses of residual risk, total degrees of mitigation, risk appetite, total current risk, and gross risk might be required according other risk management paradigms (e.g., ERM COSO, ISO 31000 and Basel III/IV). However, PEAT-DECOMM (ERM module) complies with these specifications regardless of the risk management standards followed or the company risk paradigms considered. Global Settings help customise both risk standards and paradigms to avoid confusion.

REFERENCES

API. (2000a). 580-Risk-Based Inspection - Base Resource Document. American Petroleum Institute.

API. (2000b). 581-Risk-Based Inspection Base Resource Document. American Petroleum Institute.

Avanesov, E. (2009, November). Risk management in ISO 9000 series standards. In *International conference on risk assessment and management* (Vol. 24, p. 25).

Clarin, C. (2013). Application of Layers of Protection Analysis (LOPA) for subsea production systems—A risk-based model for determination of integrity levels in a global perspective. *LUTVDG/TVBB*.

Crawley, F., & Tyler, B. (2015). *HAZOP: Guide to Best Practice*. Elsevier.

ISO. (2018). International Organisation for Standardization Technical Committee. Risk Management-Guidelines (Standard No. ISO 31000: 2018). Washington, DC: International Organisation for Standardization Retrieved from https://www. iso. org/obp/u# iso: std: iso, 31000

Moeller, R. R. (2011). *COSO Enterprise Risk Management: Establishing Effective Governance, Risk, and Compliance Processes* (Vol. 560). John Wiley & Sons.

Mun, J. (2019). *Applied Analytical Enterprise Risk Management* (Applied CQRM Book Series, Volume IV). IIPER Press.

Thomas, P., Bratvold, R. B., & Bickel, J. E. (2014, April 1). The Risk of Using Risk Matrices. Society of Petroleum Engineers. doi:10.2118/166269-PA

Woodhouse, J. (2014). Briefing: Standards in asset management: PAS 55 to ISO 55000. *Infrastructure Asset Management*, *1*(3), 57–59.

APPENDIX: PROJECT VALUATION

All companies have projects with differing sizes, investment requirements, returns, risks, and strategic and tactical value. The Project Economics Analysis Tool (PEAT) software is used to illustrate how various project economics and financial results, including Net Present Value (NPV), Internal Rate of Return (IRR), Modified Internal Rate of Return (MIRR), Profitability Index (PI), Return on Investment (ROI), Payback Period (PP), and Discounted Payback Period (DPP), can be computed.

This appendix describes the main techniques (NPV, IRR, MIRR, PI, ROI, PP, and DPP) that are used in capital budgeting analysis. Each approach provides a different piece of information, so, in this age of computers, managers often look at all of them when evaluating projects. However, NPV is the best single measure, and almost all firms now use NPV. The key concepts for the main techniques covered are listed below:

- *Capital budgeting* is the process of analysing potential projects. Capital budgeting decisions are probably the most important ones that managers must make. Such decisions include whether a company should replace worn out/damaged equipment or replace or add to existing equipment to reduce cost; undergo expansion; or invest in a new project or equipment. At its most general, the capital budgeting process involves simply choosing the best project from among several alternatives.

- Once a potential capital budgeting project is identified, its evaluation usually requires the determination of project investment cost, project cash flow estimation, riskiness of the project, and cost of capital adjusting for riskiness of the project, as well as a determination of the key economic indicators.

- The *payback period* is defined as the number of years required to recover a project's cost. The regular *payback period method* ignores cash flows beyond the payback period, and it does not consider the time value of money. The payback does, however, provide an indication of a project's risk and liquidity, because it shows how long the invested capital will be "at risk."

- The *discounted payback* method is similar to the regular payback method except that it discounts cash flows at the project's cost of capital. It considers the time value of money, but it ignores cash flows beyond the payback period.

- The *net present value* (NPV) method discounts all cash flows at the project's cost of capital and then sums those cash flows. The project should be accepted if the NPV is positive.

- The *internal rate of return* (IRR) is defined as the discount rate that forces a project's NPV to equal zero. The project should be accepted if the IRR is greater than the cost of capital.

- The NPV and IRR methods present the same accept/reject decisions for independent projects, but if projects are mutually exclusive, ranking conflicts can arise. If conflicts arise, the NPV method should be used. The NPV and IRR methods are both superior to the payback method, but NPV is superior to IRR.

- The NPV method assumes that cash flows will be reinvested at the firm's cost of capital, while the IRR method assumes reinvestment at the project's IRR. Reinvestment at the cost of capital is a better assumption and is closer to reality.

- The *modified IRR* (MIRR) method corrects some of the problems with the regular IRR. MIRR involves finding the terminal value (TV) of the cash inflows, compounded at the firm's cost of capital, and then determining the discount rate

- that forces the present value of the TV to equal the present value of the outflows.

- The *profitability index* (PI) shows the dollars of present value divided by the initial cost, so this index measures relative profitability.

- Payback measures liquidity, NPV measures direct dollar benefit, IRR measures percentage return with a safety margin built in, MIRR measures a percentage return considering a better reinvestment rate, and PI measures bang for the buck.

- The post-audit is a key element of capital budgeting. By comparing actual results with predicted results and then determining why differences occurred, decision makers can improve both their operations and their forecasts of projects' outcomes.

- Small firms tend to use the payback method rather than a discounted cash flow method. This may be rational because (1) the cost of conducting a Discounted Cash Flow analysis may outweigh the benefits for the project being considered, (2) the firm's cost of capital cannot be estimated accurately, or (3) the small-business owner may be considering non-monetary goals.

- If mutually exclusive projects have unequal lives, it may be necessary to adjust the analysis to put the projects on an equal-life basis. This can be done using the replacement chain (common life) approach.

- A project's true value may be greater than the NPV based on its physical life if it can be terminated at the end of its economic life.

- Flotation costs and increased riskiness associated with unusually large expansion programmes can cause the marginal cost of capital to rise as the size of the capital budget increases.

- Capital rationing occurs when management places a constraint on the size of the firm's capital budget during a particular period.

NET PRESENT VALUE

The net present value (NPV) method is simple and powerful: *All future cash flows are discounted at the project's cost of capital and then summed.* Be aware that cash flow at time zero (CF$_0$) is usually a negative number as this may be an initial capital investment in the project. Complications include differing life spans and different rankings using IRR. The general rule is if NPV > 0, accept the project; if NPV < 0, reject the project; if NPV = 0, you are indifferent (other qualitative variables need to be considered).

The NPV is the sum of cash flows (*CF*) from time zero (*t* = 0) to the final cash flow period (*N*) discounted at some discount rate (*k*), which is typically the weighted average cost of capital (WACC):

$$NPV = CF_0 + \frac{CF_1}{(1+k)^1} + \frac{CF_2}{(1+k)^2} + \ldots + \frac{CF_N}{(1+k)^N} = \sum_{t=0}^{N} \frac{CF_t}{(1+k)^t}$$

$$NPV = CF_0 + \frac{CF_1}{(1+WACC)^1} + \frac{CF_2}{(1+WACC)^2} + \ldots + \frac{CF_N}{(1+WACC)^N}$$
$$= \sum_{t=0}^{N} \frac{CF_t}{(1+WACC)^t}$$

NPV has a direct relationship between economic value added (EVA) and market value added (MVA). It is equal to the present value of the project's future EVA, and, hence, a positive NPV usually implies a positive EVA and MVA.

INTERNAL RATE OF RETURN

Internal rate of return (IRR) is the discount rate that equates the project's cost to the sum of the present cash flow of the project; that is, setting NPV = 0 and solving for k in the NPV equation, where k is now called *IRR*. In other words, where:

$$NPV = \sum_{t=0}^{N} \frac{CF_t}{(1+IRR)^t} = 0$$

Note that there may exist multiple IRRs when the cash flow stream is erratic. Also, the IRR and NPV rankings may be dissimilar. The general rule is that when IRR > required rate of return, or hurdle rate, or cost of capital, accept the project. That is, if the IRR exceeds the cost of capital required to finance and pay for the project, a surplus remains after paying for the project, which is passed on to the shareholders.

The NPV and IRR methods provide the same accept/reject decisions for *independent* projects, but if projects are *mutually exclusive*, ranking conflicts can arise. If conflicts arise, the NPV method should be used. (The NPV and IRR methods are both superior to the payback, but NPV is superior to IRR.) Conflicts may arise when the cash flow timing (most of the cash flows come in during the early years compared to later years in another project) and amounts (the cost of one project is significantly larger than another) are vastly different from one project to another. Finally, there sometimes can arise *multiple* IRR solutions in erratic cash flow streams such as large cash outflows occurring during or at the end of a project's life. In such situations, the NPV provides a more robust and accurate assessment of the project's value.

MODIFIED INTERNAL RATE OF RETURN

The NPV method assumes that the project cash flows are reinvested at the cost of capital, whereas the IRR method assumes project cash flows are reinvested at the project's own IRR. The reinvestment rate at the cost of capital is the more correct approach in that this is the firm's opportunity cost of money (if funds were not available, then capital is raised at this cost).

The modified internal rate of return (MIRR) method is intended to overcome two IRR shortcomings by setting the cash flows to be reinvested at the cost of capital and not its own IRR, as well as preventing the occurrence of multiple IRRs, because only a single MIRR will exist for all cash flow scenarios. Also, NPV and MIRR will usually result in the same project selection when projects are of equal size (significant scale differences might still result in a conflict between MIRR and NPV ranking).

The MIRR is the discount rate that forces the present value of costs of cash outflows (COF) to be equal to the present value of the terminal value (the future value of cash inflows, or CIF, compounded at the project's cost of capital, k).

$$\sum_{t=0}^{n} \frac{COF_t}{(1+k)^t} = \sum_{t=0}^{n} \frac{CIF_t(1+k)^{n-t}}{(1+MIRR)^n}$$

$$\sum_{t=0}^{n} \frac{COF_t}{(1+WACC)^t} = \sum_{t=0}^{n} \frac{CIF_t(1+WACC)^{n-t}}{(1+MIRR)^n}$$

$$PV\ Costs = \frac{Terminal\ Value}{(1+MIRR)^n}$$

PROFITABILITY INDEX

The profitability index (PI) is the ratio of the sum of the present value of cash flows to the initial cost of the project, which measures its *relative profitability*. A project is acceptable if PI > 1, and the higher the PI, the higher the project ranks. PI is mathematically very similar to return on investment (ROI), however it is a relative measure whereas ROI is an absolute measure. It returns a ratio *(the ratio is an absolute value, ignoring the negative investment cost)* while ROI is usually described as a percentage.

$$PI = \frac{\sum_{t=1}^{n} \frac{CF_t}{(1+k)^t}}{CF_0} = \frac{Benefit}{Cost} = \frac{PV\ Cash\ Flows}{Initial\ Cost}$$

$$ROI = \frac{\sum_{t=1}^{n} \frac{CF_t}{(1+k)^t} - CF_0}{CF_0} = \frac{Benefit - Cost}{Cost} = PI - 1$$

Mathematically, NPV, IRR, MIRR, and PI should provide similar rankings although conflicts may sometimes arise, and all methods should be considered as each provides a different set of relevant information.

PAYBACK PERIOD

Simple but ineffective by itself, the payback period (PP) method calculates the time necessary to pay back the initial cost (i.e., a breakeven analysis). It does not take into account time valuation of money, and it does not consider different life spans after the initial payback breakpoint and ignores the cost of capital. The payback period approach helps identify the project's *liquidity* in determining how long funds will be tied up in the project.

$$Payback = Year\ before\ full\ recovery + [unrecovered\ cost \div Cash\ Flow\ at\ time\ t]$$

DISCOUNTED PAYBACK PERIOD

The discounted payback period (DPP) method is similar to the payback period method, but the cash flows used are in present values. This solves the issue of cost of capital, but the disadvantage of ignoring cash flows beyond the payback period still remains.

Discounted Payback
$$= Year\ before\ full\ recovery + [unrecovered\ cost \div PV\ Cash\ Flow\ at\ time\ t]$$

EXAMPLE COMPUTATIONS

Payback Period (PP)

Suppose you are to choose between two projects, A and B. Project A costs $442 but pays back $200 for the next 3 years, while B costs $718 and pays back $250, $575, and $100 for the next 3 years.

The manual calculations are shown below and in Figure A.1.

Payback A is between years 2 and 3, as
$$-\$442\ pays\ back\ between\ \$200$$
$$+ \$200\ in\ year\ 2\ and\ \$200 + \$200 + \$200\ in\ year\ 3$$

2 years is $200 + $200 or $400 paid back, with $442 − $400
$$= \$42\ remaining\ to\ be\ paid\ back\ in\ year\ 3$$

$$Payback\ A = 2 + [\$42 \div \$200] = 2.21\ years$$

Payback B is between years 1 and 2, as
$$-\$718\ pays\ back\ between\ \$250\ in\ year\ 1\ and\ \$250$$
$$+ \$575\ in\ year\ 2$$

1 year is $250 paid back, with $718
$$-\$250\ remaining\ to\ be\ paid\ back\ in\ year\ 2$$

$$Payback\ B = 1 + [(\$718 - \$250) \div \$575] = 1.81\ years$$

	A	B	C	D	E	F	G	H	I	J	K	L	M	N
1														
2							**PAYBACK PERIOD**							
3	Suppose you are to choose between two projects, A and B. Project A costs $442 but pays back $200 for the next 3 years while													
4	Project B costs $718 and pays back $250, $575 and $100 for the next 3 years:													
5														
6		Project A:							Project B:					
7			Time	0	1	2	3			Time	0	1	2	3
8			Cash Flow	($442)	$200	$200	$200			Cash Flow	($718)	$250	$575	$100
9														
10	We compute the cumulative positive cash flow and find the year prior to payback, and then add the proportion of unpaid balance to the cash flow													
11	of the following year:													
12														
13		Project A:							Project B:					
14			Time	0	1	2	3			Time	0	1	2	3
15			Cash Flow	($442)	$200	$200	$200			Cash Flow	($718)	$250	$575	$100
16			CUM +CF		$200	$400	$600			CUM +CF		$250	$825	$925
17														
18		Year prior to payback:			2					Year prior to payback:			1	
19		Unpaid Amount:			($42)					Unpaid Amount:			($468)	
20		Proportion of Following Year:			0.21					Proportion of Following Year:			0.81	
21		**Payback Period (Years):**			**2.21**					**Payback Period (Years):**			**1.81**	

Figure A.1: Payback Period Manual Computations

Disadvantages of Payback Period

- *Neglects time value of money.* To solve this, use present values instead of cash flows, that is, use a discounted payback period instead. This means that in the example above, the $200, or $250, $575, and $100 cash flows are first discounted to present values. See the Discounted Payback Period example below.

- *Cash flows and length of time remaining are left out after the payback period.* As an example, suppose we have two new projects, X and Y with cash flows as shown below. Both have identical payback periods but clearly, project Y is superior as it has additional cash flows. These cash flows post payback period are ignored.

Project X

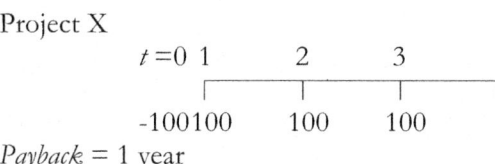

Payback = 1 year

Project Y

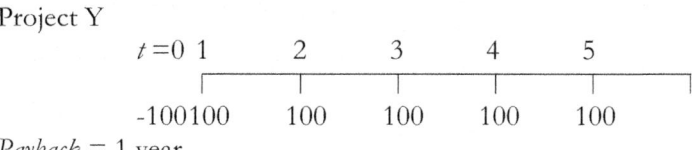

Payback = 1 year

Discounted Payback Period (DPP)

Suppose you are to choose between two projects, A and B. Project A costs $442 but pays back $200 for the next 3 years, while B costs $718 and pays back $250, $575, and $100 for the next 3 years. Further suppose that the WACC discount rate is 12%. The manual computations are shown below and in Figure A.2.

Discounted Payback A = 2 + [($442 − $338.0) ÷ $142.4]
= 2.73 *years*

Discounted Payback B = 2 + [($718 − $681.6) ÷ $71.2] = 2.51 *years*

DISCOUNTED PAYBACK PERIOD

Suppose you are to choose between two projects, A and B. Project A costs $442 but pays back $200 for the next 3 years while Project B costs $718 and pays back $250, $575 and $100 for the next 3 years. Now suppose the WACC discount rate is 12%.

Project A:

Time	0	1	2	3
Cash Flow	($442)	$200	$200	$200

Project B:

Time	0	1	2	3
Cash Flow	($718)	$250	$575	$100

We compute the cumulative positive cash flow and find the year prior to payback, and then add the proportion of unpaid balance to the cash flow of the following year:

Project A:

Time	0	1	2	3
Cash Flow	($442)	$200	$200	$200
PV Cash Flow	($442)	$178.6	$159.4	$142.4
CUM +CF		$178.6	$338.0	$480.4

Year prior to payback:	2
Unpaid Amount:	($104)
Proportion of Following Year:	0.73
Payback Period (Years):	**2.73**

Project B:

Time	0	1	2	3
Cash Flow	($718)	$250	$575	$100
PV Cash Flow	($718)	$223.2	$458.4	$71.2
CUM +CF		$223.2	$681.6	$752.8

Year prior to payback:	2
Unpaid Amount:	($36)
Proportion of Following Year:	0.51
Payback Period (Years):	**2.51**

Figure A.2: Discounted Payback Period Manual Computations

Net Present Value (NPV)

Of the projects A and B below, which is better assuming a 12% WACC discount rate? Use the NPV method.

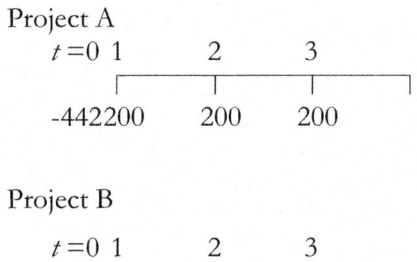

$$NPV = CF_0 + \frac{CF_1}{(1+k)^1} + \frac{CF_2}{(1+k)^2} + \cdots + \frac{CF_N}{(1+k)^N} = \sum_{t=0}^{N} \frac{CF_t}{(1+k)^t}$$

$$NPV_A = -\$442 + \frac{\$200}{(1+0.12)^1} + \frac{\$200}{(1+0.12)^2} + \frac{\$200}{(1+0.12)^3}$$

$$NPV_A = -\$442 + \$178.6 + \$159.4 + \$142.4 = \$38.37$$

$$NPV_B = -\$718 + \frac{\$250}{(1+0.12)^1} + \frac{\$575}{(1+0.12)^2} + \frac{\$100}{(1+0.12)^3}$$

$$NPV_A = -\$718 + \$223.2 + \$458.4 + \$71.2 = \$34.78$$

Comparing A and B, A has a higher NPV, therefore A should be chosen before B although both projects should be undertaken if there exist sufficient funds; otherwise, only undertake project A. Rank remains the same but NPV values differ using different discount rates. Figure A.3 shows the computations in Excel using the NPV function. Note that Excel's NPV function starts from Year 1, which means you need to set the function for cash flows from Years 1 to N, and add the cash flow of Year 0, as illustrated in Figure A.3's two NPV functions.

NET PRESENT VALUE (NPV)

Suppose you are to choose between two projects, A and B. Project A costs $442 but pays back $200 for the next 3 years while Project B costs $718 and pays back $250, $575 and $100 for the next 3 years. Now suppose the WACC discount rate is 12%.

Project A:

Time	0	1	2	3
Cash Flow	($442)	$200	$200	$200

Project B:

Time	0	1	2	3
Cash Flow	($718)	$250	$575	$100

Manually:: We compute the Present Value (PV) of the Cash Flows (CF) and sum them to obtain the Net Present Value (NPV):

Project A:

Time	0	1	2	3
Cash Flow	($442)	$200	$200	$200
PVCF	($442.0)	$178.6	$159.4	$142.4
SUM (NPV)	$38.37			

Project B:

Time	0	1	2	3
Cash Flow	($718)	$250	$575	$100
PV Cash Flow	($718.0)	$223.2	$458.4	$71.2
SUM (NPV)	$34.78			

Using Excel's NPV Function:

NPV $38.37   << =NPV(12%,E14:G14)+D14>>   NPV $34.78   << =NPV(12%,L14:N14)+K14>>

* Be careful as Excel's NPV function requires the starting CF be from year 1 and not year 0, which means you need to add back CF at Year 0, otherwise you will obtain incorrect results (e.g., instead of $38.37, you get $34.26, and instead of $34.78 you get $31.05).

Figure A.3: Net Present Value Manual Computations

Internal Rate of Return (IRR)

Using the same scenario above, calculate the IRR for projects A and B assuming a 12% WACC discount rate (this will now be used as the hurdle rate). Should we accept both projects again, and which project is better?

$$NPV = \sum_{t=0}^{N} \frac{CF_t}{(1+IRR)^t} = 0$$

$$NPV = CF_0 + \frac{CF_1}{(1+IRR)^1} + \frac{CF_2}{(1+IRR)^2} + \ldots + \frac{CF_N}{(1+IRR)^N} = \sum_{t=0}^{N} \frac{CF_t}{(1+IRR)^t}$$

$$-\$442 + \frac{\$200}{(1+IRR_A)^1} + \frac{\$200}{(1+IRR_A)^2} + \frac{\$200}{(1+IRR_A)^3} = 0$$

$$-\$718 + \frac{\$250}{(1+IRR_B)^1} + \frac{\$575}{(1+IRR_B)^2} + \frac{\$100}{(1+IRR_B)^3} = 0$$

Using trial and error, simple optimisation, or search function (Goal Seek in Excel), we obtain an IRR for project A of 16.99% and 14.99% for project B. The decision should be to choose project A over B as it has a higher return (IRR) and IRR > k for both. Figure A.4 shows the manual computations of IRR using Excel's IRR function (unlike the NPV function that starts with Year 1 cash flow, the IRR function starts with Year 0's cash flow, as illustrated in the figure).

Multiple Internal Rate of Returns

When cash flows are both + and −, there may exist multiple IRRs. For instance, consider a project costing −$1.6M with returns of +$10M in the first year and a loss of −$10M in the second year. What is the project's IRR?

$$NPV = -\$1.6 + \frac{\$10}{(1+IRR)^1} + \frac{-\$10}{(1+IRR)^2} = 0$$

Solving yields $IRR = 25\%$ and 400%

The conclusion is that one should use all the methods at one's disposal to see which makes more sense. In regular situations, they should all have similar results. Figure A.5 shows how multiple IRR errors can exist with a simple fluctuating cash flow.

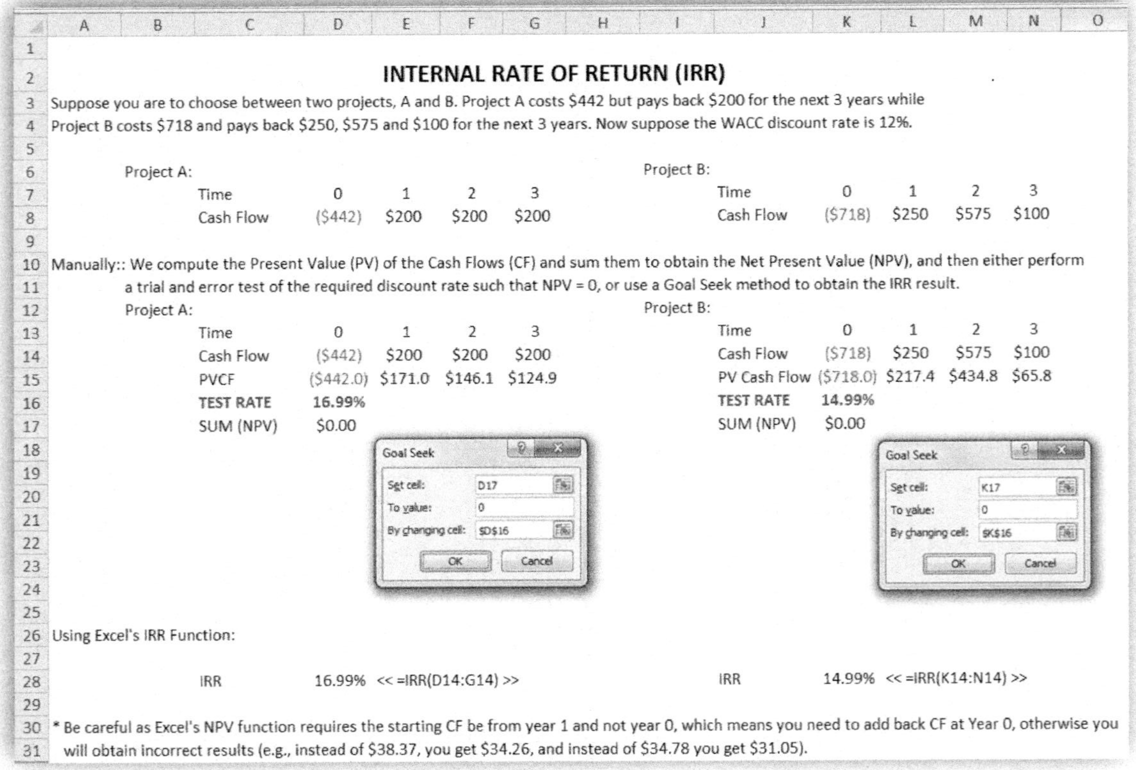

INTERNAL RATE OF RETURN (IRR)

Suppose you are to choose between two projects, A and B. Project A costs $442 but pays back $200 for the next 3 years while Project B costs $718 and pays back $250, $575 and $100 for the next 3 years. Now suppose the WACC discount rate is 12%.

Project A:

Time	0	1	2	3
Cash Flow	($442)	$200	$200	$200

Project B:

Time	0	1	2	3
Cash Flow	($718)	$250	$575	$100

Manually:: We compute the Present Value (PV) of the Cash Flows (CF) and sum them to obtain the Net Present Value (NPV), and then either perform a trial and error test of the required discount rate such that NPV = 0, or use a Goal Seek method to obtain the IRR result.

Project A:

Time	0	1	2	3
Cash Flow	($442)	$200	$200	$200
PVCF	($442.0)	$171.0	$146.1	$124.9
TEST RATE	16.99%			
SUM (NPV)	$0.00			

Goal Seek
Set cell: D17
To value: 0
By changing cell: D16
OK   Cancel

Project B:

Time	0	1	2	3
Cash Flow	($718)	$250	$575	$100
PV Cash Flow	($718.0)	$217.4	$434.8	$65.8
TEST RATE	14.99%			
SUM (NPV)	$0.00			

Goal Seek
Set cell: K17
To value: 0
By changing cell: K16
OK   Cancel

Using Excel's IRR Function:

IRR   16.99%   << =IRR(D14:G14) >>   IRR   14.99%   << =IRR(K14:N14) >>

* Be careful as Excel's NPV function requires the starting CF be from year 1 and not year 0, which means you need to add back CF at Year 0, otherwise you will obtain incorrect results (e.g., instead of $38.37, you get $34.26, and instead of $34.78 you get $31.05).

Figure A.4: Internal Rate of Return Manual Computations

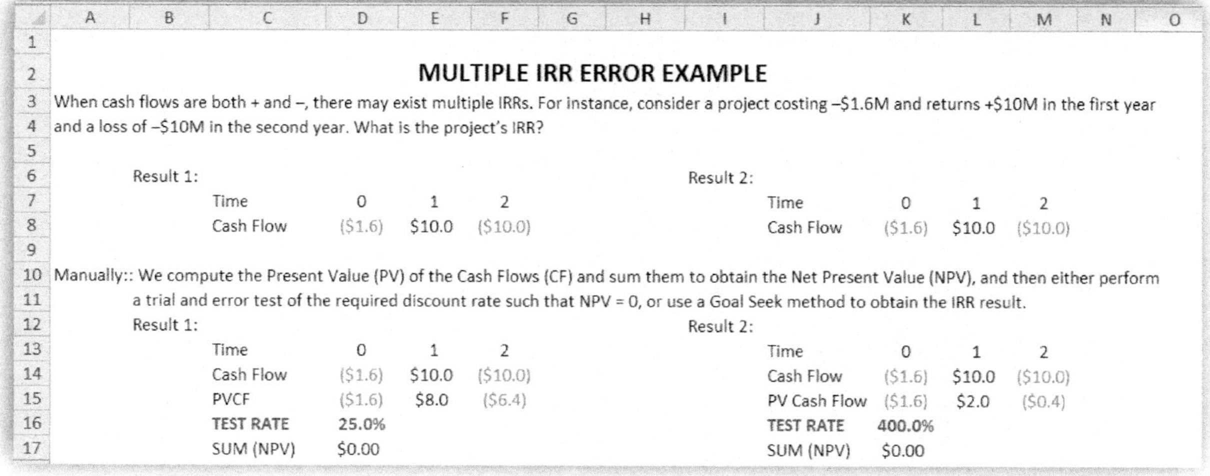

MULTIPLE IRR ERROR EXAMPLE

When cash flows are both + and −, there may exist multiple IRRs. For instance, consider a project costing −$1.6M and returns +$10M in the first year and a loss of −$10M in the second year. What is the project's IRR?

Result 1:

Time	0	1	2
Cash Flow	($1.6)	$10.0	($10.0)

Result 2:

Time	0	1	2
Cash Flow	($1.6)	$10.0	($10.0)

Manually:: We compute the Present Value (PV) of the Cash Flows (CF) and sum them to obtain the Net Present Value (NPV), and then either perform a trial and error test of the required discount rate such that NPV = 0, or use a Goal Seek method to obtain the IRR result.

Result 1:

Time	0	1	2
Cash Flow	($1.6)	$10.0	($10.0)
PVCF	($1.6)	$8.0	($6.4)
TEST RATE	25.0%		
SUM (NPV)	$0.00		

Result 2:

Time	0	1	2
Cash Flow	($1.6)	$10.0	($10.0)
PV Cash Flow	($1.6)	$2.0	($0.4)
TEST RATE	400.0%		
SUM (NPV)	$0.00		

Figure A.5: Multiple IRR Error

Modified Internal Rate of Return (MIRR)

Calculate the MIRR for the two projects A and B as specified previously. Figure A.6 shows the manual computations of the modified internal rate of return (MIRR) using cash out-flows (COF) and cash in-flows (CIF):

$$\sum_{t=0}^{n} \frac{COF_t}{(1+WACC)^t} = \sum_{t=0}^{n} \frac{CIF_t(1+WACC)^{n-t}}{(1+MIRR)^n}$$

which is equivalent to

$$|PV\ Costs| = \frac{Terminal\ Value}{(1+MIRR)^n}$$

$$PV\ Costs = \frac{-\$442}{(1+0.12)^0} = -\$442$$

$$Terminal\ Value_A = \frac{\$200}{(1+0.12)^2} + \frac{\$200}{(1+0.12)^1} + \frac{\$200}{(1+0.12)^0}$$

$$= \$250.9 + \$224.0 + \$200.0 = \$674.9$$

$$|PV\ Costs_A| = \frac{Terminal\ Value_A}{(1+MIRR_A)^n} \quad means \quad \$442 = \frac{\$674.9}{(1+MIRR)^3}$$

Solving yields MIRR = 15.15% for project A.

$$Terminal\ Value_B = \frac{\$250}{(1+0.12)^2} + \frac{\$575}{(1+0.12)^1} + \frac{\$100}{(1+0.12)^0}$$

$$= \$313.6 + \$644.0 + \$100.0 = \$1057.6$$

$$PV\ Costs = \frac{-\$718}{(1+0.12)^0} = -\$718$$

$$|PV\ Costs_A| = \frac{Terminal\ Value_A}{(1+MIRR_A)^n} \quad means \quad \$718 = \frac{\$1057.6}{(1+MIRR)^3}$$

Solving yields MIRR = 13.78% for project B.

Profitability Index and Return on Investment (PI and ROI)

Compute the profitability index (PI) and return on investment (ROI) on projects A and B as previously specified. Figure A.7 shows the manual computation of the PI and ROI.

$$PI = \frac{\sum_{t=1}^{n} \frac{CF_t}{(1+k)^t}}{CF_0} = \frac{Benefit}{Cost} = \frac{PV\ Cash\ Flows}{Initial\ Cost}$$

$$PI = \frac{\sum_{t=1}^{n} \frac{CF_t}{(1+k)^t}}{CF_0}$$

$$PI_A = \frac{\frac{\$200}{(1+0.12)^1} + \frac{\$200}{(1+0.12)^2} + \frac{\$200}{(1+0.12)^3}}{\frac{\$442}{(1+0.12)^0}} = \frac{\$480.4}{\$442.0} = 1.0868$$

$$ROI = \frac{\sum_{t=1}^{n} \frac{CF_t}{(1+k)^t} - CF_0}{CF_0} = \frac{Benefit - Cost}{Cost}$$

$$ROI_A = PI - 1 = 1.0868 - 1 = 8.68\%$$

$$PI_B = \frac{\frac{\$250}{(1+0.12)^1} + \frac{\$575}{(1+0.12)^2} + \frac{\$100}{(1+0.12)^3}}{\frac{\$718}{(1+0.12)^0}} = \frac{\$752.8}{\$718.0} = 1.0484$$

$$ROI_B = PI - 1 = 1.0484 - 1 = 4.84\%$$

We see that the ROI and PI of project A exceeds that of project B, so we would recommend going ahead with project A instead of project B.

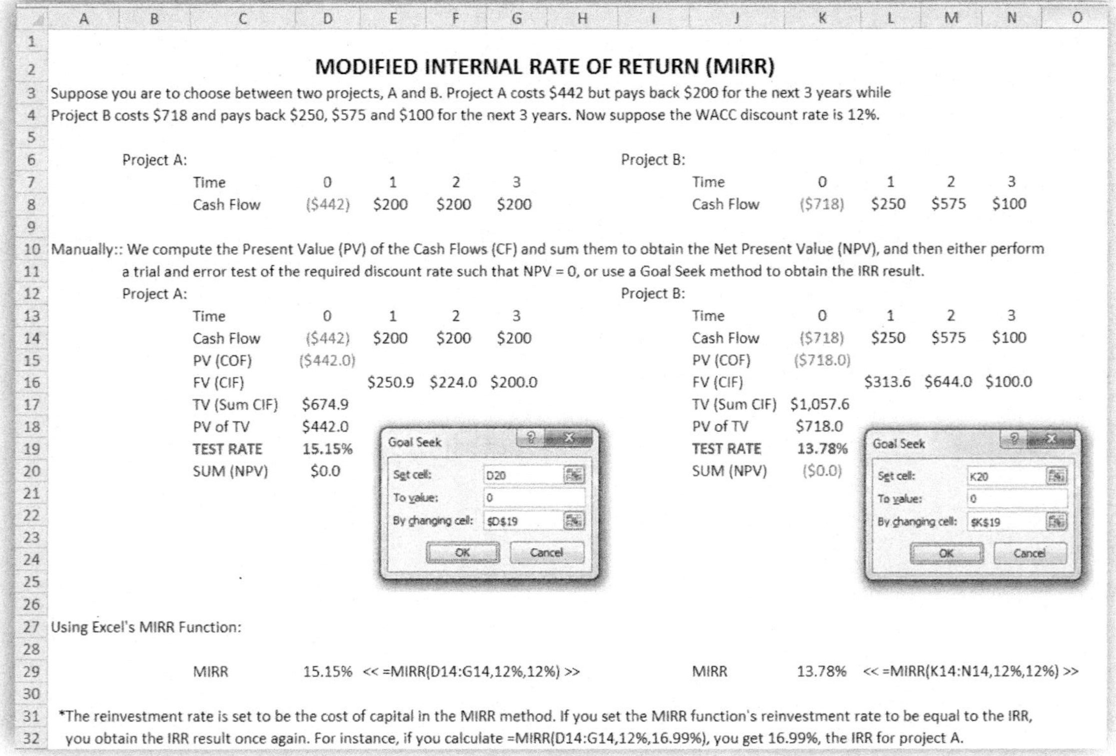

MODIFIED INTERNAL RATE OF RETURN (MIRR)

Suppose you are to choose between two projects, A and B. Project A costs $442 but pays back $200 for the next 3 years while Project B costs $718 and pays back $250, $575 and $100 for the next 3 years. Now suppose the WACC discount rate is 12%.

Project A:

Time	0	1	2	3
Cash Flow	($442)	$200	$200	$200

Project B:

Time	0	1	2	3
Cash Flow	($718)	$250	$575	$100

Manually:: We compute the Present Value (PV) of the Cash Flows (CF) and sum them to obtain the Net Present Value (NPV), and then either perform a trial and error test of the required discount rate such that NPV = 0, or use a Goal Seek method to obtain the IRR result.

Project A:

Time	0	1	2	3
Cash Flow	($442)	$200	$200	$200
PV (COF)	($442.0)			
FV (CIF)		$250.9	$224.0	$200.0
TV (Sum CIF)	$674.9			
PV of TV	$442.0			
TEST RATE	15.15%			
SUM (NPV)	$0.0			

Project B:

Time	0	1	2	3
Cash Flow	($718)	$250	$575	$100
PV (COF)	($718.0)			
FV (CIF)		$313.6	$644.0	$100.0
TV (Sum CIF)	$1,057.6			
PV of TV	$718.0			
TEST RATE	13.78%			
SUM (NPV)	($0.0)			

Using Excel's MIRR Function:

| MIRR | 15.15% | << =MIRR(D14:G14,12%,12%) >> | | MIRR | 13.78% | << =MIRR(K14:N14,12%,12%) >> |

*The reinvestment rate is set to be the cost of capital in the MIRR method. If you set the MIRR function's reinvestment rate to be equal to the IRR, you obtain the IRR result once again. For instance, if you calculate =MIRR(D14:G14,12%,16.99%), you get 16.99%, the IRR for project A.

Figure A.6: Modified Internal Rate of Return Manual Computations

PROFITABILITY INDEX (PI) AND RETURN ON INVESTMENT (ROI)

Suppose you are to choose between two projects, A and B. Project A costs $442 but pays back $200 for the next 3 years while Project B costs $718 and pays back $250, $575 and $100 for the next 3 years. Now suppose the WACC discount rate is 12%.

Project A:

Time	0	1	2	3
Cash Flow	($442)	$200	$200	$200

Project B:

Time	0	1	2	3
Cash Flow	($718)	$250	$575	$100

Manually:: We compute the Present Value (PV) of the Cash Flows (CF) for the negative CF (investment cost) and positive CF:

Project A:

Time	0	1	2	3	
Cash Flow	($442)	$200	$200	$200	
PVCF	($442.0)	$178.6	$159.4	$142.4	
ABS(CF(0)) Cost	$442.0	<<=ABS(D15) >>			
SUM CF(i)	$480.4	<<=SUM(E15:G15) >>			

| Profitability Index (PI) | 1.0868 | <<=D17/D16 >> |
| Return on Investment (ROI) | 8.68% | <<=(D17-D16)/D16 >> |

Project B:

Time	0	1	2	3	
Cash Flow	($718)	$250	$575	$100	
PV Cash Flow	($718.0)	$223.2	$458.4	$71.2	
ABS(CF(0)) Cost	$718.0	<<=ABS(K15) >>			
SUM CF(i)	$752.8	<<=SUM(L15:N15) >>			

| Profitability Index (PI) | 1.0484 | <<=K17/K16 >> |
| Return on Investment (ROI) | 4.84% | <<=(K17-K16)/K16 >> |

* We usually convert the initial investment cost (a negative value) into a positive absolute value to simplify the calculations, otherwise it is difficult to keep in mind which values are positive and which are negative. The *ROI* value is simply *PI - 1* in percent.

Figure A.7: Profitability Index and Return on Investment Manual Computations

GLOSSARY

asset integrity: the ability of an asset (e.g., oil/gas well and platform) to perform its required function reliably and safely. An evaluation of asset integrity is especially important in offshore asset decommissioning because the asset is going to be lifted out, cut, and removed from its normal standing position and transported for disposal.

capital allowances: capital expenditures (CAPEX) that can be claimed as expenses against the annual pre-tax income.

conductor pipe removal: the main structure of an oil or gas well between the asset and the seabed. The removal of this pipe and its associated casings is done to ensure that the casings do not interfere with marine activities and to meet the requirements of the license, which normally states that the seabed should be returned to its original condition.

counterparty risk: the likelihood that a company or an asset's operator, having a decommissioning liability, defaults on its contractual obligation. As a last resort, the decommissioning liability falls on the taxpayers.

decision analytics: a set of systematic, quantitative, and visual decision-making techniques to addressing and evaluating the important choices that businesses sometimes face to provide different Applied Analytics to run static analysis on performance indicators. For instance, tornado analysis provides static approaches to identify the most influential risk factors by examining one variable at a time, while scenario analysis allows determining the impact on the main economic criteria of one or two variables at once.

decommissioning: a complex process that involves the safe disposal of the oil/gas well's production equipment as well as the safe isolation of the hydrocarbons or any remaining products within the earth's surface, which also includes environmental remediation or land restoration; also known mothballing or dismantling.

decommissioning auditing: the process of examining estimations, assumptions, and measurements of decommissioning costs, asset depreciation, and residual values, including provisions, decommissioning funds, adjustment factors (interest and inflation rates), tax regime, etc.

decommissioning management: a process involving the identification of and the planning for the many responsibilities, liabilities, activities, and so forth related to the decommissioning project. It generally starts three to five years before the end of production by an asset, but that can be shorter or longer to suit the schedule set and depending on the size of the asset and the organisation's work team and project management strategy.

decommissioning provision: an accounting procedure to recognise, measure, and quantify the decommissioning obligations (liability) arising after the asset's construction and when removal (at the end of its lifespan) is required (including site restoration).

decommissioning risk management: a process for dealing with uncertainty and the potential hazards and losses of an asset's dismantling. It relies on experience, data vendors, contractor estimations, previous projects, and decommissioning norms, and also considers uncertainty analysis, probability estimations, and cost and time forecasts and contingencies, while enhancing risk modeling and quantification based on Monte Carlo simulations.

depreciation: in accounting, a technique to measure and disclose the reduction in the value of a tangible asset over time, due in particular to usage.

early decommissioning: decommissioning (e.g., well plugging and facilities abandonment) an asset before the final stage of its life cycle. A choice that might be made because of marginal fields, low flowrates, or low production levels.

emerging decommissioning strategy: an approach to decommissioning of assets encompassing alternatives to outright disassembly and removal as well as ways to maintain a balance between decommissioning timing and managing business performance (i.e., savings, profits). For example, it considers secondary usage of the facilities (e.g., CCUS, hydrogen production, or electrification) or new integrated business to delay decommissioning.

internal decommissioning strategy: a plan needed when owners maintain both assets and their decommissioning liabilities for managing operational conditions to maximise recovery value, enhance revenues, and develop in-house decommissioning capabilities.

late decommissioning: decommissioning an asset in its late stage (i.e., cold stacked, no production) because decision makers wanted to postpone their decommissioning obligations.

liquidity maximiser: in decommissioning, a strategy to sell or lease an asset looking for liquidity, where a buyer acquires the asset to increase the value of their business. However, the seller usually retains the decommissioning liability in the balance sheet while it is expected they are creating future capabilities to reduce decommissioning costs.

option awareness: when decision makers understand their decommissioning choices in terms of cost, schedule, safety, regulations, and potential risks. They should be aware that it is impossible to know all options and should overthinking them, which would result in delays and additional cost.

outsourcing decommissioning: transferring risks on asset operations and subcontracting decommissioning activities to third parties. It provides significant flexibility for assets' owners to generate liquidity and manage cash opportunities.

portfolio analysis: a process of reviewing or assessing multiple projects (i.e., current and potential), business lines, market strategies, and decommissioning strategies (early and late stage, conventional, and emerging) and selecting the most suitable or feasible ones according to the most relevant constraints (financial and nonfinancial).

project risk management: in decommissioning, a process that not only deals with planning, design, engineering, permitting, plugging and abandonment (P&A), mobilisation, demobilisation, reuse of facilities, legal requirements, and other activities, but also involves identifying uncertainty factors and managing the risks associated with these activities.

real options analysis: the application of different decision-making techniques (economics, finance, statistics, mathematics, etc.) to help organisations manage uncertainty and acquire flexibility in business decisions and strategies. Real options incorporate valuation models to identify and quantify investment decisions and projects in highly uncertain business conditions.

residual value: the estimated value of an asset (tangible or intangible) at the end of its lease term or useful life cycle.

risk profile: a quantitative evaluation of risks or threats used to guide decision analysis by assessing, reporting, and monitoring key performance indicators based on assumptions, data, and experience, in the form of confidence intervals (e.g., 99%, 95%, 90%) and descriptive statistics (mean, median, standard deviations, skew, kurtosis, etc.).

risk: the possibility of harm or loss; it is something one bears as the outcome of uncertainty, and it may remain constant while uncertainty increases over time. In decommissioning, risk encompasses exposure to physical hazards, schedule delays, cost overruns, losses, and so forth. Its management can be used to detect or create opportunities (i.e., savings, cost reduction, reliability, benefits, and so on).

risk registers: a record of risks (may include causes and consequences) and the actions taken in response to them. A simple analogy for a risk register and its elements would be a to-do list or a checkbook (presented in Excel files or spreadsheets) with potential risks or opportunities identified.

risk simulation: a risk analysis technique using Monte Carlo risk simulations comprised of hundreds of thousands of scenarios and trials to help managers analyse how uncertainty on projects' inputs impacts key economic indicators and their risk profiles, probabilities, charts, and statistics, to make better decisions.

shareholder: in decommissioning, any person, company, or group who has an interest in or could be impacted by the activities undertaken within a decommissioning project—for example, communities, environmental representatives, fishing organisations, and so on.

supply chain management (SMC): in decommissioning, the approach to dealing with different contractors and service companies, especially for platform removal, heavy material, waste management, talent management, land restoration, safety management, and continued monitoring after closure.

timing decommissioning: deciding to trigger the option to decommissioning, early or late, based on economic and market fluctuations, infrastructure obsolescence, technical challenges, regulatory pressure, and financial requirements.

traditional asset sales: a divesting strategy implying a transfer of an asset's ownership (production assets and decommissioning liabilities, including site restorations). The seller mostly receives cash to finance its other projects (shares or mixed payments can also be used), while the buyer maximises the economic value on assets that are not at the end of their life cycle.

uncertainty: not fully known or clearly identified. It involves variables that are unknown and changing, but uncertainty will be become known and resolved through the passage of time, events, and action.

well plugging and abandonment (P&A): the activity whereby offshore wells (oil or gas) are permanently closed. Part of a decommissioning project's management strategy, it involves some of the highest risks in terms of safety, environment, cost, and schedule. Completing this stage of decommissioning is important for ensuring that no fluids, including hydrocarbons, can resurface once the asset has been removed.

SOFTWARE DOWNLOAD & INSTALLATION

For **PEAT-DECOMM**, we highly recommend that you visit the OSL Risk Management Ltd. website and follow the instructions below to install the latest software applications.

- Visit www.oslriskmanagement.com/solutions/project-economic-analysis-tool and click on "DOWNLOAD A TRIAL VERSION" (Figure A). You will be prompted to log in. Please register your interest, and an automated e-mail will be sent to you shortly with the downloading link. (If you do not receive a registration e-mail after you register, then please send a note to support@oslriskmanagement.com or support@realoptionsvaluation.com.) While waiting for the automated e-mail, browse this page and see the free getting started videos, case studies, and sample models you can download.

For **Risk Simulator** and **Real Options SLS**, we highly recommend that you visit the Real Options Valuation, Inc., website and follow the instructions below to install the latest software applications.

- **Step 1**: Visit **www.realoptionsvaluation.com** and click on **Downloads** and **Download Software** (Figure B). You will be prompted to log in. Please first register if you are a first-time user (Figure C) and an automated e-mail will be sent to you shortly. (If you do not receive a registration e-mail after you register, then please send a note to support@realoptionsvaluation.com, or support@oslriskmanagement.com.) While waiting for the automated e-mail, browse this page and see the free getting started videos, case studies, and sample models you can download.

- **Step 2**: Return to this site and LOGIN using the login credentials you received via e-mail. Download and install the latest versions of **Risk Simulator** and **Real Options SLS** on this Web page. The download links, installation instructions, and Hardware ID information are also presented on this page (Figure D).

- **Step 3**: After installing the software, start Excel and you will see a Risk Simulator ribbon. Follow the instructions provided on the Web page to obtain your Hardware ID and e-mail it to support@realoptionsvaluation.com. Mention the code "**MR3E 30 Days**" and you will be sent a free extended 30-day license to use both the Risk Simulator and Real Options SLS software.

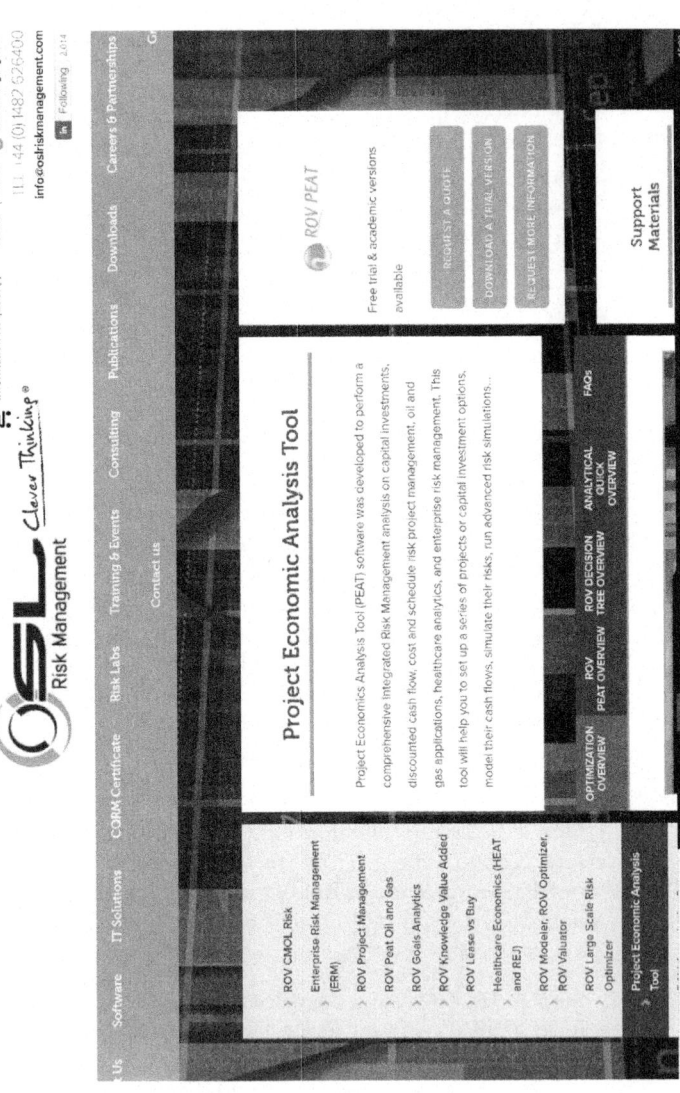

Figure A: PEAT-DECOMM Solution Download Site

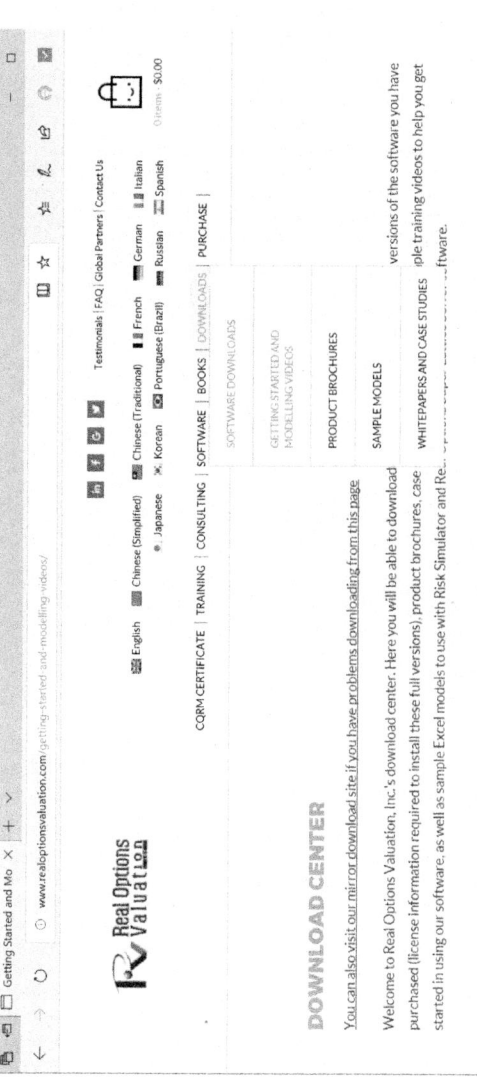

Figure B: Step 1 – ROV Software Download Site

DOWNLOAD CENTER

You can also visit our mirror download site if you have problems downloading from this page

Welcome to Real Options Valuation, Inc.'s download center. Here you will be able to download trial versions of our software, full versions of the software you have purchased (license information required to install these full versions), product brochures, case studies and white papers, and sample training videos to help you get started in using our software, as well as sample Excel models to use with Risk Simulator and Real Options Super Lattice Solver software.

YOU ARE REQUIRED TO LOGIN TO VIEW THIS PAGE.

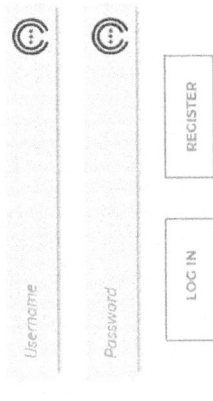

Figure C: First-Time Visitor Registration

English | Chinese (Simplified) | Chinese (Traditional) | French | German | Italian
Japanese | Korean | Portuguese (Brazil) | Russian | Spanish

CQRM CERTIFICATE | TRAINING | CONSULTING | SOFTWARE | BOOKS | DOWNLOADS | PURCHASE

FULL & TRIAL VERSION DOWNLOAD:

Download Risk Simulator 2018 – Auto Installer
Download Risk Simulator 2018 – Auto Installer (mirror site)
Download Risk Simulator 2018 – For 32 Bit Excel
Download Risk Simulator 2018 – For 32 Bit Excel (mirror site)
Download Risk Simulator 2018 – For 64 Bit Excel
Download Risk Simulator 2018 – For 64 Bit Excel (mirror site)

Download OLDER version of Risk Simulator 2014 | WIN x64 and Excel x32 edition)
Download OLDER version of Risk Simulator 2014 | WIN x64 and Excel x32 edition) (mirror site)

This is a full version of the software but will expire in 15 days, during which time you can purchase a license to permanently unlock the software. Please first uninstall all previous versions of Risk Simulator before installing this newer version.

To permanently unlock the software, purchase a license and e-mail us your Hardware ID (after installing the software, start Excel, click on Risk Simulator License, and e-mail admin@realoptionsvaluation.com the 16 to 20 digit Hardware ID located on the bottom left of the splash screen). We will then e-mail you a permanent license file. Save this file to your hard drive, start Excel, click on Risk Simulator License, Install License and point to the location of this license file, restart Excel and you are now permanently licensed. Installing the license only takes a few seconds.

SYSTEM REQUIREMENTS, FAQ, AND ADDITIONAL RESOURCES:

- Windows 7, 8, and 10 (32 and 64 bits)
- Microsoft Excel 2010, 2013, or 2016
- 2GB RAM Minimum (4 GB recommended)
- 600 MB Hard Drive
- Administrative Rights to install software
- Microsoft .NET Framework 2.0, 3.0, 3.5, or later
- MAC OS users will require either Virtual Machine or Parallels running Microsoft Excel

Figure D: Download Links and Hardware ID Instructions

INDEX

abandonment, 31, 37, 42, 44, 71, 72, 74, 82, 89, 95, 98, 100, 144, 145, 168, 193, 252, 253
abandonment option, 71, 74, 82, 89
accounting, 23, 67, 93, 107, 108, 109, 111, 112, 113, 119, 142, 252
acquisition, 82, 114
agency, 53, 54
airline, 79
ALARP, 189
American option, 77
amortisation, 111
Asian option, 77
assessment, 24, 28, 30, 34, 57, 60, 108, 124, 189, 191, 230, 235
asset, 26
asset integrity, asset integrity management, AIM, 22, 34, 40, 83, 84, 85, 95, 97, 98, 102, 103, 105, 107, 111, 113, 119, 122, 129, 142, 152, 191, 199, 251
assurance, 44, 69, 95, 102, 105
AT&T, 80
auditing, 23, 93, 107, 117, 119, 142, 251
bang for the buck, 61, 62, 63, 233
barrier, 31, 74, 80
barrier option, 74
Bermudan option, 77
blackout, 77
blowout preventers, 31
Boeing, 79, 89
bond logging, 42
campaign, 42
capability, 40, 45, 52, 75, 77, 194, 201, 217, 218
capital, 68, 69, 80, 94, 103, 107, 108, 115, 116, 124, 126, 149, 167, 189, 190, 228, 231, 232, 233, 234, 235
capital allowances, 115, 251
capital budgeting, 68, 69, 91, 124, 231, 232, 233
capital expenditures, CAPEX, 69, 81, 82, 91, 102, 103, 107, 111, 114, 124, 125, 126, 129, 167, 190, 191, 199, 200, 202, 204, 205, 208, 209, 210, 213, 214, 215, 220, 222, 224, 226, 251
capital investment, 68, 69, 234
carbon capture and storage, CCS, 60
carbon capture, utilizations and storage, CCUS, 67, 68, 74, 75, 80, 81, 95, 100, 102, 105, 128, 130, 190, 252
cash, 19, 21, 25, 68, 81, 82, 85, 90, 91, 94, 95, 96, 97, 98, 100, 104, 105, 107, 116, 118, 124, 125, 126, 143, 186, 189, 190, 232, 233, 234, 235, 236, 237, 239, 241, 243, 246, 253, 254
cash flow, 68, 81, 82, 90, 94, 105, 116, 118, 124, 125, 190, 232, 234, 235, 236, 237, 239, 241, 243
casing, 31, 33, 42, 43, 100, 103
cement, cementing, 31, 32, 42, 43, 79, 102
chooser option, 74
communication, 23, 24, 48, 51, 56, 146
comparative risk, 34
conductor pipe removal, 32, 79, 251
constraints, 95, 97, 129, 149, 199, 218
contract, contract manager, 41, 50, 74, 89, 101, 102, 104, 190

contraction option, 74, 82, 105, 129
contractor, 50, 51, 158, 167, 168, 252
corrosion, 34, 39, 40, 46, 102
cost of capital, 124, 125, 232, 233, 234, 235, 236, 237
counterparty risk, credit risk, 94, 96, 97, 98, 116, 117, 142, 251
critical success factors, 65
current prices, 109
customised, 73, 126
cutting, 37, 43, 75, 79, 104, 118, 149, 167, 174, 190, 191, 199
decarbonisation, 21, 26, 68, 95, 100, 101, 102, 103, 108, 118, 128
decision makers, 19, 22, 23, 24, 26, 59, 63, 67, 75, 78, 83, 93, 94, 95, 105, 107, 109, 111, 113, 115, 118, 122, 124, 126, 127, 129, 142, 146, 147, 151, 153, 156, 157, 168, 174, 175, 186, 189, 190, 192, 193, 194, 199, 200, 208, 215, 216, 233, 252, 253
decision sciences, 69
decommissioning costs, 94, 96, 97, 104, 108, 109, 110, 111, 116, 117, 118, 119, 120, 124, 128, 251, 252
decommissioning liabilities, decommissioning provisions, 30, 80, 81, 82, 93, 96, 97, 102, 107, 109, 110, 118, 252, 254
decommissioning management, 251
decommissioning risks, 37, 95, 105, 107, 108, 123, 142, 189, 192, 194, 200, 228
deep clean, 29
deferment option, 75
depreciation, 101, 107, 109, 110, 111, 112, 113, 114, 115, 117, 126, 251, 252
directors, 48, 49, 80

discounted, discounted cash flow, 68, 81, 82, 85, 90, 110, 125, 143, 232, 233, 234, 237, 239
dismantle, 115
disposal, 21, 22, 26, 31, 33, 36, 40, 53, 113, 118, 217, 243, 251
distribution, 72, 112, 123, 151, 152, 215, 217
drill rig, 31, 44
drilled, 42, 87
drug development, 69
dynamic sensitivity, 67, 69, 105, 123, 128, 154, 168, 169, 192, 216, 228
early decommissioning, 74, 75, 79, 252
e-commerce, 69, 82
economic value, vii, 23, 39, 69, 85, 93, 94, 95, 96, 97, 100, 101, 105, 110, 112, 117, 118, 124, 126, 127, 128, 130, 142, 192, 231, 232, 233, 234, 251, 254, 255
efficient frontier (*see also:* Markowitz efficient frontier), 61, 63
electrification, 97, 100, 104, 105, 128, 130, 252
emerging decommissioning strategies, 98
energy companies, iv, 92, 199
energy projects, iv, v, 21, 26, 60, 72, 76, 78, 81
engagement, 22, 48, 53, 56, 57, 95, 111, 151, 175, 192
environment, environmental remediation, 21, 22, 25, 26, 27, 30, 31, 33, 34, 36, 39, 40, 42, 44, 53, 56, 69, 83, 84, 93, 97, 100, 103, 104, 105, 108, 113, 119, 121, 142, 145, 146, 150, 167, 186, 191, 199, 251, 254
equipment, 21, 26, 27, 29, 30, 42, 89, 93, 94, 103, 113, 122, 149, 217, 218, 231, 251

European option, 77
exercise, 77, 124
exotic option, 74
expansion factor, 87, 130
expansion option, 76, 82, 85, 86, 87
external stakeholders, 22, 52
extrapolation, 85
fail, 41, 73, 85
fair market value, 72
fatigue, 39, 40
fixed assets, 93
flexibility, 68, 72, 74, 77, 83, 91, 98, 105, 129, 130, 145, 146, 148, 149, 174, 175, 186, 190
flow zones, 31, 32
forecasting, 73, 108, 118, 124, 143
funding, 49, 101, 116, 142
gas-to-wire, GTW, 74, 78, 80, 81, 95, 101, 102, 105, 128, 129, 130, 144
General Motors, 78
hazard and operability, HAZOP, 189, 193, 230
hazardous, 19, 39, 40
health, 19, 22, 37, 44, 53, 69, 91, 95, 97, 100, 105, 117, 119, 142, 145, 186, 189, 218
health, safety, environment, and quality, 100, 189
health, safety, environment, and quality, HSEQ, 100, 101, 105, 113, 120, 189, 190, 191, 194, 200
heat maps, 157, 209
historical costs, 109
historical, historical data, 67, 109, 115, 120, 128
hurdle rate, 235, 243
hydrocarbon, 21, 26, 29, 30, 251, 254
implementation cost, 85
importance, 22, 48, 216, 229
influence, 23, 46, 47, 48, 52, 95, 209

inspections, 29, 40, 82, 104, 113, 119, 142
intangible, 69, 103, 111
integrated risk management, IRM, 158, 167, 191, 192, 193, 200, 201, 208, 216, 217, 228
integrity, 37, 40, 67, 100, 110, 112, 144, 230, 251
intellectual property, 74, 82
interaction, 48
internal stakeholders, 22, 49, 52
inventory, 53, 78
investment, 67, 68, 69, 70, 75, 76, 80, 81, 82, 85, 97, 101, 103, 105, 111, 124, 127, 231, 232, 236
land remediation, land restoration, 37, 45, 82, 94, 142, 145, 251, 254
late decommissioning, 70, 79, 96, 102, 252
layers of protection analysis, LOPA, 189, 193, 230
leadership, iii, 24, 49, 146, 200
liabilities, 96, 97, 107, 109, 111, 118, 119, 251
lifting, 29, 30, 33, 37, 40, 41, 44, 75, 79, 104, 118, 167, 174, 190, 191, 199, 201, 218
liquidity, 19, 21, 25, 91, 97, 98, 118, 125, 128, 232, 233, 236, 252, 253
maintenance, iii, 29, 40, 67, 84, 85, 95, 100, 104, 108, 113, 189
manager, iii, 50, 60, 61, 85, 208
manufacturing, 69, 76, 77, 78, 88, 89
marine, 19, 33, 40, 82, 146, 209, 251
market, 27, 33, 44, 45, 71, 74, 75, 77, 79, 80, 87, 94, 95, 101, 108, 109, 111, 113, 114, 118, 122, 127, 128, 129, 234
market risk, 75
Markowitz efficient frontier (*see also:* efficient frontier), 61

models, 28, 40, 43, 51, 72, 73, 79, 83, 87, 95, 118, 253, 255
moment, 71, 90
monitor, 50, 116, 167, 175, 215, 217
monitoring, 22, 33, 36, 45, 50, 84, 98, 147, 157, 169, 174, 175, 176, 186, 191, 200, 217, 228, 253, 254
Monte Carlo simulation, 40, 67, 73, 86, 118, 120, 122, 123, 124, 127, 128, 142, 143, 146, 149, 151, 153, 155, 167, 186, 192, 215
multiple, 67, 68, 78, 79, 81, 87, 126, 127, 128, 142, 147, 149, 150, 152, 153, 174, 194, 234, 235, 243
net present value, NPV, 81, 90, 98, 124, 125, 127, 128, 129, 133, 136, 137, 231, 232, 233, 234, 235, 236, 241, 243
objective, 62
offshore, iii, 19, 21, 25, 26, 27, 30, 32, 37, 39, 40, 44, 46, 52, 53, 55, 57, 59, 74, 75, 76, 100, 101, 102, 104, 115, 128, 129, 130, 144, 146, 187, 251, 254
offshore drilling unit, 30
oil and gas, iii, iv, 21, 25, 26, 36, 43, 44, 45, 46, 57, 69, 70, 78, 79, 80, 81, 83, 86, 87, 93, 94, 100, 102, 103, 104, 107, 112, 113, 115, 117, 124, 128, 129, 156, 187, 193
operational, 19, 25, 41, 51, 67, 84, 93, 94, 95, 97, 98, 103, 108, 109, 113, 122, 124, 126, 129, 130, 142, 158, 189, 190, 193, 201, 208, 217, 252
operational expenditures, OPEX, 124, 126, 127, 129, 208
operational risk, 41, 51, 193
operators, 26, 36, 37, 43, 51, 53, 55, 70, 75, 76, 78, 79, 80, 81, 91, 93, 98, 100, 101, 102, 103, 115, 119, 122, 142
opportunities, 21, 25, 36, 39, 69, 70, 76, 80, 96, 97, 98, 101, 104, 105, 124, 146, 199, 200, 253, 254
optimal, 70, 72, 80, 87, 89, 90, 91, 152, 158
optimisation, 63, 73, 129, 143, 243
option to abandon, 81
option to contract, 102
option to expand, 81, 82, 102, 103, 104
option to switch, 78, 80, 102
option to wait, 70, 75, 78, 81
options, 44, 45, 59, 67, 68, 69, 70, 71, 72, 73, 74, 75, 76, 77, 78, 80, 81, 82, 83, 85, 86, 88, 89, 90, 91, 93, 95, 96, 97, 100, 101, 102, 103, 105, 106, 120, 124, 125, 126, 128, 129, 130, 141, 142, 143, 174, 175, 190, 228, 255
out-of-the-money, 74
outsourcing decommissioning, 253
payback, 82, 232, 233, 235, 236, 237, 239
PEAT, 124, 125, 126, 127, 128, 129, 130, 142, 151, 154, 155, 156, 157, 167, 174, 175, 193, 194, 195, 199, 200, 208, 209, 215, 217, 228, 229, 231
perforating, 43
performance, 19, 48, 51, 71, 78, 84, 95, 96, 100, 101, 105, 107, 110, 123, 124, 125, 126, 127, 129, 130, 142, 151, 153, 156, 167, 174, 190, 191, 193, 201, 215, 216, 251, 252, 253
permits, licences, authorisations, notifications, and consents, PLANC, 27
permitting, 22, 26, 28, 29, 145, 253
pharmaceutical, 69, 76, 81

pipeline, 21, 25, 27, 29, 34, 35, 54, 55, 103, 112
platform, iii, 21, 25, 26, 29, 33, 36, 44, 51, 69, 74, 75, 76, 81, 87, 88, 100, 101, 102, 103, 109, 110, 121, 126, 130, 149, 155, 156, 157, 168, 176, 200, 201, 209, 218
platform preparation, 22, 26
point estimate (*see also:* single-point estimate), 63
portfolio, 61, 63, 82, 124, 126, 128, 130, 142, 143, 175
portfolio analysis, 126, 253
power, 26, 34, 45, 48, 69, 81, 101, 102, 103
power cable, 26, 34
preparation, 29, 30
price, 70, 71, 74, 77, 78, 80, 81, 87, 88, 90, 150
pricing, 75, 78
probability, 67, 71, 72, 128, 151, 153, 155, 156, 167, 174, 215
project management, iii, v, vii, 22, 24, 26, 27, 69, 96, 97, 98, 101, 104, 119, 120, 142, 146, 149, 151, 157, 158, 168, 186, 192, 200, 216, 217, 252
project manager, iii, 50, 73, 91, 145, 147, 148, 149, 153, 158, 191, 199, 208
project team, 24, 28, 49, 50, 52, 56, 208
provisions (*see also:* liabilities), 74, 107, 108, 116, 117, 119, 120, 142, 251
qualitative, 69, 189, 191, 192, 199, 201, 208, 228, 234
qualitative risk, 189
quality, 44, 113
quality assurance, 44
range, 45, 151, 153, 186
recovered, 31, 42
regulation, 104, 116, 199
regulatory bodies, regulator, 27, 28, 29, 34, 53, 75

renewables, iv, 19, 70, 105, 119, 128
representatives, ii, 48, 56, 216, 254
reserves, 26, 95, 110, 112
reservoir, 31, 32, 42, 86, 87, 88, 101
residual, 94, 95, 104, 107, 111, 113, 114, 117, 120, 122, 123, 126, 142, 190, 199, 215, 229
residual value, 95, 104, 107, 111, 112, 113, 114, 117, 120, 122, 123, 126, 142, 190, 251, 253
returns, return on investment, ROI, 72, 80, 81, 124, 127, 231, 232, 233, 234, 235, 236, 243, 246, 247
rigless, 30, 44
risk manager, 51, 194, 199
risk profile, 67, 123, 124, 127, 128, 129, 149, 150, 153, 154, 168, 175, 191, 194, 216, 253, 254
risk quantification, 186, 189, 191, 192, 193, 194, 200, 201, 217, 228
risk registers, 24, 67, 189, 191, 192, 193, 199, 200, 208, 254
running in hole, 42
safety, 19, 21, 22, 23, 25, 30, 33, 37, 39, 40, 41, 42, 44, 45, 51, 54, 71, 72, 91, 93, 94, 95, 97, 100, 101, 104, 113, 119, 142, 143, 145, 146, 151, 167, 174, 175, 186, 189, 190, 191, 199, 233, 253, 254
sales, 78, 83, 85, 95, 96, 97, 104, 112, 113, 122
salvage, 74, 96, 97, 107, 112, 113, 114, 115, 122, 124
sample, 255
scenario, 64, 65, 98, 157, 192, 208, 209, 243
section milling, 42, 43
sensitivity, sensitivity analysis (*see also:* dynamic sensitivity), 65

sequential compound option, 76, 81, 85, 88
severing, 33
shareholder, 47, 67, 103, 105, 125, 130, 254
Sharpe ratio, 62
simulations, 24, 41, 91, 118, 120, 122, 123, 124, 127, 128, 129, 130, 142, 146, 149, 150, 153, 167, 168, 175, 186, 192, 215, 216, 252, 254
single, 33, 128, 145, 148, 149, 152, 231, 235
single-point estimate (*see also:* point estimate), 63
stakeholders, 19, 22, 47, 48, 49, 51, 52, 55, 56, 95, 191, 193, 199
static, 68, 122, 127, 128, 157, 208, 209
statistics, 67, 69, 120, 123, 127, 128, 129, 130, 167, 176
steelwork, 39, 40
stochastic, 71, 149
strategic, iv, vi, 23, 48, 67, 68, 69, 70, 71, 74, 75, 76, 77, 78, 81, 82, 85, 86, 87, 88, 89, 90, 91, 92, 93, 96, 105, 118, 129, 143, 146, 175, 190, 231
structural load, 40
structures, structural, 21, 25, 29, 34, 39, 40, 41, 75, 76, 88, 108, 209, 218
subsea, 26, 101, 230
supply chain, 22, 45, 46, 93, 95, 104, 111, 113, 254
switching option, 76, 78, 87, 190
tactical, 231
tangible assets, 82, 111
tax reliefs, 94, 96, 115, 116, 117
taxes, 93, 94, 95, 96, 97, 101, 108, 112, 115, 116, 117, 119, 142

technological development, 36
technology, 22, 24, 43, 63, 68, 69, 75, 76, 82, 87, 89, 90, 108
timing decommissioning, 67, 94, 105, 128, 129, 254
traditional, 30, 33, 68, 72, 81, 82, 85, 89, 104, 117, 120, 129, 130, 142, 143, 146, 148, 151, 186, 192, 201, 208, 228
trials, 66
trigger, 26, 70, 72, 80, 81
tubing, 30, 31, 42, 43, 103
tubing hanger, 30, 31
uncertainty, 19, 22, 23, 51, 59, 64, 67, 68, 69, 77, 82, 83, 86, 90, 91, 94, 105, 109, 111, 118, 119, 120, 123, 127, 130, 142, 145, 146, 148, 149, 150, 152, 153, 156, 167, 168, 174, 186, 191, 201, 208, 215, 252, 253, 254
utilities, 29, 81, 93, 100
valuation, 69, 89, 130, 142, 236, 255
vesting, 77
volatility, 70, 71, 90, 101, 105
waste management, 45, 53, 105, 254
well bore, 42
well head, 36
well plugging and abandonment, well P&A, iii, 22, 24, 26, 28, 30, 31, 32, 42, 44, 59, 63, 68, 82, 94, 102, 103, 108, 109, 115, 118, 128, 145, 146, 147, 148, 149, 151, 152, 153, 154, 155, 156, 157, 158, 167, 168, 170, 171, 172, 173, 175, 186, 193, 194, 198, 199, 200, 201, 202, 203, 204, 205, 206, 207, 208, 209, 210, 211, 212, 213, 214, 215, 216, 217, 218, 228, 253, 254

Printed in Great Britain
by Amazon